WHAT'S YOUR
MONEY
PERSONALITY?

WHAT'S YOUR **MONEY** PERSONALITY?

Changing the way Black families manage their finances

VANGILE MAKWAKWA

MACMILLAN

First published in 2023
by Pan Macmillan South Africa
Private Bag X19
Northlands
Johannesburg
2116

www.panmacmillan.co.za

ISBN 978-1-77010-886-8
eISBN 978-1-77010-887-5

Text © 2023 Vangile Makwakwa
Illustrations © 2023 Larissa Elliott

All rights reserved. No part of this publication may be reproduced, stored in or introduced into a retrieval system, or transmitted, in any form, or by any means (electronic, mechanical, photocopying, recording or otherwise), without the prior written permission of the publisher. Any person who does any unauthorised act in relation to this publication may be liable to criminal prosecution and civil claims for damages.

The views and opinions expressed in the text that follows do not necessarily reflect those of the publisher. The author's commentary and advice are based on extensive practical experience, research and work with clients, but no financial outcomes can be guaranteed.

Editing by Sean Fraser and Zodwa Kumalo-Valentine
Proofreading by Nkateko Traore
Design and layout by Nyx Design
Cover design by Larissa Elliott

*In many ways I am truly my ancestors' wildest dream.
This book is dedicated to all the men and women in
my bloodline who came before me.*

Contents

Introduction   1

Part 1: Setting Out
Chapter 1: Digging deeper   17
Chapter 2: What is trauma?   22
Chapter 3: An African perspective   34
Chapter 4: The impact of oppression   43
Chapter 5: Understanding our parental wounds   57
Chapter 6: Understanding money archetypes   68

Part 2: The Shadow Archetypes
Chapter 7: The Sweet One   85
Chapter 8: The Destroyer   110
Chapter 9: The RunAway   142
Chapter 10: The Fixer   165
Chapter 11: The Eternal Child   196
Chapter 12: How archetypes interact   226

Part 3: The Golden Archetypes
Chapter 13: The Sweet One becomes the Boundaried One   245
Chapter 14: The Destroyer becomes the Renovator   258

Chapter 15: The RunAway becomes the Grounded Seeker   273
Chapter 16: The Fixer becomes the Sovereign One   289
Chapter 17: The Eternal Child becomes the Evolving Adult   305
Chapter 18: Using ancestral money wisdom   324

Conclusion   331
Glossary   336
References   339
Acknowledgements   349

Introduction

I am fortunate in that I am not the first in my family to have attended university. And by 'family', I mean in the traditional African sense, including extended family, such as aunts, uncles, cousins, and grandparents, for instance.

My dad is a pharmacist and my mom a nurse, and both my maternal and paternal families include professionals such as teachers, doctors, nurses, and engineers, so I was exposed to a variety of career options from a young age. However, this exposure also made me aware that obtaining an education does not necessarily lead to financial freedom.

My relationship with money was shaped mainly by my maternal family simply because I spent more time with them as a child and in my teens, even though my father paid for most of my education. Throughout my childhood, I observed the adults around me struggle with finances. They never seemed to have enough money, living pay cheque to pay cheque, which meant that emergencies caused great anxiety in the family.

I noticed, too, how adults' behaviours changed when they discussed money, always with a sense of fear, frustration, and anger. As a teenager, I became hyper aware of the role of money in our family dynamics, the cause of much of the conflict between my mother,

her siblings (my aunt and uncles) and her mother (my maternal grandmother).

In my childhood, my mother was the primary provider in my maternal family, taking care of three adults and four children (her two daughters and two nephews). And yet, despite being the breadwinner, she still felt unappreciated and resentful, and believed that people only tolerated her because of what she was doing for them financially.

As I got older I started to understand that, even though my mom had a helper, my grandmother and great-grandmother also helped by looking after us, cooking and making sure that the house was running well. Never once did my mom have to worry about our safety because she knew that we were well looked after.

As a child, I witnessed my mom's explosive arguments with family members about money. It was a recurring theme and sometimes it even got physical. It was scary to witness such events, and in the process I learnt that money causes fights and I started associating money with arguments and tension. By the time I was in my teens, talking about money or handling money felt unsafe.

When my uncle came back from exile in the early nineties, my mom helped him get set up, and asked my uncle to step in and look after the family. And so it was that, in my teens, the family dynamics changed: my mom became unemployed and suddenly lost decision-making power and respect in the family, and my uncle became the breadwinner and was given most of the decision-making power.

I witnessed my uncle, who earned a substantial salary as an electrical engineer, struggling to support six of us (my grandmother, my mother, two adult cousins, my sister and me). Although my uncle was loved, he was not always respected, and many family members felt he should be doing more financially. I saw how he would buy furniture for his house, only for his younger brother to take it and sell it. My grandmother would often intervene and ask my uncle to forgive his younger brother, but this happened repeatedly and I

Introduction

cannot imagine how my uncle must have felt.

When I was in Grade 12, my maternal grandmother passed away, and my uncle resigned from his job, leaving us in his house, which he owned, to rent a place far from us. I realised later that he had resigned simply to free himself from the financial burden of supporting the family. With my grandmother gone, he felt he could finally live for himself.

I didn't know it then, but my grandmother's passing signalled the end of my maternal family unit because the two people who'd been the glue holding us together – my granny and uncle – were no longer able to. I think my uncle was scared to kick us out of his house and feared setting financial boundaries because he thought the family would stop loving him and react in the same way they had with my mother. In the end it was simply easier for him to quit his job and use his unemployed status to force all the adults to support themselves.

Growing up in this environment was challenging, with constant fights, sometimes physical, about money. My mother was vocal in her resentment, to the extent that my uncle banned my sister and me from openly talking about money. The constant conflict and persistent anxiety about money affected our mental health; I was depressed throughout my teens and would even run away from home, disappearing for days on end.

I observed how some members of the family protected themselves financially and dealt with our family trauma by avoiding all financial responsibility (for themselves and others), attending only important family functions. Other well-educated and able-bodied adults never left home and relied entirely on the main breadwinner to take care of them – financially and emotionally – and, as a result, never had a voice in family decisions. Even with their degrees and diplomas, they battled to earn a living. These differing personalities would often clash when it came to money.

When it was time for me to choose a career, I decided to study finance at the University of Cape Town, 2 000 kilometres away, in order to earn my own money and avoid the conflict that inevitably came with it. Growing up in my maternal family, I had seen the people I loved continue to struggle financially, with no knowledge of how to manage their finances or make their money grow. I was also terrified that my family would expect me to take care of them as soon as I began earning a salary, because that's what I had seen happen to both my mom and my uncle.

After graduating with an honours degree in Finance, I thought my financial future would be secure. However, when I started working as a mining and energy analyst, I spent my first pay cheque within days and struggled to hold onto money. Although I had a good understanding of finance theory, I found it challenging to apply what I had learnt to my own life.

I had a deep understanding of finance theory and could talk about anything from budgeting to economics, supply and demand, inflation, derivatives, shares, and investing, but I was struggling financially. And so, even though I had two other jobs, I decided to go travelling so that I could earn US dollars or pounds and pay off my student loans. I found work on a cruise liner and thought it would be an easy way to save money since my rent and food were paid for. Instead, I ended up becoming a shopaholic and, despite drafting several budgets, I found it difficult to save money.

I later decided to write my Graduate Management Admission Test – commonly referred to as GMAT – and got accepted into the Simmons School of Management in Boston, Massachusetts, to do my Master of Business Administration (MBA). At the time, I believed that my money issues were related to education, and that a master's degree would change my life and my relationship with money. I graduated with US$60,000 in debt and started suffering panic attacks whenever I had to handle or talk about money.

At the same time, my uncle called to inform me that the family had been waiting for me to graduate and start earning money so that I could look after them. I was only 25, with no kids and no husband,

Introduction

and was being asked to take responsibility for seven adults and five children. I started a business, but it failed because I found myself unable to charge for my services, invoice people, or talk about money. I even watched *The Secret*, tried visualisation techniques, recited affirmations, and practised gratitude, but nothing seemed to work. There seemed to be no way out of my financial crisis.

It was at this point that a friend introduced me to vipassana meditation, a meditation practice where you take a vow of silence for 10 days to focus on meditating. During this time, I saw how every thought triggered an emotion and sensation in my body. I realised, too, that I spent most of my time worrying about money and finally understood what that worry was doing to my body.

After vipassana, I read theses on behavioural finance and economics and focused on understanding the link between emotional intelligence and money. I started writing blogs, creating money exercises, and sharing them. People started coming to me for money coaching, and the more shifts they saw, the more people they referred. Finally, I landed a publishing deal for my first book, *Heart, Mind & Money: Using Emotional Intelligence for Financial Success*, and paid off my $60,000 debt in three and a half years.

And so it was then I became debt-free, went back to travelling, became a nomad, and started running my business on the road. However, I found myself struggling to increase my income and lived in constant fear of my maternal family turning to me for money. This fear wasn't unfounded, however, because my uncle and one of my aunts, both of whom were career professionals, often alluded to the fact that it was now my turn to look after the family. My aunt had even tried to shame my sister and me at a family gathering for setting financial boundaries.

I would have nightmares of being rejected by my family, enduring fights about money and being shouted at for not doing enough. I would wake up shaking and scared, convinced that the only way to keep myself safe from the fighting and to be loved by my family was to make very little money so I could always say I don't have any money. After all, both my mom and uncle had gotten out of the cycle of family drama by quitting their jobs.

I realised then that my view of family was tainted by violence and the trauma around money, and this was affecting my ability to grow financially. The mindset that had helped me get out of debt couldn't help me create a consistent stream of income, grow my business, or create passive income streams.

I started questioning why I felt the way I did about making money and how my family dynamics and history impacted my earning potential and business. I went back to my research on emotions and money and noticed that finance and economics theses looked at money through an individual, Western lens and rarely explored family dynamics around money, especially in Black families. Of course, this made sense, because traditional finance and economics works on the premise that we are rational human beings and, as a result, we make rational financial decisions. But the reality is that humans are also emotional beings, especially when it comes to our family and friends. That's why I found myself struggling with financial boundaries and focusing on wealth creation when it came to my family – setting boundaries seemed like I was risking family rejection and going against tradition.

It also became obvious to me that most financial advice ignores family dynamics, especially in Black families, where emotions, ancestors, racial trauma, and family ties play a crucial role in financial decisions. And so I started to realise that there was a need for conversations about money and family dynamics, especially in marginalised communities, and decided to focus on this in my coaching and writing.

It wasn't until a friend suggested that some of my fears might be ancestral that I began exploring my own family history and ancestral trauma. While researching epigenetic inheritance I found studies showing that we inherit more than our looks from our ancestors –

Introduction

we also inherit their memories and thought patterns and store these in the body, which affects our nervous systems and psyche. These memories and patterns are then triggered by certain events in our lifetimes and, when they are activated, we repeat ancestral cycles. So, it was possible that some of my money fears were inherited and were in fact not mine, but it was up to me to break those cycles. To do that I needed to work with the body, regulate my nervous system, use my education and knowledge of money, know my ancestors and delve into the spiritual realm.

I intuitively understood that healing my relationship with money was a holistic endeavour and that there was a link between the body, the mind, the spiritual and the physical. And so I went back home and asked my mom (who is healer and herbalist) to teach me how to phahla (communicate with my ancestors, the individuals in my bloodline who came before me) and how to recite our clan names, and she in turn helped me understand my family history. She explained that one of my female ancestors was doing caesarean sections long before hospitals were built in South Africa, that my maternal great-grandfather was one of the most well-known healers of his time and that I was named after my great-great-grandmother – the one who held most of the healing gifts in our bloodline – and that I could call on my ancestors to teach me all they knew about making money, healing the body, the womb and our bloodline in the spiritual plane. She explained that her gift as a herbalist and healer came from simply communicating with the ancestors and asking them to guide her on herbs and access that wisdom in her DNA.

My sister is a sangoma (or shaman) and I started doing her courses in which she teaches people how to build relationships with their ancestors and so connect deeper with my ancestors and ask for guidance.

Through these experiences, I came to understand that I was truly the sum total of those who came before me, and that who I am today has been impacted by the lives I lived in other lifetimes and galaxies before I came to this plane.

Yes, my deceased family members no longer walk this plane, but that doesn't mean they have completely gone; they exist in the spiritual realm and I could continue building our relationship and ask for help. I realised, too, that this relationship was a symbiotic one – I could help my ancestors heal and they, in turn, could help me heal and pass on knowledge and wisdom so that I could make changes and help our bloodline do better in the future.

The truth is that these family dynamics predated my and my parents' generation, so I would need help from the people with whom it started.

Being able to talk to my ancestors and tell them my grievances has been life changing, and at times I have had what I can only call miraculous experiences. I called on my ancestors and spirit guides to walk with me and help me understand how our family got here and how I could heal myself and break the cycle, and my ancestors channelled very specific meditations for me to write, record and practice so that I may heal them, myself and versions of me across lifetimes.

I started to see how money and setting income goals would take me back to my painful past by triggering the childhood parts of me that were still struggling to integrate or process my family trauma with money. This would make me feel like a kid again, making illogical decisions and panicking when I made more money than usual. What I saw as a child was that money leads to arguments and arguments scared me (most children fear conflict), so when I had to deal with money as an adult, I would be transported back to those painful memories and start shaking and freaking out; my reaction would be to go into fight-or-flight mode, which would impact both my body and my mental state.

The only examples I had seen on how to stay safe with money was to get rid of money or not make money at all. So I would end up spending it as quickly as possible, energetically blocking it, or refusing income-generating opportunities, which led to me recreating my family's financial patterns and repeating the cycle of money trauma in my adulthood.

I started recording my own guided meditations and the more I followed these, the more realisations I had about trauma and the more I started to change the way I behaved with money. A lot of these meditations are unique to my courses, particularly the Money Magic course, and involve us calling on our ancestors and/or spirit guides to help us heal specific traumas and wounds that sit in the body and energy plane. We, in turn, share our pain and fears with our ancestors and they see how their actions when they were alive have contributed to these traumas and wounds in this present moment. Our ancestors then begin to heal and give guidance to us and other family members in dreams or waking life (unfortunately, I am not an expert on how these messages are delivered – I just know everyone receives them in different ways).

When we heal ourselves and go into our bodies, our nervous system starts to regulate, we breathe deeper, our heart rate starts to slow down, our digestion improves radically, we find it easier to pause and relax; in this space of relaxation, we reflect more, look at situations from different angles, become less reactionary and, in so doing, start to react differently to the people around us and to situations that arise, including financial situations. When we react differently to how we've been taught to react to money and to family dynamics or other situations, we start to change the way we behave with money and with our families. And, as our family dynamics start to change for the better, we start to feel more supported, which increases our sense of confidence within ourselves. Which changes the way we show up in our environment, which alters the way we see ourselves, which leads to increased income and investments.

Over time, I started sharing these meditations with other entrepreneurs and some family members on my paternal and maternal side, and before I knew it, I was discussing wealth creation and womb work with my aunts, cousins, and siblings. My mother even gifted my sister and me land as an investment for future generations and asked us to build apartment buildings there so we could have passive income for the future.

I thus went from being someone who didn't dare talk about money with her family to one who hosts retreats for her family so they can heal their money and relationships. But for this to happen I had to understand the persona or money profile I had adopted in order to survive the trauma within my family and how that influenced how I interacted with family members.

My clients also experienced powerful changes and we realised that the guidance we were working on was not just about money. It was also about healing ourselves and our relationships, which ultimately led to a better relationship with money.

The more I did the meditations (and, by default, the ancestral work on money) the more I was led to other healing modalities – past-life regression therapy, plant medicines, and a variety of other practices – and I began to understand the ways that trauma plays out within families and how it affects our relationship with money.

This journey of money, self-discovery and personal growth has taken me down many paths, including: behavioural finance and economics, meditation, communicating with my ancestors (I come from a lineage of sangomas/shamans), acupuncture, spirit guides, tantra/yin/vinyasa yoga, tantra/yoni massages, vipassana meditation, weekly full-body massages, chi nei tsang (abdominal healing massage), karsai nei tsang (genital healing massage), trauma coaching with different coaches, conventional therapy, breathwork, my mother's herbs and healing methods, sweat lodges, ayahuasca (psychoactive tea), cacao ceremonies, mushroom journeys, cannabis oil, past-life regression, epigenetic research, polyvagal theory (study of the nervous system's responses to the environment), living in ashrams, EFT tapping (Emotional Freedom Technique – essentially acupuncture without needles), travelling, fasting (sometimes eating

Introduction

only grapes and drinking only water for 21 days), and taking a vow of silence for days/weeks/months on end so that I can go within and understand myself and the way money trauma works with the body.

My study of ancestral money trauma is part of a body of work that I've developed in my online school, Wealthy Money Academy, over the past eight years, and it's helped me not only increase my own income and start buying properties, but also helped hundreds of clients, particularly women of colour, increase their income and savings, heal their ancestral money trauma and change their family dynamics.

My work on ancestral trauma is about understanding how trauma travels through the bloodline and across lifetimes and how that trauma impacts us mentally, physically, psychologically, spiritually, and financially in the present.

I am not a psychologist or sangoma (even though some clients may think that I am one); I work with ancestors predominantly through guided meditations and breathwork meditations that are channelled by my ancestors and guides. In these meditations people learn to connect with their ancestors and learn to feel the sensations and emotions in their bodies. The meditations take people through past-life and present-day memories, into the akashic plane (a metaphysical library of all experiences, past and present) in order to heal ancestral patterns and access ancestral wisdom. If your ancestors need more specific rituals performed, they often let you know who to consult or talk to in the meditations.

I also use my degree in finance and my MBA to help people start (and scale) businesses and create additional streams of income, and this is heavily supported by the emotional and spiritual work I do in the meditations.

One thing I've learnt is that my family's story is not unique and emotions are particularly charged when it comes to our families and friends. Our loved ones' reactions – or lack of reaction – to our success can deeply impact us, and we often take on certain money profiles or personas that help us survive within our families. But the identities we develop out of survival don't always serve us in the long run, and can in fact hold us back from building wealth, creating healthy family relationships and building generational wealth.

Experiencing trauma can have a profound impact on our family dynamics. This can then extend beyond our family and start to impact our money profile, our personal profile, and even our mission in life. This is because our family is often where we first experience trauma, and this trauma can shape how we respond and how we operate in the world.

Each profile has a specific mission within the family, and understanding this is crucial when it comes to unpacking how different family members respond to trauma. In this book, I explore the role of each family member and how their role, or lack thereof, can affect how they respond to trauma. It's important to note that each profile outlined here has a unique way of responding to money and finances, and this can have an influence on how a family grows financially.

Once we understand each person's money profile, we begin to see that each has a different role and a particular way of contributing to the family's financial success. Unfortunately, society often places the most value on those who bring in the most money, but not everyone is cut out for this. Some profiles are just not meant to follow the traditional path to success.

This is where things get tricky. When we praise one type of intelligence, such as academic intelligence, we risk overlooking the special intelligence of other profiles. This can lead to a sense of inadequacy and even trauma for those who don't fit the conventional mould. This is especially true for Black people, who have endured centuries of trauma through slavery, colonisation and apartheid. In many cases, Western ways of thinking and being are elevated above all else, leaving some profiles behind and affecting their relationship with money and self-worth.

Introduction

Overall, understanding how trauma impacts our family dynamics, as well as our money profile, is essential for creating a healthy and prosperous family unit. It's also important to recognise and celebrate the distinctive intelligence of each profile to ensure that everyone is able to thrive.

In 2020, when I started writing this book, I shared a list of money archetypes within Black families on Facebook – the Fixer, the Destroyer, the RunAway and the Eternal Child/Spoiled Brat – to help others understand the ways trauma plays out within their own families and the response was overwhelmingly positive. I realised I was dealing with a significant and widespread phenomenon that needed more research, exploration and discussion.

PART 1

Setting Out

CHAPTER 1

Digging deeper

We've been taught that money centres entirely on the individual, that wealth-building is a personal matter, but this is not true. Having money and making money affects not just us as individuals but the people around us. One person's financial habits can have an impact on the whole family.

Financial success is not just a result of individual choices, but also of collective efforts and historical events. Our finances are often influenced by the people and circumstances in our lives. Many of us put our own aspirations on hold to support our family members, such as siblings or parents. Some even go into debt simply to gain approval from others. It's therefore important to recognise the impact that our relationships and societal pressures can have on our financial decisions and outcomes. Building generational wealth requires not only individual effort, but also a collective effort from our families and communities.

Healthy family dynamics can help individuals develop healthy coping mechanisms for financial challenges. On the other hand, dysfunctional family dynamics can contribute to problems such as overspending, debt, and conflicts over money.

The impact of family dynamics on our financial decision-making can be seen in a study conducted by Xolile Antoni (2023) in which the influence of the family on financial decision-making was explored. The author conducted a study on 360 students at a university in the Eastern Cape, South Africa, and found that family structures play a significant role in shaping financial behaviour.

According to this study, major life events such as the death or separation of parents can have a significant impact on a child's transition into important life roles and shape their behaviours as they grow older. The research also found that students from single-parent households tend to have lower levels of financial literacy and self-confidence compared with those from two-parent households.

The study also suggests that students from households with higher income and education levels have better financial socialisation techniques and behaviours, such as saving and investing, compared with those from lower-income and less-educated households. This highlights the importance of family structure and socioeconomic status in shaping financial behaviours among young adults in South Africa.

Antoni suggests that financial educators should thus consider family variables and involve other family members, such as parents, when providing financial education to students. The author found that parents' financial literacy and education have a significant impact on students' financial behaviour. This study therefore highlights the need for a more comprehensive approach to financial education that considers the role of family dynamics in shaping financial behaviour.

Money is also the source of many fights and arguments in families and can even tear them apart, thus impacting generational wealth; but good money management can also bring peace to a family and change family dynamics.

A study by Sandra Titus et al. (1979) looked at family conflict over inheritance of property. The research included interviews with 14 families (the authors are American and don't specify the race or ethnicity of the families) and found that inheritance isn't just about passing on wealth, but also 'a matter of conflict', and even when there is a will, families – in particular, siblings – still end up fighting because they don't believe the money and assets are divided fairly. In some cases, inheritance disputes may be the last straw, with the result that siblings no longer speak to each other.

The study identifies several factors that contribute to family conflict over inheritance: differences in expectations and perceptions of fairness, the emotional attachment of family members to the property in question, and the role of family dynamics in shaping the conflict. (Most family members in the study couldn't articulate why the other side was upset and understood only their own point of view.)

Some of the conclusions drawn by the study were that conflict over inheritance often arises due to unresolved family tensions, poor communication, and feelings of exclusion. The authors suggest that consistent and effective communication within families about money and inheritance could help prevent such conflicts in the future. This would not only save families time and money, but also prevent emotional strain and stress.

As we can gather from the studies discussed here, family dynamics play a critical role in shaping our relationship with money and financial outcomes. While traditional teachings on money focus on earning, saving and spending, they do not cover navigating family dynamics, especially within extended or Black families, friendships, and romantic relationships around money. This can lead to associating success with loneliness or even a fear of increased financial pressure from family when our incomes increase.

In extended or Black families, individuals play different roles to ensure the survival of the family or community, including as emotional support, financial provision, and even questioning our core values and ethics as a family. However, as families move from extended to nuclear, these roles become more complex, and money and finances can become a source of resentment between family members. Some may shoulder more of the financial load, while others only show up for weddings and funerals, and some even cause friction.

I've witnessed individuals quitting their jobs and giving up work as a way to avoid financial pressure from family. At first, I thought this was uncommon, but as I travelled and worked with people from different countries, I discovered that this was not a unique occurrence.

In Japan, the combination of societal, family and financial pressure has resulted in a significant number of individuals disappearing without a trace each year. This phenomenon is so prevalent that the Japanese have a term for it: *johatsu*, or the 'evaporated people' – individuals who choose to vanish and become anonymous, cutting off all contact with their loved ones, never to be seen again (Mauger & Remael, 2016). In fact, there are books and an entire industry dedicated to assisting Japanese individuals to disappear without a trace.

The lack of communication about societal and family pressures when it comes to money, especially within relationships, can lead to broken family units with little understanding of how it happened. So, it's essential to acknowledge and address family trauma and heal it so that we can involve or at least talk to other family members, such as parents, when making financial decisions.

In this book, I explore four key questions:

1. Why do some family units continue to thrive from one generation to the next?
2. Considering the oppression and violence we've had to endure, what do money profiles in Black families look like?
3. How does trauma affect each family member and influence their financial behaviour?
4. Why is it difficult for families to work together and advance as a unit?

Ancestral trauma often lies at the heart of our family dysfunction and inability to progress financially. In order to survive trauma, we learn to embody specific archetypes within our family structure. These archetypes are carried into our adult lives, impacting our finances, romantic relationships and parental roles, which can hinder our ability to accumulate wealth.

Imagine if we had a deeper understanding of trauma and why family members behave and react the way they do.

How would having a better understanding of our families' driving forces make it easier to communicate with them and build harmonious relationships?

How can understanding each other's financial motivations and needs help in accelerating the process of building generational wealth or family legacies?

My hope for this book is that it serves as a launching pad, particularly for members of the Black community, to begin delving into the ways in which our family dynamics have shaped our identities and influenced the archetypes or money profiles we embody.

By understanding these money profiles, we can start to comprehend how they impact our relationship with money and our ability to create generational wealth.

CHAPTER 2

What is trauma?

Trauma occurs when we encounter something we are unable to comprehend or manage in the moment, and it then lingers with us, influencing our actions and reactions to stimuli or events.

It doesn't have to be a major event either; it could be something as apparently insignificant as not receiving the support and celebration we deserved from siblings or friends when we did something exceptional. This can cause us to downplay our successes simply to feel accepted by them or gain their approval.

Trauma can also leave us feeling helpless and powerless, which can affect our nervous system, bodily functions and lead to overwhelming traumatic stress. According to Bessel van der Kolk (1994), trauma lives in the body and impacts the nervous system, changing the neural synapses of the brain (Bremner, 2006), which can be seen on brain scans. The way we think and process events change due to trauma, prolonged trauma, or childhood trauma. Trauma is one of the reasons people behave in ways we see as unreasonable or irrational. Trauma has even been linked to digestive issues (Liisa Hantsoo et al., 2019), as well as a reduction of synapses within the brain (Bennett & Lagopoulos, 2018).

What is trauma?

As we can see from some of the research, trauma is a complex issue that can't be healed simply by trying to change one's mindset or listening to motivational speeches. It requires a combination of physical and psychological intervention to help individuals overcome its deep-rooted effects.

People with complex trauma often find it difficult to be motivated because their entire system, including their brain, is wired for survival. The brain is continually scanning the environment, looking for potential threats that may harm them. This can lead to feelings of anxiety, hypervigilance and avoidance.

So you can see why telling someone to 'think positively' may not be effective in addressing their trauma. When people force themselves to think positively without addressing the underlying trauma, they may end up feeling more stuck, angry, numb or dissociated.

We all respond to trauma and traumatic events in different ways – this is called a trauma response. According to Schauer & Elbert (2010), there are six ways in which we respond to trauma: Freeze, Flight, Fight, Fright, Flag and Faint.

People also talk about 'the four Fs': Flight, Fight, Freeze or Fawn. I would like to add another response that I have encountered that is rarely mentioned and which we will discuss later: Force (I am trying to keep with the Fs theme). By 'force', I mean the need to be in control, especially when one has experienced a traumatic event that leaves one feeling powerless.

Research shows that because trauma is stored in the body, it can be passed down from one generation through family stories, and emotional and behavioural patterns. A new body of research is now dedicated to exploring the impact of historical and cultural trauma on the next generation; these studies show that traumatic experiences endured by the previous generation impact the way people parent and communicate with the next generation, and in turn, the way future generations interact with the world.

To understand the transmission of intergenerational trauma,

Berckmoes et al. (2017) spent five months observing and interviewing 41 mothers who lived through the 1994 Rwandan genocide, as well as their teen children. According to the study, the aftermath of the Rwandan genocide affected family dynamics in various ways. One of the effects was an increase in family conflict, which can be attributed to the trauma experienced by the survivors. Additionally, the genocide left mothers with an increased workload and higher stress levels, which affected their productivity and economic status.

The study also found that the children of survivors continued to experience the effects of the genocide in their daily lives. Communication breakdowns between parents and children were common, with some parents remaining silent and others being verbally abusive towards their children. The children could feel their mothers' pain and suffering, causing them emotional distress even though their mothers tried to protect them by staying silent.

The research also revealed that the children of survivors faced financial disadvantages, heavy family responsibilities, and a sense of missing out on opportunities and rights. They often struggled with the dilemma of staying loyal to their families or leaving to look for better opportunities.

In the mid-2000s, a researcher by the name of Brent Bezo conducted a study on three generations of 15 Ukrainian families who had lived through Holodomor (intentional mass starvation of Soviet Ukrainians during the Stalin regime from 1932 to 1933). In this study, people shared how the experience lead to increased anxiety and shame, and how it affected or changed parenting styles, sexual behaviour, relationships with food and community trust; even more interesting was how each generation taught the next not to trust other people or the world at large (DeAngelis, 2019).

The studies conducted in the Ukraine and Rwanda provide important insights into how trauma can affect not only the generation that experiences it directly but also the next generation. They show how trauma can impact family dynamics, which can have lasting effects on future generations.

Ancestral trauma

According to the University of Utah, 'Epigenetic inheritance is an unconventional finding. It goes against the idea that inheritance happens only through the DNA code that passes from parent to offspring. It means that a parent's experiences, in the form of epigenetic tags, can be passed down to future generations.' What this means is that we carry our parents', grandparents' and great-grandparents' experiences and emotions within us.

Dias & Ressler (2014) conducted an experiment with mice where they trained male mice to be afraid of the scent of cherry blossoms. Every time they introduced the smell of cherry blossoms, they would electrocute the mice. Three days later, they had the mice mate with female mice. The resultant pups were not electrocuted or introduced to the scent of cherry blossoms until adulthood. When they eventually introduced the offspring to the scent of cherry blossoms, the pups started shaking and displaying other symptoms of anxiety. These pups could also pick up subtle traces of cherry blossoms in the air, which changed the anatomy of their brains and certain areas lit up when monitored digitally. This same behaviour was observed in the following generation of the mice even though they had never been electrocuted. This led researchers to understand how we, as humans, carry our ancestors' emotional reactions to traumatic situations and events.

These understandings are supported by research that has found that many children of apartheid, slavery and Holocaust survivors experienced post-traumatic stress disorder (PTSD), possibly linked to events that occurred in their family's history two or three generations previously.

A study by Kim et al. (2022) investigated the psychological

impact of South Africa's apartheid violence on the mental health of the next generation. The study, which included 304 pregnant women in Soweto, in 1990, who had experienced apartheid violence, studied their children's mental health in 2007 and 2008. Researchers found that the prenatal stress (stress during pregnancy) caused by apartheid negatively impacted the mental health of children born to young or teenage mothers in 1990, concluding that children born to young mothers during apartheid were likely to experience mental health issues. These findings support existing research showing that a mother's emotional state during pregnancy can impact the physical and emotional health of their children as they grow.

Other studies, such as those by Vivian Rakoff (1966), have looked at how the Holocaust impacted the children of survivors and found that the majority of those children were more likely to struggle with mental health disorders. A Canadian study by Amy Bombay et al. (2014) found that children whose parents and grandparents had suffered serious mental health issues were most likely to struggle with their mental health and be suicidal.

These studies help us understand how our ancestors' experiences can have a significant impact on future generations. This means that the experiences we have today will likely be passed down to future generations and shape their lives, just as our ancestors' experiences have shaped ours. And the same is thus true for how money trauma can be inherited and impact our lives. It is, therefore, important to acknowledge how our ancestors' experiences with money have shaped us and our families over generations and recognise that we carry these experiences with us.

Time does *not* heal wounds and it certainly doesn't heal trauma. In fact, with time, trauma can be passed down from generation to generation and start to shape the family and the way people relate to each other in those families. It can even destroy families.

Growing up in my maternal family, I was baffled by how family members could be highly educated but still carry so much pain and throw tantrums that beat mine (as a teen) by a mile. How was it that I was often more rational than the adults around me who responded to everything in anger?

I was confused by how people who were otherwise so mature and educated would still cry over things that happened when they were 10. I would see my mom bring up things that happened to her as a teen and shout at my grandmother about them. Time had not erased her pain. I also saw how my cousins, as grown men, refused to move out of home and demanded to be mothered like children.

I swore never to be like them, but then in my early twenties I found myself doing the same: crying every night about things that I experienced in my teens and that my parents were not supporting me financially. And because I was in pain, 20-something me would be calm for a few days, but as soon as I encountered challenges I would react with anger and self-destruction in much the same way teen me had. I would, for instance, call home and blame my mom and remind her of all the verbal, emotional and physical abuse, waiting for an apology that never came.

I couldn't understand why I was repeating the same patterns. I mean, I was practising positive thinking and affirming and visualising and sending love and light. But all that positivity only lasted as long as things were good; when things went bad, I would be back to square one and sometimes feel even worse.

I didn't understand it then, but I do now – I, like everyone else in my maternal family, was entrapped in a time loop, hijacked by the wounded parts of me, not to mention the wounded *ancestral* parts of me. Those parts were reacting in a way that a child or teen would react, so even though I was a full-grown adult, my four-year-old or 16-year-old self was running my life.

It is clear then that trauma affects the way we process information and changes the way we respond to events, so when we heal ancestral trauma, we work on healing our ancestors, our nervous systems and our psyche in order to change the way we respond to external events and process information. This, in turn, changes the stories and beliefs we pass down to the next generation, as well as the way we parent the next generation, thus breaking the cycle of trauma.

Have you ever felt like you're having an out-of-body experience when something triggers you, like being swept back to a painful moment in your past, and you react in a crazy way but can't seem to stop it? That's what being triggered and being hijacked by the younger versions of you looks and feels like. Your inner child or inner teen takes over your psyche, dominating your reactions and behaviour. That's what trauma does – the parts of us that are stuck in the past and can't process the pain they experienced will come to the surface when we experience similar events that remind us of that pain, and those parts of us will hijack our psyche and start to run the show by taking us right back to childhood or teenage behaviour.

Linking ancestral trauma, family dynamics and money

Ancestral money trauma refers to the inherited trauma our ancestors experienced and passed down through generations. This trauma includes their thoughts, emotions, behaviours and actions around money that became part of our family lineage. As a result, we often take these patterns for granted and don't realise how they influence our own behaviours and attitudes towards money. This trauma can be passed down through our physical DNA, through emotional reactions or via stories that are shared within our families. We absorb these beliefs and behaviours about money without realising it, and they can lead to anxieties and fears around money. Essentially, our ancestral money trauma affects the way we think about and approach money.

Growing up, we learn how to handle money by observing our parents and their behaviour when it comes to money. Our parents, in turn, learnt from their parents, who learnt from their parents, and so on. Unfortunately, not all these behaviours were helpful or beneficial, but the good news is that our ancestors also had a wealth of knowledge and wisdom when it came to money, which they also passed down. Examples can be found in skills such as cooking, entrepreneurship, farming, managing people, healing and listening. So, in the same way that trauma is passed down to us via our ancestors, so is their innate wisdom.

Ancestral trauma is why the current generation responds in much the same way to money (at a nervous system and emotional level) as the previous generation did. You may find yourself behaving out of sorts in relationships or the way you deal with money, repeating your family's financial patterns, or even attracting the same type of partner as your ex or father or mother, no matter what you do.

For example, if your mom exhibited a fear of not having enough money and always spent all her money by the end of the month, you may find yourself scared and spending your money as if you have no control over it. That's because nervous systems interact with each other and, as children, we learn to co-regulate (positively interact) or co-dysregulate (negatively interact) with our caregivers' or parents' nervous systems, including when it comes to money. Our parents' nervous systems also reacted with that of their parents and so on. Our nervous systems learn to react to money in the same way.

Having a dysregulated nervous system means that the system in our body responsible for coordinating all functions and responses to stress is not working properly and cannot properly process stressful situations as they happen, making it difficult to concentrate and remember things, which can lead to mental health challenges and even physical illness.

A regulated nervous system means that the system that controls and coordinates all the functions of our body, including our response to stress, is functioning smoothly and efficiently, leading to a sense of calmness and emotional stability, as well as physical health.

According to Murray et al. (2015), co-regulation is when caregivers provide the necessary coaching and nurturing so that their children are able to perform day-to-day activities.

Children learn how to behave and react to tasks and activities by watching the adults around them. They observe the little nuances and either take them on or rebel against them. In fact, children so readily co-regulate the nervous systems of adults in their environment that I believe it is important for parents to do their own work on money trauma before trying to change a child's behaviour when it comes to money.

So if our parents' or caregivers' nervous systems were dysregulated, or imbalanced, when dealing with money, we will most likely have dysregulated nervous systems when dealing with money.

As relayed in the introduction of this book, I had my own money issues; I struggled to make money and hold onto money and even now, when I am deeply triggered, I can resort to these old money habits that come from childhood.

As mentioned, I was 10 years old when my mom's brother, my uncle, returned to South Africa from exile. I was too young to understand it then, but his homecoming – with his degrees and a number of high-profile friends – had financial implications for many in the family. For my mom, it was a relief – it meant that she had someone who was able to share the financial load. Up until then, my mom had been supporting most of her family, including my sister and me, entirely on her own.

My uncle soon found a job and within a few years everyone – and I mean *everyone* in the family – moved in with him: my grandma, my cousins, my other uncle, my sister and me. Until that point, we'd never really lived with the family; my sister and I had always been in boarding school, but my uncle insisted we move in with him.

It was the late 1990s and my uncle held a high-profile position in Transnet and made a lot of money. He bought a 21-hectare plot in Johannesburg, with several buildings, a park, swimming pool and orchard and we all lived there. Eventually, my mom decided she needed to move to Johannesburg to be with us, so she quit her job and moved in with us too.

He had a master's degree in electrical engineering from Germany, had lived in different countries, spoke multiple languages and had no boundaries when it came to money, so he would just give and give and give. He was a spender and was praised by the family for his generosity.

When payday came around, our house became a party haven. My uncle hosted some of South Africa's top politicians and celebrities; it was nonstop braais, alcohol and gifts, and the party did not stop until the money ran out – think *The Great Gatsby*, except people went home every evening.

When my uncle had money, he was on top of the world, and you couldn't tell him anything. We just had to wait out this phase, which would go on until, at about the fifth of the month, there would be no money left to buy food, pay for water or electricity, or pay the bond, for example. At this point, my uncle would become withdrawn, frustrated and sad, and ask my grandmother (a pensioner) for money for petrol, food and electricity.

It was a life of feast or famine; what I didn't know at the time was what it was doing to my nervous system. All I knew was that I didn't like how my body felt in that house and how it felt when my uncle had money. What we, as a family, saw as excitement about having money was actually anxiety about having money (excitement and anxiety have the same physiological response so people often confuse the two).

When we feel unsafe when we have money, we feel anxious; our nervous system becomes dysregulated, and there's a seemingly inexplicable urge to get rid of the money. When we feel anxious about having money, the parts of us that feel unsafe focus on getting us to feel safe again – and, in this case, we will get rid of money. And one of the easiest ways to get rid of money is to give it away. When my uncle had money, we could barely talk to him let alone reason with him, because he was being hijacked by his sub-personalities, which were freaking out about having money, and intent on spending and giving away money as quickly as possible.

By co-dysregulating with my uncle's nervous system, my own nervous system learnt that having money was not safe. And, as I got older, my natural instinct was to protect myself by getting rid of money, and my teen self, stuck in that trauma, would hijack adult me, even with all my finance education, because the role of the mind is to keep us safe, not to keep us wealthy, and if keeping us safe means getting rid of money, then that's what our psyche will work towards. So what we often see as people's excessive spending and them being overly generous are often a trauma response to having money and feeling unsafe with money.

To change my response to money and stop reacting the way I had learnt to react to money in my teens, I had to connect with those scared younger parts of me and regulate my nervous system and train my brain (the amygdala, the emotional centre of the brain) to remain calm when dealing with money. The more I regulated my nervous system and the calmer I remained, the easier it became for me to change my financial behaviour – I was able to hold onto money and say yes to more income opportunities, which led to different financial outcomes than those experienced by my family.

There's still a part of me that feels like money is synonymous with violence and represents danger. This trauma sometimes manifests physically and makes me feel unsafe and uneasy, even when I'm expanding financially. I've thus had to learn to differentiate between the trauma and the reality of a situation.

It's often hard to tell when a person (lover, family member or friend) is being naturally generous or just getting rid of money, but being in your body and noticing how its sensations change when you are in their space or when they are gifting you is often a good indicator. The only issue with this is that if your nervous system is dysregulated where money is concerned you won't know whether you're co-dysregulating with the other person's nervous system or if it's just your own trauma response to being gifted.

My need to be safe always overrode all my fancy MBA knowledge, because like all humans, I'm hardwired to survive. In the past, I would blame myself for my inability to save and chastise myself for my lack of financial discipline. I didn't realise that my nervous system was constantly on edge and in a state of heightened alertness as a result of my teen experiences with my uncle, and that led me to spend money quickly.

CHAPTER 3

An African perspective

I had the pleasure of interviewing my sister, Honey Makwakwa, who is not only a sangoma but also the founder of Sangoma Society, an academy that teaches people about African spirituality and the ancestral realms, both online and offline. Her insights on ancestral trauma are particularly relevant to this book as it explores how ancestral trauma shapes our family dynamics, which in turn affects our financial situations. It's worth noting that consulting with ancestors or sangomas is a common practice for many on the African continent when it comes to business and financial decisions. I find Honey's perspective invaluable because much of my work on trauma and money profiles has been channelled to me via meditation by my guides and ancestors. I have then done additional research and studies on money, family dynamics, and trauma to create a body of work and exercises that can help others transform their lives.

Below is a transcript of our conversation:

VANGILE: How would you define ancestral trauma from a sangoma's perspective, and how does it come to be that we carry ancestral trauma?

HONEY: Ancestral trauma would imply that it is trauma that we've inherited from our ancestors, which would then be epigenetic inheritance, which we would carry in our bodies, nervous systems, and our neural pathways. So, effectively, whatever stage of life development and experience, healing, pleasure, and joy that the two individuals who conceived us had experienced until the time we were born would then be encoded into our DNA. Scientifically speaking, what becomes encoded – epigenetic memory that we just subconsciously act out on – is what was actually inherited by our parents at the time of their own conception. We are an egg in our mother's womb from the time of her conception, so at the time our mother is born, we're already in her body. We already exist. So then when we're born, we're born with all this subconscious code for how we experience the world around us. The child born before their parent became a graduate and the child born after their parent became a graduate is going to have a very different epigenetic inheritance for themselves and the children they will have.

VANGILE: This sounds like a very Westernised way of explaining ancestral trauma ...

HONEY: See, the thing is that every time somebody explains something with logic and patience, we attribute that to Western thinking. But, if you look at medical history, for instance, the Caesarean section is something that was developed in Africa out of pure need because Africans' precolonial diet meant that our babies were enormous. If you're delivering a baby that is anywhere up to 70 centimetres in height, that is not a baby that is going to be born vaginally. And it just makes sense that you're going to have to find a way to cut into the womb and restitch it because you're going to need the mother alive for this enormous child to have a better bearing on life and to breastfeed. That's your best bet for that child making it through their first five years in life. We weren't doing things based on the shape of a tail feather. We have ubungoma, ubunyanga, ubuthandazeli – all these things that are extremely scientific. We tend to misconstrue what we don't understand as unnecessarily mysterious. It is not mysterious.

It's just that we don't have the context for the knowledge. Ubunyanga is essentially astrology, African Astrology. Do you know ubuthandazeli? It goes with everything, from counselling right into emotional wellbeing and mental health – faith development as well as the development of emotional tools. Then ubungoma concerns governance and how we interact with each other as individuals: protocols of governance, personal governance, familial governance, governance of agency, personal agency, familial agency, democratic agency. These things are all governed within what we now term African spirituality. We've mysticised a way of being.

VANGILE: Why do you think, when we talk about ancestral trauma or ancestors, people expect to hear something mystical, especially when it encapsulates African healing?

HONEY: I think any time someone hears the term 'African', or 'ancestor' in the context of the African, we have that lens that I can only frame as the trend of those movies in the 1980s that were all about voodoo. It was people in white robes, in caves, thousands of candles and chanting, and it was made to look like this nonsensical thing. If you look at the movies or TV shows like *Shaka Zulu* and how those were framed, African sangomas were just doing weird things that had absolutely no frame of logic or reason. It was completely unhinged.

All this content has been created through the Western gaze and then superimposed on the Black spiritual experience as something that is real to us. It's got no context in the broader scope of what African spirituality stems from. If you think about the realities that science has trailed, what African spirituality has foretold for centuries … If you just look at the festival of the Dogon people, every 52-and-a-half years, during the Lionsgate, they celebrate

Sirius B as an origin planet for humanity on Earth. Science didn't discover Sirius B until 70 years ago. But these people have been doing this celebration for millennia.

The thing is that we [need to] preserve information, how we relay information, and how it has been possible for us to relay it for thousands of years ... the entire process and its reality exist for the preservation of knowledge and for it to be passed on. It is not that the dead do not want to rest; it is that the knowledge needs to be passed on. But because the knowledge keeps disappearing, they need to keep being invoked in order to reteach us this knowledge. Today we have different means. We now have ways of recording that, which we didn't have before. It can be argued that even this level of technology is not the first time that humanity reached this peak in our cycle of being on this earth as much as it is scientifically being recorded right now, that humanity is approaching extinction. In the next 300 years, it is very likely that if we don't change our patterns of being on this plane, we're going to 'extinct' ourselves. It's not going to be the first time that such a thing happens. But it's like we're going to keep repeating this thing of colonialism and having this Western gaze, the superior inferior inability to see humanity as a singular being. It's just when we talk about Western ancestors, when we talk about the ancestors of philosophy, astrology, and science, and what we read on the periodic table in that context, we see the ancestors as very different to how we read it when it is African and Black.

It comes down to one thing. If race is all that is affecting these perspectives, then it comes down to racism. Because how is it different for me to invoke an ancestor to ask them to give me knowledge? How is that different to when any other scholar interrogates Michelangelo's work to understand how he reached the conclusions he reached? You use the resources you have available to tap into that understanding.

VANGILE: So, when we invoke ancestors, we are actually just calling them. Would you say that this is just another form of record-keeping?

HONEY: It is absolutely a form of record-keeping, knowledge seeking. All the ancestors can do is guide us, inform us. The actions that we take in response to the information we're given are what make this such a powerful way of living – to live under the guidance of the ancestors. But if a person receives guidance from the ancestors and takes no action, then there is obviously no power in it.

VANGILE: You work with a lot of clients and some of them ask about their business success and how the ancestors and ancestral rituals/rites play a role in that.

HONEY: Look, when we talk about having relationships with the ancestors, or about things that come to us from the ancestors, think about it like a broken telephone. If there are things that were supposed to be done, rites of passage that were supposed to be performed for you during your upbringing but were not, then it can be that there are breaks in communication between yourself and your ancestors.

If you are looking at things like rites of declaration that were not performed with regards to your parents' union, then it can be an issue with the passing of a family member. These things can cause issues. Basically, anything that can cause a break in communication between yourself and your ancestors can be a hindrance to how you find yourself being able to perform in this world. And then also when you go further when pursuing something to bring about a certain outcome. Now, if you're going to invoke your ancestors and ask for their assistance with something, you're going to need to have someone in your bloodline who has possibly done the same thing before.

There are patterns that we could inherit, right? But now the thing is that there might be a pattern of behaviour that somebody started. This is what we call umkhokha. Somebody started the pattern of behaviour, perhaps of meditation, in the family, and then we all naturally adapt to it. Perhaps somebody started a detrimental pattern, and then we all adapt to it. We don't necessarily have to be beholden to that. We can change it. We have agency. When people say, 'Oh, they spend money recklessly because of the ancestors,' I have to disagree to some extent unless you're speaking in the context of an ancestral calling – and even then, just because you have an ancestral calling does not mean that you have a calling specifically related to an ancestor governing providence – that doesn't dictate that you would be reckless with your finances. It is absolutely not as black and white as that.

VANGILE: How have you seen family dynamics impact ancestral money trauma and, in turn, success in people's lives?

HONEY: So when certain rites aren't ratified by agreements, then you sit outside of those agreements and you can find yourself in a place of deep frustration when you're trying to bring certain things to fruition. And that's then when we say, you know what, people, izinhlanhla zabantu azifani – our luck is not the same. It's absolutely true. I have seen it with my own eyes.

When a person has been declared at the time of birth, it's been reported to the ancestors that you were born, this is who you are, and all those rites of passage are observed. And then the rites of passage when it comes to school-going age and graduation, for instance. When that person comes into my practice and their parents were married and have observed those ancestral rites, you cannot compare that person's good fortune and how easily they move through the world with someone who's born out of wedlock, and maybe third or fourth generation of people born out of wedlock – the two just do not compare. Honestly, so many people have come into my practice and said it just feels like the other shoe is supposed to drop at any moment in time. This is not the reality for people around me.

And it's like, well, you're comparing apples and oranges because you're coming from six, seven generations where we can actually record very clearly that marriage rites were performed. You've had every single rite of passage observed in your lifetime. And you're comparing what you view as a stroke of good luck that can break at any time with someone who comes from a long line of parents born out of wedlock.

People dealing with broken telephones have deeper challenges on their hands compared to you. That also then creates this other dynamic that people seldom understand because it then also plays out romantically. We understand that marriage – even before it is a romantic thing in the Western concept – is a business thing. It is the same, ancestrally in the African context. The ancestors will make agreements with regard to the marriage with other bloodlines because the unification of your bloodlines fortifies the mutual bloodlines and their coexistence in the long run.

Each and every ancestor has his or her own role to play in the afterlife. Now, when we're sitting here and seeking a wisdom that isn't in our direct line – maybe it wasn't your great, great-great-great grandfather who had it, but rather his fourth cousin, and now you're waiting for that fourth cousin to be the person who comes to bring that knowledge – it's going to be a little bit more challenging than the person who's a direct descendant of that fourth cousin. But you still have that same knowledge within the bloodline. But now, if you're looking at trying to reach that fourth cousin, and that fourth cousin was related to you by marriage, but it's not really marriage because that marriage was never ratified through the actual observation of the rites of marriage, then you're not going to be able to reach that ancestor. You're going to find yourself cut off at the knees. You're going to be frustrated because there isn't that agreement in place that should bind you to the person who bears that knowledge. So, when it comes to the ancestors, everything is governed by agreements and the rites that ratify those agreements.

Do you understand? It's political, it's spiritual, it's business –

but business that extends beyond this realm of existence. And it is no different from how you could look at it in arranged marriages in the East and how the royals would marry in the West. Because, at the end of the day, we are all looking for what will ensure our survival, for the longevity of our bloodline. And then that's where you can now see that, oh goodness, there are certain families where people get married somewhere between the ages of, say, 23 and 30. And maybe now it's sliding a bit later and, say, 27 and 35. But these people don't get divorced. That's it. And you look and it's generations of this – and it's that epigenetic inheritance. But it's also what we normalise by our lived experience. If I have lived seeing people go through different challenges within the context of marriage, if I've experienced a challenge in marriage, I'm more likely to overcome it.

It's the same in business and employment.

It's easy for a person who has seen people waking up every day to go to a job to experience that as how life in adulthood is. A person who hasn't experienced that – hasn't heard about a boss, or the rigours of being employed – is going to have a much harder time staying employed because they don't have a context or a template for how to deal with that reality.

A person who has seen the ups and downs of what entrepreneurship is like is going to find it very easy to absorb the shocks of entrepreneurship themselves if that's the path they choose.

So it's a combination of things. It's about that telephone being intact as well as what you've been exposed to. And, of course, when we speak about the ancestral, that doesn't just mean that the ancestors are dead. Your living ancestors count greatly as well. So what you've seen your parents and your grandparents go through is going to be what's also normalised to you.

VANGILE: Thank you so much for your time, Honey. This has been eye-opening, and I now understand why sangomas address family dynamics and ancestral rites when it comes to helping people clear money blocks. I can see how we, as African people, have been doing this work for millennia.

CHAPTER 4

The impact of oppression

It's impossible to have a proper or fruitful conversation about money, trauma or family dynamics without considering systems of oppression. We need to recognise how historical systems of oppression, such as sexism, slavery, colonisation and apartheid, have been designed to tear apart Black and indigenous families.

The legacies of slavery, colonisation and apartheid have left us with broken family structures and, as a result, some of us have grown up in single-parent households, which could potentially impact our financial literacy and ability to create generational wealth. It's crucial to acknowledge this reality and its impact on our lives, both communally and individually in the present moment.

As mentioned in the study by Xolile Antoni (2023), children from single-parent households in South Africa tend to have different financial behaviours than those from two-parent households, and that can't be ignored.

A study by Budlender & Lund (2011) looked at the impact of historical and present events on family structures in South Africa. The authors argue that the apartheid government engineered this broken family system, which has resulted in high rates of unemployment, an increase in HIV/Aids infections, poverty, inequality, and limited access to resources and opportunities.

They analysed data from the *Time Use Survey* of 2000 as well as household surveys to find that only a small percentage (35%) of children in South Africa live with both parents. They also looked at data from 1996 to 1999 and found that few women were married. This was done by reserving cities for white people while relying on poorly paid labour from African people who were only allowed to live in cities and towns on a migrant basis without their families. As a result, men had to leave their villages, wives and children to work in cities and only returned home for one week a year.

The authors argue that this created women-headed households, and men sometimes stopped sending money home to support their children, which led to women having to work as domestic workers, leaving most of the children in parentless households with only grandparents to look after them. This changed family dynamics, and also created a situation where women are the main breadwinners but not the key decision-makers in the family. All these factors have had a huge impact on wealth creation within Black families in South Africa.

Studies in the US have shown that slavery had a similar impact on African-American families. The breakdown of family units among people of African descent has spiritual ramifications, as explained in the interview with Honey.

The apartheid system contributed to a 'broken telephone' system between us and our ancestors, which also has financial ramifications since many of us cannot easily call on our ancestors to receive the knowledge and wisdom we need to succeed financially and emotionally. Racism is a significant part of the trauma that needs to be processed by people of colour (and even white people who have been the main benefactors of this system), and it is at the core of our money wounds.

It's important to acknowledge that our society is not always fair, and that systems that promote racism, sexism and ableism can make it difficult for certain individuals to achieve financial success. Unfortunately, this often leads to emotional trauma for many people from marginalised communities.

The effects of slavery, discrimination and displacement are still felt today, especially when it comes to how people approach money. These experiences have shaped people's beliefs and behaviours, which can lead to mental health issues and financial hardship. This is highlighted in a study by Adonis (2016) that delves into the impact of apartheid-era human-rights violations on subsequent generations. Adonis conducted interviews with 20 participants, who were either the children or grandchildren of victims of gross apartheid-era human-rights violations, in order to explore the extent to which they experienced intergenerational trauma as a result of their family experiences.

Adonis found that the trauma experienced by family members who were direct victims of human-rights violations during apartheid was passed down to following generations, affecting their mental health and wellbeing. Many of the interviewees experienced trauma symptoms such as anxiety, panic attacks and depression that stemmed from observing and watching their grandparents and parents' pain and suffering.

Many of the participants also believed that apartheid had had a financial and material impact on them and their families' ability to survive because many of the breadwinners had been killed during apartheid. Some participants also experienced a constant sense of powerlessness and helplessness that stemmed from their inability to deal with the traumatic and financial impacts apartheid had had on their families. The study thus argued that the passing down of trauma from one generation to the next is an inherent psychological consequence when one group intentionally hurts or oppresses another.

Looking at the study by Adonis, we can see that experiences of discrimination, oppression or displacement can and do affect an individual's mental health and sense of power. Racial trauma also affects how we interact with money because it affects how we see ourselves in this world and can lead to lower self-esteem (Williams et al., 2021).

When a person's self-esteem is impacted, the way they show up in the world is affected, which affects their ability to negotiate salaries and/or price their products and services, which decreases their income and wealth (Makwakwa, 2013).

In essence, constantly dealing with stressors like racism and microaggressions (in other words, subtle racism or racist undertones) can overload the body, making it tough for the nervous system to handle these situations. This is called allostatic load and refers to how the body responds to stress. Sadly, the effects of colonisation, apartheid, racism and slavery have had a huge impact on the allostatic load of Black people, affecting their health, nervous system and finances. Experiencing daily microaggressions and overt racism only adds to this load, making it even more challenging for our nervous systems to function properly. In fact, Weinreb (2019) argues that trauma-exposed Black people have a higher risk of developing trauma-related symptoms than other racial groups.

Racism is a constant presence in our lives, which means that we are always on edge and activating our nervous systems, which takes a toll on our physical health. This constant activation can be exhausting and makes it difficult to process other life events. As a Black person, feeling constantly exhausted is thus common. It's not as simple as just relaxing and manifesting things, as so many people suggest. We don't always have the privilege to sit back and unwind because we are often in situations where we need to be on high alert, dysregulating our nervous systems almost all the time. This alertness may well have been learnt from our ancestors (who were also always on alert) and passed down through generations.

Research by Geronimus et al. (2006) found that Black women bear a large burden of allostatic load, even when compared to Black men and white women. This is worse when Black women have minimal or no financial resources.

A higher allostatic load caused by experiences of racism can lead to various health issues, mental health problems, and accelerated cellular ageing, which all affect the quality of our relationships (Lewis & Van Dyke, 2018). As a result, racism has an impact on the way we interact with our family members, creating complex family dynamics and contributing to family trauma and financial challenges, which is why I strongly believe that trauma and money work should include a decolonisation approach.

Just like systemic racism, systemic sexism also exists and it's important to understand how these two systems intersect and perpetuate trauma in different ways. Systemic sexism is a gender-based discrimination that is deeply ingrained in society's structures, leading to unfair treatment of people based on their gender.

According to the World Economic Forum's *Global Gender Gap Report 2022*, it will take another 132 years to close the global gender gap if we continue at the current rate. Moreover, gender inequality, especially in the workplace, is at a high risk of worsening. This report highlights that societal expectations, family demands, employer policies, and geopolitical conflicts affect women differently, resulting in women earning less money and accumulating less wealth than men globally. The report also suggests that women across the world reported 4% higher stress level than men, leading to greater emotional and mental disorders that affect women's wellbeing.

The National Business Initiative (NBI), in collaboration with the Southern Centre for Inequality Studies (SCIS) at the University of the Witwatersrand (Wits), conducted a study in 2021 that revealed that women in South Africa earn R72.44 for every R100 men earn for the same amount of work, despite the fact that 42.6% of households in the country are headed by women. The study also disclosed that white men are the highest earners and that men, regardless of race, make up most of the employees at all levels in companies in

South Africa. The report also stated that the majority of low-level employees are Black and female, while top management is white and male.

Women are often overworked and underpaid due to 'invisible labour' and what is termed the 'second shift'. Invisible labour refers to the work women do at home, such as cooking, cleaning and childcare, which is essential but undervalued and ignored. The *Global Gender Gap Report 2022* looked at data from 33 countries worldwide, representing over half of all working-age individuals, and found that men only spend 19% of their total work time on unpaid work like childcare, housework and caregiving, while women spend a much higher proportion of their work time (a total of 55%) on unpaid work. This inequality limits women's ability to pursue career and leadership opportunities. And, with the cost of childcare on the rise, there's a danger that women will continue to be expected to do more of this unpaid work than men.

The 'second shift' refers to the extra work women do, such as taking care of kids and running errands, after they knock off from their paid jobs because many women are still expected to take on most of the responsibility around the home (which is invisible labour). This can be stressful and makes it hard for women to succeed in their careers because it creates additional demands on their time and energy outside the workplace. As with invisible labour, this additional workload also restricts most women's ability to pursue opportunities, thus limiting their earning potential and ability to create wealth.

Bleiweis et al. (2021) looked at pay disparity in the US and found that Black women lose an estimated $964,400 to the wage gap over a 40-year career, Native American women lose $986,240, and Hispanic women lose $1,163,920. Black women face discrimination based on their race and gender, making it difficult for them to succeed in their careers and earn a fair wage. This perpetuates financial instability in Black households, leading to stress and tension within families, increasing the likelihood of conflict and arguments, as well as feelings of anxiety and depression, which affects trust and communication between family members, leading to further intergenerational trauma.

Furthermore, being consistently underpaid for work can create feelings of frustration, resentment and disillusionment, which can negatively impact a person's motivation and confidence in their abilities. This makes it even harder to negotiate for better pay or pursue higher-paying job opportunities in the long run.

In addition, the experience of being undervalued and underpaid can create a sense of inferiority and usher in the imposter syndrome (I call this the not-good-enough wound), which can impact the message passed on from one generation to the next, affecting the next generation's relationship with money and the money profiles they adopt.

Reading all this, one may wonder, so what's the point of addressing money trauma when we have to continue dealing with systems of oppression? The reality is that these oppressive systems have deeply impacted our overall health, emotional wellbeing, family dynamics and identity.

Healthy family dynamics are important for financial success because they tend to provide a supportive environment that fosters positive beliefs and attitudes towards money. When family members communicate effectively and support each other, it can lead to greater financial stability and success.

Racism has also affected our nervous systems and our ability to handle stressful situations, particularly financial stress. This, too, has been passed down through generations and continues to affect us today. The way we view wealth and money has been shaped by these systems, leading us to embody money archetypes/profiles in order to survive.

Unfortunately, we were born into a world of structural inequalities, but it is up to us to do the inner work to heal ourselves, our families, and our communities. By doing so, we can break the cycle of trauma and create positive change for future generations.

As the saying goes, 'It ran in the family, until it ran into me.'

Linking financial success to positive thinking

It is crucial to understand how the popular 'New Age' language around money, frequency, positive thinking, 'high vibe' and manifestation can unconsciously perpetuate systems of oppression and trigger feelings of inadequacy in marginalised groups. It's thus important to be mindful of these issues and strive towards creating safe and inclusive spaces for healing and growth.

In the world of personal development, you often hear people talking about the importance of raising your frequency or being in a high vibe state in order to attract money and success. This belief can, however, be problematic and even harmful because it assumes that only people with high frequencies can attract wealth. This can create a false sense of hierarchy and promote the idea that those who struggle financially are not on a high-enough frequency.

The idea that having a high frequency or being 'high vibe' is the key to accumulating wealth is not only flawed, but also dangerous. It creates a belief that wealthy individuals have achieved a certain level of consciousness or spirituality, making it difficult to hold them accountable for their actions. And yet history shows us that many wealthy individuals and countries have done terrible things, responsible for any number of atrocities, including colonisation, oppression and dictatorships. To reduce money to a purely spiritual concept is dangerous and perpetuates the idea that those who are poor are not spiritually advanced enough or don't have the right mindset. While mindset is indeed important when it comes to wealth building, it's not the only factor and we should never equate money with spiritual enlightenment. How can someone living in abject poverty be expected to constantly think positively and ignore the systemic inequalities and racism they face every day, just to achieve a so-called 'high-vibrational' state or develop the right mindset for financial success?

The truth is that there are people who are poor and conscious with an incredible outlook on life, just as there are wealthy individuals who are unconscious and wealthy with a tainted outlook on life, and vice versa. Wealth does not equate to spirituality, just as poverty does not negate it.

Money cannot be used as a measure of our worthiness or how much the universe loves us. It's also not an indication of how well we are able to use the law of attraction, because there are other universal laws that come into play, as well as many factors that can contribute to our financial success or lack thereof.

For example, karma may play a role in our financial situation, and we could be reaping the benefits of good karma or paying off debts from past lives. Additionally, our privilege and access to resources can give us a significant advantage when it comes to building wealth. It's worth acknowledging that many of those who teach or equate wealth with being 'high vibe' are usually individuals in so-called developed countries with access to more opportunities and resources than others.

No matter how much good karma we invite or how many opportunities come our way, dealing with intense trauma, crippling anxiety, fears of rejection and/or systemic oppression can hinder us from taking advantage of those opportunities.

Financial success is influenced by a complex interplay of factors, including, but not limited to: inherited wealth, white privilege, institutional racism, patriarchy, classism and class mobility, the country of our birth, our social status during our upbringing, our religious upbringing, access to basic resources like education, social networks (often determined by class), an ancestral history of colonisation, an ancestral history of slavery, and ancestral history of apartheid, for example. All these factors make it harder for most of us to make money and/or save money. The influencing factors listed above are not excuses – many behavioural economists have proven that these structural impediments affect our finances. Hahn & Simms (2021), for instance, argue that poverty results from structural barriers, not individual choices, so it's important to acknowledge the challenges of dealing with oppressive systems while managing our personal finances.

Systemic oppression and systemic poverty are interlinked and often reinforce each other. Systemic oppression refers to the ways in which systems and institutions (such as the government, and the education and financial systems) maintain discrimination and inequality based on race, gender, class and other social identities. This can lead to systemic poverty, where individuals and communities face ongoing obstacles or barriers to accessing resources and opportunities, such as education, employment and financial stability.

For example, if a certain racial group is historically excluded from quality education (which was the case with Black South Africans during apartheid and African-Americans during the Jim Crow era), they and their descendants may not have the same job opportunities and access to higher-paying careers as those who have received a better education. This can lead to systemic poverty for that group. Additionally, discriminatory lending practices (again, common during apartheid and Jim Crow) that prevent people from accessing loans and other resources also contribute to systemic poverty for generations to come.

Systemic poverty can be near impossible to break free of and can change not just the make-up of our brain, but also the way people behave with money, because people living in poverty face unique challenges and may not have access to the same resources as others.

A study by Natalie Holz et al. (2015) found that poverty trauma can have a negative impact on children's brain development. This is because poverty is a traumatic experience and the brain registers it as such, leading to different ways of processing information.

Moeini-Jazani et al. (2019) found that, due to limited options and immediate needs, individuals in poverty may prioritise short-term needs over long-term planning. This can lead to decisions that result in more debt, fewer savings, and unhealthy habits. The study explains that the reason behind poor people's tendency to make short-term financial decisions is not because of any inherent flaw in their character or intelligence, but rather because they often face significant financial stress and have limited resources to work with. This stress can make it difficult for them to focus on long-term goals and can impact their sense of personal power and self-worth. As a result, they may feel that they are unable to overcome challenges and achieve their desired outcomes. It's thus important that we acknowledge and address systemic factors that contribute to financial stress and inequality, rather than blaming individuals for the challenges they face.

Linking Black Tax, ancestral trauma and oppression

Trauma and systemic oppression are deeply intertwined, and it's impossible to discuss one without the other. When we examine the ways in which these forces intersect, we begin to understand how they can impact family dynamics within Black communities, ultimately resulting in the concept of Black Tax.

Our financial behaviour and attitudes are influenced by our cultural and familial values, our experiences when it comes to systemic barriers, and our desire to support and uplift our loved ones. Black Tax refers to the financial burden Black families bear due to systemic oppression, colonisation, apartheid and racial inequality. It's a term that describes the additional financial responsibilities that Black families are expected to shoulder, which are often beyond what's expected of other groups.

These responsibilities include supporting members of the extended family, paying for further education or training, and dealing with the negative impacts of institutionalised racism and discrimination. This can put a significant strain on Black families' finances and can make it almost impossible to build wealth, especially when a single person is responsible for most of the expenses.

A study by Mangoma & Wilson-Prangley (2019) explores the concept of Black Tax and its impact on the emerging Black middle class in South Africa, defining Black Tax as the financial obligations that Black professionals and entrepreneurs have towards their families and communities that go beyond their personal needs and wants. (Although, of course, Black Tax impacts many more individuals than the study's definition of 'Black professionals and entrepreneurs' suggests.) The study focused on understanding the financial 'transfers' (obligations) of the emerging Black middle class. The researchers used a combination of six semi-structured interviews and a questionnaire with 23 questions, which they shared with a network of emerging Black middle-class friends and colleagues via social media platforms such as Facebook and Twitter. The study received 118 usable responses, with coloured, Indian, and white respondents being excluded.

The data analysis revealed that 75% of the participants sent money home monthly, 5% sent money weekly, and 5% sent money quarterly. The recipients of those funds used the money for education, funerals and general living expenses, and many of the responders indicated that they felt the recipients expected more than what was sent.

The participants felt either privileged or obligated to help, and while 71% believed that financially supporting their relatives delayed their own financial success, 60% still felt happy to help because it strengthened their relationships with family members. The study also found that Black Tax is shaped by culture and tradition, and the transfers are relational, material and emotional. Different people respond to requests and interpret financial obligations differently, and individuals are constantly trying to balance individualism and collectivism at a family level.

The impact of oppression

Black Tax has a rich history rooted in compassion, love, and wisdom on how to get out of poverty. It's important to understand that it wasn't always referred to as 'tax', and is not unique to African people – it is also practised in Asia and other collective cultures.

The concept is simple yet effective: families prioritise the education of the most talented or eldest child in the family to secure a better-paying job and so elevate the family's income. The family will often make sacrifices to ensure the education of that child, and when they graduate and start earning an income, they will help educate the next sibling or cousin. The cycle continues until everyone in the family has received an education and has moved into a higher income bracket, building a strong support system in the process.

This practice highlights the importance of giving and paying it forward within our communities, and how it can have a powerful impact. Unfortunately, there are some who have forgotten the original intent, and siblings who were meant to be allies in building and elevating the family have checked out. It's, however, essential to recognise and honour the history and original intent behind Black Tax in order to continue building strong and supportive families and communities.

In some cases, Black Tax can result in one highly educated family member carrying most of the financial responsibility, which can cause resentment and ultimately lead to broken families. Unfortunately, this is something I can relate to from personal experience.

On my mother's side, our family was torn apart because of the burden of Black Tax. My mother was left to take care of not only her own children, but also her sister's children, her siblings and her mother. She felt used and unappreciated, leading to feelings of resentment and envy within the family. Eventually, my mother had to separate from her family, and it was only recently, after 17 years, that I reconnected with some of my maternal family. I was shocked to find out that my cousins had children I had never even met.

One of the reasons why Black Tax can cause resentment in

today's world is because the dynamics of family financial responsibilities have shifted due to globalisation and economic changes. Unlike in the past, earning a degree does not guarantee a good job or a decent income. The cost of living has risen sharply across the world, making it even harder for young graduates to support themselves, let alone their extended families.

This pressure and financial strain can lead to feeling overwhelmed and detached from family members who were once seen as a safety net. Many young graduates may even distance themselves from their families in an attempt to avoid the burden of financial obligations, leaving the most successful family member to shoulder the responsibility alone.

As Black people, our relationship with money is shaped by a number of factors, including Black Tax and systemic oppression. These factors have a significant impact on the money profiles and archetypes we adopt. The financial values we carry can be overwhelming, but they can also be an opportunity for us to examine and redefine our relationship with money and how we use it to support ourselves and our communities.

CHAPTER 5

Understanding our parental wounds

When I was 13, my mom's fancy car got repossessed, and it came as a huge shock to me. I had always believed that my family was financially stable and that we could afford anything we wanted. But seeing the car being driven away made me realise that we weren't as well off as I had thought.

This was the first time that I became aware of the value of money and how it could run out. It was a traumatic experience for me, and I couldn't help but feel helpless and lost. The trauma of watching my mom lose her car has stayed with me and has influenced the way I buy cars.

The second time I realised we were struggling financially was when my mom's old van broke down on the way to school. I could sense the anxiety in my mom's voice as she tried to flag down passing cars for help so she could get me to school on time. It was a scary experience, and I couldn't help but feel that we were completely alone in the world, when it came to our financial issues. My mom had moved us to Johannesburg to give us a better education, but in that moment it felt like we were more isolated than ever.

I remember making a promise to myself never to abandon my

mom to her pain and to help her shoulder her burden by never making her feel alone or that she had suffered needlessly. Subconsciously, I made the decision to protect my mother by making sure she never doubted her financial decisions as a parent. I reasoned that if she saw me struggling in adulthood, then she would know that other people struggled too, no matter how much they'd been given.

I learnt to stop asking for anything or even talking about money because I didn't want to stress my mother any further. I also decided not to trust money because it always seemed to run out when we needed it most.

These experiences had a profound impact on my relationship with money. As an adult, I found myself constantly spending money as soon as I earned it because I needed to reject it in order to keep my loyalty to my mother alive. I couldn't trust money, so I never felt I had enough of it. I listened to affirmations about having more money in my sleep, but it only made me panic and feel half-crazed.

Part of me also felt like becoming financially free was a betrayal to my mother. She had struggled so much, and I felt as though my success would invalidate the struggles we had shared. It just felt wrong to be doing well when she had suffered so much.

I couldn't earn money in my business, I couldn't get a proper job that paid me a good salary, and I couldn't save. When I started integrating these memories and healing the versions of me still stuck in that trauma I was able to start healing my relationship with money and start saving, investing and making money.

In the process of my healing journey, I started to understand that the way our parents raise us and the kind of people they are was influenced enormously by how they were raised by their own parents or caregivers, who in turn were influenced by their parents or grandparents, which has a profound impact on our behaviour as children. This, in turn, affects how we relate to money, our family, ourselves, our children and our romantic partners. It can also result in the development of mother and father wounds, which can have lasting effects on our emotional wellbeing and relationships.

The mother wound

Gaba (2019) describes the mother wound as a loss or lack of mothering passed down through generations in mother-daughter or mother-son relationships and shows up in our parenting styles.

According to Gaba, some signs of the mother wound include: not feeling like you have your mother's approval or acceptance, never feeling loved, difficulties in connecting with your mother, uncertainty about your relationship with your mom, trying to be perfect in order to get your mother's love, and feeling like you have to protect and care for her, instead of her protecting and caring for you.

I define the mother wound as the emotional pain and psychological trauma a person experiences as a result of their relationship with their mother. It's not about blaming or shaming our mothers, but rather understanding how our mothers' own wounds, patterns and conditioning can impact us deeply. This, in turn, can lead to four different scenarios:

First, we may become adults in childhood, taking on a lot of responsibility at a young age, which can cause deep resentment towards our mothers. This resentment can show up in our lives as anger, depression, or sadness, and can also impact our finances.

Second, we may feel like we are not good enough, unlovable, and unworthy of love. Since we didn't receive the love we needed as children, we may have weak boundaries and give too much of ourselves to others. This can result in us not feeling worthy of actually being paid (quite literally) or feeling invisible.

Third, we may rebel against our mothers by checking out of the family and relationship dynamic or becoming the opposite of our mothers in every way. This can be detrimental because our mothers may have qualities that can serve us in our lives, and by rebelling, we may miss out on embracing these qualities.

Fourth, we may struggle with finding our own sense of self and power by remaining connected to our mothers' wounds. We may fear what could happen if we dream bigger or achieve more than our mothers, and this can lead to guilt, self-sabotage, and doubt about our future.

It's important to recognise these patterns and work through them in order to heal the mother wound and create a healthier relationship with ourselves and our mothers.

My relationship with my mother has always been complex, and it wasn't until I reached my thirties that things started to improve. It was only when I travelled to India to complete my tantra yoga teacher training that I finally started to understand how my mother's relationship with her own mother (my grandmother) had influenced her parenting style and how that had affected our own relationship. And how my grandmother's relationship with her mother (my great-grandmother) had impacted how she parented my mother, and so on. It was like a chain reaction that stretched back generations.

When I began to delve into the importance of the mother wound and how it is passed down from generation to generation, I learnt that the mother-daughter dynamic was influenced by the environment in which I and all the women who came before me were raised and how that influenced our relationship with our bodies, our wombs and, ultimately, money. It was a revelation to see how everything was interconnected, an understanding that gave me a new perspective on my own life and relationships.

Interestingly, as I began to focus on developing my work around trauma and focused on going into my body during my tantra yoga training, I experienced a strange and powerful sensation in my womb and would sometimes fall asleep in between sequences so my body could process the sensations.

After a few weeks, I received guidance to record a series of meditations that would make it easier for me to connect to my body and my womb and understand the ancestral memories I was carrying in my body. Whenever I tried to release memories related to money that were stuck in my body, I would suddenly feel intense pain in my womb and ovaries. At the same time, memories that seemed to be tied to that pain would come flooding back.

These, however, weren't my own memories, and they didn't feel like past-life memories either. Instead, what I felt was an intense fear and sense that, as a woman, it was not safe to have money or be powerful. In fact, the fear was so great that I panicked at the very thought of having money and attracting unwanted attention from men – a feeling of 'unsafety' that had been passed down to me from generations of women who came before me.

I realised that this fear of visibility and safety had a direct correlation to our finances and survival. Back in the day, our foremothers worried about what others would say or think about them, which in turn affected the men they could attract and marry, and thus their very financial survival. It also wasn't safe for Black people (and other people of colour) to be seen enjoying their wealth and living in joy by white people, because if they were seen, white people may have taken what they had or even harmed them. An example of this can be seen in the history of Sophiatown in the 1950s and District Six in 1966 during apartheid in South Africa. During those times, the police forcibly removed Black and Brown people who were living in community with white people and relocated them to remote and underdeveloped areas, without any compensation for their homes (Davids, 2018). Sadly, these incidents are not unique to South Africa. In the US there are the infamous Tulsa race riots of 1921, where a thriving African American community known as 'Black Wall Street' in Tulsa, Oklahoma was completely destroyed on 1 June 1921 (Madigan, 2021). According to Madigan, 'Estimates of losses in property and personal assets, by today's standards, range from $20 million to more than $200 million.' None of the victims received any compensation from the city or insurance companies. The impact of this massacre has been felt for generations, leaving lasting trauma among Black families, and the true history of the event was suppressed for many years. It's evident that based on these historical events, it hasn't always been safe for Black people to be noticed or seen by white people.

In these meditations, I felt and saw how my women ancestors learnt to survive by making themselves invisible, shrinking themselves and putting their needs last (in their families and communities) just to stay safe. This is something that was passed down from generation to generation, and unfortunately, their daughters were taught to do the same.

I realised that I had unknowingly picked up the survival tactic of being invisible from the women in my family – a way for them to protect themselves in a world where they were not always safe. However, this behaviour was negatively impacting my finances because it prevented me from seeing myself (making me invisible to myself) and communicating the value of my work to others. As a result, I found it challenging to price my products and services fairly, which in turn affected my income and ability to build wealth.

As I explored the parenting styles and what had been taught to my mother and then subsequently to me and my sister, I began to understand how this cycle continued. And I realised that to heal and break this cycle, I needed to go back and explore where the women in my family had started giving up their power and shrinking within themselves to remain safe.

This required me to connect with them and enquire about their pain and talk to the one or many who had started it all, so that they could heal and, in turn, heal the bloodline. I used the meditations that were channelled to me to work on asking each woman to mother herself so that she could heal herself and not rely on her daughters to do that for her.

Through this work, I gained a better understanding of my mother and her struggles and was able to let go of my loyalty to her and release the feeling of betrayal so that I could live my own life and break the cycle of fear and invisibility.

During this time, I began to share the multitude of meditations I had created and recorded, over 100 in total, in my online academy with my clients and have had the privilege to witness how many of them have transformed their relationship with their mothers and their money by connecting with and healing their female lineage.

Ask yourself ...

Before you move on to the next section, I invite you to take some time to reflect on these questions:

1. What role have you taken on in your relationship with your mother? Have you been the caretaker, the mediator, the rebellious child, or something else?
2. How do you think stepping out of this role might shift the power dynamics in your relationship with your mother? Are you willing to take that risk?
3. How do you believe earning more money could impact the power dynamics in your relationship with your mother? Are you willing to explore this possibility?
4. How does playing small help you empower your mother in your relationship? Is that something you want to continue, or do you want to shift the balance of power?
5. How might expanding and living your dreams affect your relationship with your mother? Are you willing to take that risk?
6. How might expanding and living your dreams fully impact your mother as an individual, beyond just the relationship between the two of you?
7. How is playing small and the current relationship you have with money keeping you close to your mother? Is that a

healthy dynamic for you, or is it holding you back?
8. How are you remaining loyal to your mother's sacrifices, pain and struggles? How is your inner child remaining loyal? Are there ways in which this loyalty is no longer serving you and, if so, how can you begin to release it?

The father wound

Interestingly, there are quite a few studies on absent fathers, but not many that define the father wound (a Google search for *father wound* leads you to religion and God) – unlike the extensive research defining and unpacking the mother wound.

A study by Salami & Okeke (2018) looked at how growing up without a father in South Africa can affect a child's development, especially in terms of their social and economic situation. The researchers randomly chose 300 Education students from the School of General and Continuing Education (SGCE) at the University of Fort Hare in East London and conducted an observation on them. They noted two important issues related to fatherhood in South Africa from previous research: the problem of absent fathers and the issue of fathers' involvement in their children's lives.

They explained that just because a father is not present in the home doesn't mean they are not involved in their children's social and educational development. Similarly, a father's presence in the home doesn't guarantee the holistic development of the children.

The researchers found that children who grow up without fathers are more likely to face developmental challenges such as lower self-esteem, poorer academic performance and behavioural problems. They also found that the economic and social status of the child's family played a role in how the absence of the father affected them. Looking at Salami & Okeke's findings, it becomes clear that a father's absence impacts children's educational levels and sense of self, which then impacts finances and financial behaviour in the long term.

The role of the father has changed with every step of our evolution, and in recent times, the role of the father has been considered one of protector and provider (Kraemer, 1991). As a result, when the father is emotionally and/or physically absent, the family unit is left without a protector, and our inner child can feel unprotected, unsafe and impoverished. This can lead to us feeling anxious about physical safety and money as adults. This can affect our grounding, as the widely accepted role of a father is to protect and provide. In women, the father wound may impact the masculine aspects of our lives, such as feeling protected in our finances and our relationships with men. Our relationship with money – including how we receive, ask for, and relate to it – is thus often influenced by our father wound.

Jed Diamond, writing for *The Good Men Project* (2017), outlines several ways in which a broken relationship with our fathers can have a negative impact on women.

Firstly, if we didn't receive the love and affection we need from our fathers, we may try to find it elsewhere, seeking love and validation from men throughout our lives. This can lead to us constantly striving for male approval, even if it means upholding the patriarchy or engaging in behaviours that don't align with our values. Ultimately, this stems from mistaking approval for love.

Secondly, if our fathers hurt us, we may develop a filter through which we see all men, causing us to feel anger towards them and blame them. This can be detrimental to our relationships with other men and prevent us from forming meaningful connections.

Thirdly, if our fathers left us when we were young, we may develop a deep fear of abandonment. This fear can manifest in one of two ways: either we close ourselves off from the world to protect ourselves from being hurt again, or we become clingy, going to great lengths to please those around us in the hope they'll never leave us.

Lastly, those who carry a father wound may be attracted to partners who also have father wounds. Like attracts like and, without realising it, we may be drawn to people who have similar unresolved issues.

In my opinion, the father wound, or absent father, would impact a Black man's relationship with money in the following ways:

- **Overspending or underspending:** If a boy grew up in a household with financial instability or received no financial guidance from someone who looks like him, he may develop unhealthy spending habits as an adult. For example, he may overspend in order to compensate for a sense of lack that stems from not having a father figure, especially in a world that teaches Black men that they are less than their white counterparts, or they may underspend out of fear of never having enough.
- **Lack of financial knowledge:** Without a father figure to teach them about finances, boys may lack basic financial knowledge and struggle with financial literacy as adults. This can result in difficulty managing their finances, making sound investments, or saving for the future.
- **Issues with defining masculinity:** Some boys may associate financial success with masculinity and, without a father figure, they may struggle to understand what it means to be a successful Black man. This can lead to a distorted relationship with money, in which financial success becomes a measure of self-worth.
- **Impulsive decisions:** Boys who grew up without a father figure to teach them how to move through this world as men, especially in a racist patriarchal system, may have difficulty regulating their emotions and making sound decisions. This can lead to impulsive financial decisions, such as taking out loans or making risky investments without fully considering the consequences.

Growing up without a father figure can thus have a profound impact on a boy's relationship with money, and it may require a conscious effort to overcome these challenges and establish healthy financial habits. For some children (boys and girls), growing up with a single mother means taking on the father role and learning to rely solely on themselves for protection and financial stability. They become their own father figure and often assume responsibilities typically reserved for fathers in the household, like co-parenting their siblings and sharing their mother's emotional burdens. They may become their mother's sidekick and feel obliged to start managing the household expenses or earning money to supplement the mother's income. In this case, their relationship with money is deeply tied to their mothers, and their dreams intricately linked to them too. They learn to be independent and strong, but have a tough time asking for Divine (spiritual being that you deem as sacred, transcendent, or exceptionally extraordinary) support and trusting that things will work out and they have the power to change things. There is also a fear of allowing money in if the source of that money is unknown and beyond their control, leading to subconscious blocking of money.

From all of this, it is clear then that our mother and father wounds impact our family dynamics, our sense of self and the money profiles we adopt with our families.

CHAPTER 6

Understanding money archetypes

Archetypes are universal symbols that exist in our collective conscious and unconscious. They are often reflected or embodied in our stories and characters. The mother is, for example, an archetype. If you mention the term 'mother' anywhere in the world, people tend to have the same image of the mother as nurturing, compassionate, sweet and loving. Money archetypes are much the same: universal themes relating to money, wealth and finances – think of the spendthrift or miser archetypes, often depicted in caricatures like Scrooge McDuck.

Archetypes (or profiles) may be shaped by experiences and attitudes, and are not fixed in stone; they can evolve and change over time in response to cultural and historical influences. Cultural experiences can shape archetypes and the way individuals respond to these archetypes. The wife, for example, is an archetype, but the way a wife is portrayed differs across cultures, centuries and decades.

A study by Pong (2022) argues that people's attitudes towards money differ according to culture, age, gender, religion, ethnicity, nationality, education level, income and past experience; these money attitudes then affect self-image, happiness and mental health.

Given this study and others like it, it makes sense that Black people would have different money archetypes, based on their family dynamics and their lived experiences. This book explores money archetypes within Black families, which evolve in response to trauma experienced within a family and outside a family.

Different personalities respond to traumatic events differently. Weinberg et al. (2021) conducted a study of 249 individuals with different personality traits to see how different personalities respond to traumatic exposure and found that personality traits affect how people respond to trauma and stress. Another study by Preedy (2015) suggests that personality traits may even influence the amount of coffee consumed. The study argues that it's possible that what we consume helps shape our personalities. For example, one theory indicates that when regularly consumed, coffee can change personality traits related to psychiatric disorders and affect the central nervous system.

So, if food can affect our personality, why can't money do the same? And if our personalities affect the food we eat and drink, why can't our personalities affect the way we relate to money?

My theory is that children (who eventually become adults) are born with certain traits and into families with a specific role. Their personality profiles will impact the archetypes they adopt, which will then impact their behavioural patterns and core trauma responses (fight, flight, freeze, fawn, or force), which will then impact their relationship with money if these behavioural patterns and trauma responses are left unchecked.

Based on this theory and the work I have done over the years, I've come up with a list of archetypes and the role each plays in the family. I have explored how these profiles behave when they are in their 'shadow' state and triggered, as well as when they are reacting from their 'golden' state and have integrated their trauma. I must note here that my focus has been predominantly on families of colour, so I have limited my analysis to the context of Black people. I also need to state up front that these money archetypes are not the original archetypes of Black people and have evolved out of the need for us to survive the trauma of capitalism, systemic oppression and violence that have seeped into our family lives.

These archetypes are also not set in stone and we can move between archetypes; we may have a predominant Primary archetype and a Secondary archetype and, as we start to heal, we edge towards our Golden archetypes or move between our Golden and Shadow archetypes.

Here's a quick overview of the archetypes we explore in more detail in the upcoming chapters. In order to provide a real-life case study for each profile, I conducted real-life interviews with 10 individuals, all of whom (except for that of the Sweet One) were clients I have worked with over the years. I've taken steps to protect the privacy of everyone I interviewed, and have thus changed their names to keep them anonymous.

I reached out to each person individually, told them about the book and asked permission to use their story as a case study, sharing with them a concise summary of the Shadow archetypes. Additionally, I provided a four-page summary of the Golden archetypes and informed them of my analysis of their individual profiles based on our previous coaching work we had done together. I asked them to read through the summaries and provide feedback on whether they agreed with my assessments. I then conducted in-depth interviews with each of them and transcribed the interviews into case studies; I have made sure to keep their responses as true to their own words and expressions as possible. This allows their personal stories to shine through, making them more powerful than anything I could have written myself.

1. The Sweet One

The Sweet One will fawn (flatter) and pretend everything is good. They will shut down and numb themselves because their nervous system is too overwhelmed to process what's happening around them, so they respond by fawning.

Children tend to co-regulate according to the nervous system of their caregiver and simply do not have the tools to process continuous trauma. If the caregiver's nervous system is dysregulated that will completely dysregulate the child's nervous system as well. Dysregulation sometimes looks sweet and pleasing, but because they are numb, disconnected from their bodies, and are not able to come to terms with their feelings, it appears that the child never gets angry. If they are not able to break this pattern, they can become adults who people please, are scared to rock the boat and struggle to set boundaries.

2. The Destroyer

The Destroyer acts out the family trauma in living colour. They tend to become the external embodiment of the family's trauma by mirroring the family's dirty laundry, responding to whatever is happening by going into fight mode.

I was this child: foul-mouthed, angry, rude, depressed and in pain. Ironically, sometimes the most sensitive children are Destroyers, burning down entire villages in anger or grinding the family to a standstill with their grief and sadness. They are here to get us to pay attention to the things we want to hide and, as a result, as adults, they are often misunderstood, considered uncaring and rude, and can become the black sheep of the family.

3. The RunAway

RunAways leave home and never look back. Broadly speaking, these children check out, daydream, live in a fantasy world, party, hang out with friends, experiment with drugs and have sex at an early age, for instance. Their core trauma response is flight.

Sometimes, they will run from their feelings and being in their own bodies, so it's not a simple matter of leaving a literal environment; it's about running away from situations or themselves. This is termed avoidant behaviour.

These kids are even more sensitive than the Destroyers; they feel too much and too deeply and are often overly emotional, so they have to escape their bodies in order to survive all that they are feeling. If they don't break this pattern, they can become adults who self-medicate, feel unrooted, believe in magical thinking (in other words, fixating on fantasy rather than reality) or completely disconnect from the family. They may also have a hard time committing to projects and relationships and quit when the going gets tough.

4. The Fixer

Fixers need to fix everyone and keep everything together. These children do everything exactly right so as to keep the family from falling apart. They even parent their parents and their siblings. These are the model kids, and although they have elements of people pleasing, they are driven by the need to stay in control and be mini adults (the need for control may be referred to as the 'force response').

They often felt powerless as kids and so learnt to take back their power by controlling everything, sacrificing their childhood to become 'adults'. If they are not able to break this pattern, they can become adults obsessed with being perfect, scared of failure, driven by a need to fix/save others or situations, and have a hard time surrendering and trusting the process. They can sometimes come across as overbearing and rigid.

5. The Eternal Child

The Eternal Child is stuck in their childhood or teens. This is the child who never grows up, one who is always financially supported and looked after by everyone else, especially parents. In men, it has often been called the Peter Pan syndrome – the boy who never grows up.

These are the adults who are held captive by their childhood or teen trauma, so their core trauma response is to freeze. If they don't break this pattern, they can become adults who have a hard time taking responsibility for their actions, their lives and their finances.

Shaping family dynamics and our relationship with money

In a family, it's important to understand each person's money profile and their strengths and weaknesses. Not everyone is meant to be a breadwinner or take on financial responsibilities, and it could be harmful to overload such an individual with family responsibilities and financial burdens if they don't have the energy and skillset to handle it.

The Destroyer is here to teach us to do things differently, the RunAway shows the family how to let go of things, go exploring, and bring back new ideas, and the Fixer is the breadwinner and sets boundaries.

The issue with many families is that they don't understand that each family member has a particular role to play. Some family members may have a Sweet One profile, which is helpful financially, but they may not have the energy or skills to be a Fixer who can take on the role of a breadwinner and set boundaries. When a Sweet One is overloaded, they can break under the weight and that, in turn can cripple the entire family.

It's interesting how, in so many families, the Sweet One and the Fixer tend to be praised the most because they appear to be the 'perfect' and 'easiest' children. However, as those children become adults, I've noticed that they often struggle the most with acknowledging their trauma, processing their emotions, and speaking their truth. They seem to carry a lot on their shoulders and end up bottling up their feelings, which can be exhausting for them in the long run.

So, although the Sweet One may be the glue that holds the family together, without a Fixer, there's no one pushing people to think about finances or generational wealth. The role of the Destroyer is to uncover the things that the Sweet One and the Fixer don't want to face, while the RunAway's role is to explore new things and bring them back to the family; the Eternal Child exists to bring our attention to our wounded inner child and teen and to heal those versions of us that don't feel parented. If we don't honour each family member's role, we may force them into roles that don't match who they were meant to be, which can lead to them feeling lost and unseen within their own families.

The archetypes we develop in response to the trauma we experience in our families impact the way we show up in the world and the way we parent, which also then impacts our relationship with money and the next generation.

In my experience, people often switch between archetypes depending on the circumstances. However, most individuals tend to have a Primary and Secondary archetype that they identify with most. So, while they may shift between different archetypes, these two tend to be dominant.

Healing our archetypal patterns requires us to go into our shadows and dark spaces to do uncomfortable work so that we can start to change our behavioural patterns. While this may not seem directly related to money, it lies at the core of the work I do around money. By observing how parents behave with money, I can often guess the money stories their children will develop.

Ultimately, however, our money traumas are not just about money, but also about our deeper emotional experiences and patterns. This is why traditional approaches to personal finance, like budgeting, often fail to lead to long-term behavioural change. Trauma simply can't be intellectualised away.

Through my work with hundreds of people globally, I've found that although many people may experience similar money issues, the root cause of those issues can vary widely. For instance, both the Sweet One and the Destroyer may struggle with a fear of being seen, which can impact their business success, but the root cause of that fear may differ greatly between the two archetypes. As a result, different healing modalities may be needed for each archetype.

It's also important to note that each archetype can have children who take on different archetypes or even similar archetypes, but choose to deal with the root trauma in various ways. This is why families can have a mix of archetypes and continue to repeat the same money patterns over and over. It also explains why families may experience sudden financial success in one generation and then lose all their wealth in the next; the Fixer archetype (often the most financially responsible archetype) may, for example, not always give birth to another Fixer.

All these dynamics illustrate how deeply ingrained our money patterns can be within our families and why we need to confront our archetypal patterns in order to heal them.

CASE STUDY

My maternal family dynamics

My mom (a Fixer archetype) had four siblings, and my grandmother (a Sweet One) became a single parent when my grandfather passed on in the sixties.

My mom was the second born and once she started working she noticed the situation at home: that my grandmother, an entrepreneur selling vegetables, was really struggling with raising her siblings and couldn't make ends meet on her own. In response, my mom, at the age of 16, decided to step in to help by looking after her siblings and giving my grandmother money for the family.

Two of her siblings (my aunts) were RunAway archetypes; one had children young and left her two kids with my grandmother while she continued with her schooling, so by default, the kids ended up with my mother. By the time my sister and I came along, my mother was already looking after her own family and constantly fighting with them about money. She also decided to build a family house, which is the house she lives in now.

By this point, however, things started falling apart because my mother now had two children and could no longer support everyone and their kids, so the fights escalated. Not only that, but she also had a lot to say about how others were living and parenting, and how she saw the family progressing, which introduced a lot of friction in the family.

This radical change of heart and refusal to keep looking after others probably also felt like a kind of betrayal because she had been looking after the family for well over a decade by then, so people began to see her as selfish and started rejecting her. My mom then went from a Fixer to a Destroyer archetype.

Growing up, I watched as my mother constantly screamed about how her family had taken so much from her financially; by the time I was in my teens, my mother and my maternal grandmother were no longer on speaking terms. My mom also stopped speaking to her siblings and my cousins and stopped helping financially.

My mom was angry at everyone, especially my grandmother. She felt like everyone had taken and taken from her, and that her financial strength had been used against her and she started sharing the family drama and talking about everyone's business publicly.

In my teens, my uncle (a RunAway and Sweet One archetype) stepped in to look after the family; he bought a plot and everyone moved in with him and he took over financial responsibility for my grandmother, my younger uncle, my mom and all his sisters' kids (my sister and me included).

He, however, had no clue how to handle the various family members, especially my cousins (Eternal Child archetypes), who were adults but living at home and financially dependent on him and their parents. He battled to set financial boundaries, barely raised his voice or complained and I suspect his fear of added financial responsibilities is why he would get rid of money as soon as he made it. He was trying to keep himself safe, fearing that if he made more money, his responsibilities would increase. If he had no money, he wouldn't have to keep looking after the family.

As the Sweet One, my uncle didn't feel safe enough to set financial boundaries and, instead of kicking people out, he moved out of his own home and went to live elsewhere. And then, when my grandmother passed on, the entire maternal family structure broke down and the financial situation became dire – there was no longer a strong Sweet One archetype to hold the family structure in place.

How did things go so wrong?

My mother had been the breadwinner in her family, the sibling who ended up being her mother's sidekick, mothering her siblings, and she felt resented by everyone.

This resentment generally leads to a very tense relationship between siblings, because the responsible sibling is not just a sibling, but also a deputy mother. Female breadwinners may also not have the best of relationships with their mothers, or they may have overly co-dependent relationships with them.

The deputy parent-child is often a firstborn (the Fixer or Sweet One), but not always. They watch their mother struggle with the parenting role and, out of love, decide they don't want their mother to go through this alone and so step in to share the emotional load.

Over time, however, the responsibilities start to shift; they're no longer just listening and keeping the other kids in order, but start cooking the food and taking care of the kids. They stop being a child and start acting as a deputy parent – in other words, the child is 'parentified'. This usually happens gradually, so neither the parent nor the child is aware; but with some parents, the shift can be blatantly obvious because you have a 10-year-old looking after all the other kids, and the mom or the dad are nowhere to be found.

When this deputy parent-child starts earning, they automatically shoulder the financial load, give their parents money or help with the groceries. They may also make career decisions based on what their siblings need and what will help him or her earn enough to support everyone in the family.

You now have a child who is energetically parenting and if that child is a woman, their womb energetically feels as though they've given birth to babies that are not theirs and their womb may carry a lot of anger about this, which could lead to womb issues. If a child is a man, they may also carry a lot of anger in their lower abdomen (sometimes referred to as the sacral chakra) which can lead to sexual issues.

The relationship between the deputy parent-child and their siblings may begin to change; the other siblings start to see the sibling as a parent and they start going to the deputy parent-child with their problems, including financial and school needs. And, as the siblings grow up, they become accustomed to being taken care of and don't offer to share the financial responsibilities. This can lead to feelings of resentment and being taken for granted by the deputy parent.

Finally, when the deputy parent starts to withdraw and decides, 'I am done. I am no longer parenting you. I'm not your mother. I'm not your father. Go find your mother. Go find your father. I want to use my money for myself,' the siblings feel betrayed. Their inner child feels like they have been abandoned or rejected by a parent and they act out, rejecting their deputy parent-child. And, in turn, the deputy parent-child feels hurt, betrayed and unappreciated; sibling rivalry ensues, and deep sibling wounds start to develop in the family.

The deputy parent-child tends to carry a lot of anger and bitterness as an adult because their inner child has been completely suppressed. They may never have had the opportunity to truly be a child and, as a result, carry a lot of pain and sadness. They struggle to spend money on themselves or have fun because they have learnt to put their siblings or parents' needs before their own.

The inner child of the deputy parent-child is also angry because they have had to parent themselves and were praised for being responsible at a young age, when they were just children themselves and needed their own parents. As a result, they may find it difficult to ask for help when they need it and can feel very alone in the world. This can lead to deep mother and father wounds.

When the siblings for whom they gave up so much start to turn on them, the deputy parent-child feels betrayed, resentful and deeply sad. All that pain can turn them into a Destroyer archetype.

None of the wounds that arise in these situations were intentionally inflicted. At the heart of the sibling wound is a lack of communication around boundaries, with parents unable to discuss and set clear financial expectations and siblings not equipped with the tools to navigate these discussions. It's not about age either, because even siblings in their thirties and forties can struggle with these deep inner-child and inner-teen wounds.

In addition, the deputy parent sibling may have been praised as the perfect child by one or both parents due to the tremendous responsibility they took on. This constant praise of one sibling over the others could create a sense of competition and animosity among the siblings, leading them to take on the RunAway or Eternal Child archetypes as a coping mechanism.

PART 2

The Shadow Archetypes

A Shadow archetype is the hidden and unconscious part of a person's personality that includes traits and emotions they may not want to acknowledge or show to others because they have been deemed undesirable and shameful. These characteristics influence behaviour and thoughts in subtle and harmful ways and often lead to self-sabotage in various aspects of our lives.

CHAPTER 7

The Sweet One

As adults, the Sweet Ones are well liked in the family. They have a good relationship with almost everyone and are seen as forgiving and understanding (often seen as empathetic and sweet). Having been considered the 'good' or 'nice' children, sweet and loving, as adults they have learnt not to rock the boat and to do what is expected of them. As a result, they are people pleasers. The Sweet Ones learnt to cope with trauma by fawning, consistently abandoning their needs to serve others in order to avoid conflict and bond with their parents or caregivers (Ryder, 2022).

Fawning is a response to childhood and complex trauma and arises from repeated exposure rather than a single, once-off event. They try to do the right thing, in the right order, so even if the Sweet One is not always sweet, they are cherished. They were often unproblematic kids, the ones with 'nice' friends, and now have loving partners. The quintessential definition of 'nice', they keep the peace at family gatherings and play within societal and family rules to stay safe and keep the status quo. All they want is peace and for everyone to get along so they themselves can feel safe. This need to be liked can stem from childhood neglect or abuse from siblings, parents or other family members.

If I had to guess, I would say most family members and people fit this archetype, which is especially important, because this archetype is the glue of the family and prevents the other archetypes from going to war with each other.

Driven by their need to be liked and validated, their role within the family is to keep the peace, often to their own detriment. They rarely get angry, mainly because they are numb and have learnt that being anything but sweet may lead to conflict and so tend to avoid conflict. In fact, this is the big difference between the Fixer and the Sweet One: the Fixer is often at the centre of the conflict in the family and can keep that conflict going for a while, whereas the Sweet One resolves conflict and will often be the level-headed and calm one.

They may complain about others behind their backs, but will not willingly come right out and challenge them – in fact, they often find a diplomatic way to resolve the situation or just go along with whatever is suggested (even if they don't agree).

The truth is that no one is always sweet. It's normal to get angry and upset about things in our families, friendships and relationships, but the Sweet One learns to bury their rage and fear because they have learnt that it's not safe to upset people. And let's not even talk about their pent-up resentment ...

Their role in the family

When I reflect on the Sweet One archetype, I think of the aunts and uncles who may not have a lot of money, but are always there to offer whatever they have and lend a helping hand at funerals and weddings. They are the ones who cook, clean, dig graves, start the fire, sweep the yard, who have an extensive network at the burial society and church. They may not always be sweet, but they are kind and will always offer good, solid guidance when you need it – and, if we are honest with ourselves, a lot of family events and functions wouldn't happen without their networks and capacity to work. They are the Sweet One.

The Sweet One keeps the family together and gives them a sense of belonging and being part of the tribe, which is very important if the family is going to progress. It is the Sweet One – and the Fixer, if they don't stay at home – who tends to host family members or have extended family members come live with them for periods of time, either to visit or until they get themselves back on their feet.

If a family has strong Destroyer archetypes, the role of the Sweet One becomes very important, because Destroyers trigger everyone (that's their role), whereas the Sweet One soothes and reminds everyone that they are not their shadows. In fact, they will often change their opinions based on who they are talking to and, if they have issues they feel have to be resolved, they will call a family meeting and sort them out in a peaceful manner.

They give money when asked, and never say no because they are conflict avoidant, so their money comes with no complaints or demands due to their fear of setting boundaries. They do not volunteer to help financially, but will often be roped in to help and provide the majority of the non-financial help.

The Sweet One learns to survive by playing roles and acting them out perfectly to get love and validation, putting their wants and needs aside to service others. In doing so, however, they learn to 'invisabilise' themselves. And often, because of the roles they play and take on, they can feel as though no one truly knows them (and maybe no one really does, not even their partners) and have a deep fear of being rejected, which has deep ramifications in their finances and romantic relationships.

In the absence of a strong Fixer archetype in the family, the Sweet One will step in and fill this role, but it can be challenging for them if there are financial demands that come with it.

It can be easy to confuse the Sweet One with the Fixer (it took me a while to see the differences when working with clients and looking at various family histories) because both tend to be the backbone of the family, but I hope that, as you read more, you will start to see the big difference between these two.

In my maternal family, my uncle was a Sweet One, but was confused with being a Fixer – a mistake because the Sweet One cannot handle the full force of a Destroyer. The Sweet One's main role is to keep the peace in the family, especially when the Destroyer and the Fixer go head to head, and to provide a haven for the RunAway when they feel ready to return home.

As a child

As we now know, as a kid, the Sweet One learnt to survive trauma by fawning and people pleasing. In order to stay sweet, they had to learn to suppress their emotions by disconnecting from the body and staying in the head, thus avoiding their own feelings. As a result, they may struggle to explain what they are feeling or ask for help, because they are the ones others tend to turn to for help and they fear upsetting people or making them uncomfortable.

These were the good kids, those who did well in school and often got straight As or Bs, the ones who always did as they were told and were respectful to a fault. They rarely experimented with alcohol or drugs and were focused on all the right things. As a result, everyone had high hopes for them. They were seen as successful before they even reached university – everyone expected them to go to university before landing a respectable job. The weight of this perfection, however, holds the Sweet One back in adulthood, often financially.

As a parent

As a parent, the Sweet One can be loving and understanding, always determined to do what is right for their children. They will stress the core values of being human.

In their shadow state, they may have a tough time setting

boundaries with their kids because of their need to be liked. They may even abandon the parent role in an effort to be cool so that their children like them, often allowing their children to bully them. Alternatively – and even worse – they may smother their children with too much attention and become the overbearing parent. Children may also see how others take advantage of the sweet nature of the parent and feel the need to step in and protect them. To cope with the Sweet One as a parent, a child may adopt the following archetypes:

- **The Sweet One:** A child may decide to cause less stress for their parent by being equally sweet themselves.
- **The Eternal Child:** Because the parent has a hard time setting boundaries, the child may come to resent being 'unparented' and may then force the parent to parent them. In this case the child adopts the Eternal Child archetype and, because the parent does everything for them and can't set boundaries, this relationship can turn into one of toxic co-dependence.
- **The Fixer:** Since the parent is having a tough time being in their full parenting power, the child steps in and becomes a mini parent and may even start setting boundaries with other family members on behalf of the parent.

Managing life and finances

What keeps the Sweet One from attaining the success they desire?

Blocks to wealth and expansion

Everyone saw the Sweet One as the golden child so, as an adult, they feel an invisible pressure or need to maintain this image. They tend to feel pressured into doing the right things or doing things the right way: marry on time, have kids on time, and establish themselves in a steady career, for instance.

They tend to follow societal or family rules to be socially acceptable, and when they fall short, they feel as though they're failing or are not good enough. This presents itself as a need to be perfect, but it is, in fact, the desire to be accepted and not make anyone unhappy.

The result is that they have a crippling fear of taking financial risks because they need to be certain that their success will not make others uncomfortable or lead to their exclusion from the tribe. If the Sweet One grew up in a wealthy and/or entrepreneurial family or community, they will find it easy to launch a business and/or build wealth and even take some risks, because doing so will not lead to conflict in their social circle or family. If, however, they didn't grow up in an entrepreneurial family, they can struggle with creating multiple streams of income and can take a long time to launch any new product, service or innovation.

Needing everyone to be okay with them – and determined not to upset anyone – can lead to procrastination, putting off their own dreams as they opt for the safe path, which can affect their ability to accumulate wealth. Interestingly, however, the Sweet One is often great at saving, especially for retirement, because they want to do the right thing (or what they are told is right) and saving is considered socially accepted behaviour.

Blocks to increasing income

Of all the archetypes, the Sweet One struggles most to find their own path or voice because they depend on validation from family and friends. They have a hard time increasing their income and sticking to their salary goal because they worry about what people will say, wilfully making themselves invisible so they can be accepted by the tribe. They want people to validate their path before they get started because they do not want to do anything that may cause tension or conflict in the family, and this may, of course, block their income.

They are the most likely to stay close to the family home or where they grew up – that's where they are most comfortable and feel safe because they feel accepted there and know the rules. They also tend to network in the same circles (because of their fear of rejection), which makes it difficult to find new opportunities and to collaborate with others. This is an energy of contraction – the polar opposite of expansion energy: the willingness to expand in all areas of our lives, even the networks we have. After all, our friends and cliques know the things they know and even know the same people we know; but sometimes, in order to grow and achieve something different from the tribe, we need people who see things differently and view situations with a new set of eyes.

The more opportunities we take advantage of – in business and the workplace – the greater our chances of success and the more likely we are to boost our income.

Blocks to getting out of debt

Of all the archetypes, the Sweet One is the most likely to get into debt to save the family. They are overly helpful and if they see a family member or even a member of the community struggling, they may help them even if it means taking on debt or giving the last of their money.

In the absence of a strong Fixer archetype, the Sweet One may take on the role of supporting the family financially, but may also end up buckling under the weight because they lack the intense financial energy of the Fixer, an energy that is needed to move forward towards a common goal. And so the Sweet One ends up overextending themselves to keep up with the financial demands of looking after the family.

To fit in and gain acceptance, the Sweet One may also compare themselves to others to make sure they are doing the right thing. It is normal for us to compare ourselves to everyone else if we grew up being compared to others. This is how we gauge our progress. It is human, but it has its downfalls.

The Sweet One also has an element of doubt about themselves and their abilities, which can shape the way they manage money. If we doubt ourselves, especially when it comes to money, it will be hard to take financial action in faith and this doubt will surface yet again when we discuss money with clients, which will make it difficult to invoice people. It will also come through when dealing with financial professionals – we give up our financial power and believe that everyone knows more about money than us. This is how people fall victim to swindles and buy into the belief that they are not able to budget or invest.

There is also the risk of the Sweet One getting into debt just to keep up with the Joneses. Again, this is driven by the need to fit in and be part of the tribe.

Family dynamics around money

Because of their need to be accepted, the Sweet One is scared of the criticism from others. They get a lot of validation from being liked so they sometimes confuse criticism with anger and dislike and that threatens their sense of safety.

Criticism feels extremely unsafe to the Sweet One so to avoid criticism and keep the peace in the family, they shrink, invalidate their feelings and give whatever is asked of them. They have a hard time setting boundaries and, as a result, tend to give more than they should in terms of time and energy. They believe that if they give more and hold space for people, they will receive more, but this can often leave them feeling overburdened, especially because holding space is invisible labour and difficult to quantify.

Because they tend to make just enough money, they're often only able to financially support themselves, but will readily support other family members, especially if they see a need. They are the most likely to offer family members long-term shelter and food in tough times.

They also give emotionally and with their time. They are the peacemakers in the family, so they are the ones people (family, friends and co-workers, for instance) come to with their issues; the Sweet One makes the tea, listens and gives great advice.

In most African households, they are also the ones who cook for or host events, because they are seen as having a listening ear. The sentiment is, of course, beautiful and needed in every family or community, but it is also time-consuming and can actually exhaust the Sweet One.

Core wounds

Let's take a look at the core wounds of the Sweet One and how they affect their financial behaviour.

The not-good-enough wound

The core wound the Sweet One needs to heal is the not-good-enough wound. In the Sweet One this manifests as the obsessive need to be liked and validated, which leads to making the self invisible and often shows up as self-criticism (inner critic), the strive for perfection, and procrastination. This lies in the belief that we need to be more than we are in order to get the things we truly want in the world and to be deserving of the money we want.

This wound is very common in children who have experienced emotional, physical and verbal abuse, because they need to make sense of the abuse and, because kids don't have cognitive reasoning abilities, they jump to the conclusion that *they* are the problem, and not good enough. This leads to low self-esteem and self-doubt and permeates all elements of their life – from relationships to finances.

When we feel 'not good enough', we don't see our worth and value and rarely feel deserving of all that life is able to give. Healing the not-good-enough wound can help the Sweet One release their fear of criticism simply because the fear of criticism actually stems from the wound itself. And until the Sweet One heals this wound, they will exhaust themselves trying to prove their worth and that they deserve to be paid well, deserve money, deserve love or any of the goodness in this world.

The not-good-enough wound manifests as trying to save others financially (even people who would never try to save them). They also tend to overextend themselves, giving in abundance to those they love in romance, friendships, and family relationships, not because they love them, but because they need them to feel that they are enough.

And it is exhausting.

The Sweet One is often worn out because they are doing too much, not for themselves, but for others, and they have no boundaries. Stillness and rest will feel scary, while making money or dealing with finances will feel too daunting.

For Black people, this wound is further impacted by our experiences of racism, which impacts our mental health (Kwate & Goodman, 2015). A huge part of not feeling safe is that it changes the way we see the world, how we interact with it and see ourselves. And the core tenet of racism is that Black people are inferior and less than, in essence: not good enough. The system reinforces this in overt and subtle ways, which changes the way we see ourselves and our abilities, and thus affects our confidence and our belief in ourselves around building successful businesses, making money and even how we parent our kids.

If we can start to heal our traumas and release them on a physical level – in other words, rewire the nervous system – we can start to feel safer in our bodies, which can help us feel safer with money and start to change the way we behave with money. It will also be easier to release our vows (defined as profound spiritual promises or commitments) because part of us will see that we no longer need them to keep us safe.

When we talk about 'ease' when it comes to finances, we do not mean there will be no challenges or obstacles, but rather that we will be at ease and our reaction to the financial situation will not be worsened by our responses and fears of what others will say.

The not-good-enough wound affects the Sweet One's finances in the following ways:

- **Overcompensation:** When we believe we're not good enough, we tend to give away a lot of our products and services for free, or under-price our products and services because we doubt what we have to offer and that people will see the value, simply because *we* don't see the value.
- **Giving to the point of exhaustion or being broke:** We give even when we have very little (emotionally, mentally and financially) because we need others to like us, because our self-esteem is so low, which affects us financially because sometimes, in order to get validation, we will give our last cent even when we can't afford to.
- **Inability to say no or ask for our money from people who owe us:** We avoid any conversation that will make others uncomfortable because we need their approval and need them to make us feel that we are enough.
- **Decreased savings:** We often use money as a tool to prove that we're enough and so we overspend to our own detriment.

When the Sweet One heals their not-good-enough wound, they find it easier to set boundaries, say no and find their voice, because their sense of self is no longer tied to others' opinions – and this is a game changer for their finances.

The fear of being seen as imperfect

Perfectionism is a trait often associated with anxiety and it appears to be both psychological and biological in nature. It can, however, be changed (Antony & Swinson, 2009).

The fear of being seen as imperfect can present in the Sweet One as procrastination, an inherent fear of failure and/or a fear of criticism. This probably stems from the way our society is structured, as Antony & Swinson (2009) point out, because society rewards high standards. Doing well at school, for example, leads to higher grades and praise from teachers and parents. As kids the message we receive is: having high standards (being perfect) leads to more love and greater acceptance.

The Sweet One struggles with being seen as doing things wrongly, or imperfectly, and while they may admit as much in private, they are terrified of being seen as doing anything wrong in public. This shows up as a fear of being seen as failing, so they never get started with anything.

But it's not just a matter of reservation – it *feels* wrong or unsafe. And sometimes it may feel like they have to pretend to be someone else in order to be safe. Most of us carry stories and beliefs from childhood that it's not safe to be seen – we saw how our parents or other family members were treated when they became visible, after all. Feeling like it's not safe to be seen makes sense since we make the vow of invisibility in order to protect ourselves. The fear of being truly seen – in all their glory and all their mess – scares them. What if they are found lacking and no one likes them any more? Or worse ... What if they are seen for their greatness and they have to constantly live up to that greatness? Or worse ... They are hated for being great?

I suspect that the current school system contributes to this – many adults spent their childhood being praised for being smart and getting things right and then that praise was withdrawn when they didn't do things perfectly. As a result, most kids associate this withdrawal of approval with withdrawal of love. This is even worse if the child grew up in a household where perfection was demanded at all times and every single fault was highlighted.

This system of reward and withdrawal will play out in our adult lives and affect our finances because, in order to grow and expand, we are required to experiment, and we know that we will make mistakes and perhaps even 'fail'. That's part of the process. In fact, making mistakes and 'failing' is how we build resilience.

This fear of failing and being seen as imperfect may make it hard for the Sweet One to start a business (entrepreneurship teaches you to get used to failing, trust me), invest in new things (not all investments work out and we learn a lot from those that don't), collaborate with others, or show up on various media platforms, for instance.

On the surface this appears to have nothing to do with money, but it has a lot to do with money.

The vow of invisibility is a soul decision we make in childhood/teens/adulthood (or even past lives) not to show ourselves and/or not be seen. It can also be an ancestral vow. More often than not, though, the vow of invisibility – especially for Black women – plays out with us hiding our brilliance, our knowledge and our light. The reasoning is: If they can't see us, they can't harm us.

The vow of invisibility means that we stop seeing our own greatness and become invisible to ourselves and started saying things like: 'I don't know what I want', 'I'm not sure', 'I'm confused', or 'I'm not accomplished enough'.

We learn to hide from ourselves and, in so doing, hide our desires and soul cravings from ourselves.

We stop seeing our own Divinity.

We stop seeing ourselves and start focusing outside ourselves.

These are the effects of the vow of invisibility: It doesn't just stop us from showing ourselves publicly, it stops us from seeing ourselves privately as well. It keeps us invisible from ourselves so that we no longer see our own worth and our own deserving.

This is simple logic. In fact, most of our ancestors stayed safe by remaining invisible or just staying under the radar as much as possible.

So our vows of invisibility are tied to physical safety, especially for Black people.

The vow of invisibility is thus not just about physically showing yourself. We can be comfortable standing in front of a million people and still be invisible, because we are curating what we show people and are hiding our truth – that truth that we want to live or know could change people's lives or our own life.

I recommend thinking of visibility as vulnerability. Consider the following scenarios grounded in the notion of vulnerability:

- Constant criticism from a parent/adult, essentially instilling in us that we were never good enough, means that we learn to avoid anything that can invite criticism.
- Being bullied at school means that we learn to hide in order to stay safe, so we stay away from anything that shines a spotlight on us or exposes us to conflict.
- An insecure partner (or friend) puts down our every achievement, so we learn to keep ourselves safe by not shining or hiding our successes.
- The abuse of a thriving adult by another adult(s) demanding financial support means that we learn that making money (or others seeing us make money) is unsafe and leads to financial abuse.
- When men hit on us, sexualising us from a young age, we learn that being sexy and visible in our own bodies is unsafe, so we stay safe by hiding ourselves and denying our sexual energy, which is a magnetic energy and impacts on our money.
- Being sexually abused and then being made to feel like you asked for it (applicable to both men and women) means we feel shame.

- When experiencing constant inter-generational oppression (and even death) because of how we look – our ancestors were, for example, persecuted because of how they looked or what they believed – we may carry an ancestral vow to hide various aspects of ourselves in order to survive.

Most of these scenarios would make us feel physically unsafe, especially in childhood, because children tend not to have the resources to process such trauma so these events may overwhelm our nervous systems and remain unprocessed.

In order to protect ourselves we would conclude that it isn't safe to show our light and brilliance, and our inner child and inner teen will choose to be invisible to keep us safe. And, as we get older, this belief is continually reinforced by events in our lives, so that by the time we are adults, our nervous systems are hardwired to keep us safe by ensuring our invisibility.

We learn to keep quiet on things that matter, because speaking up could result in conflict. This feels like death to our inner child and is registered as such by our nervous system. Judgement and criticism, while logically understood by our conscious mind, is registered as almost deadly by our nervous system, because of inner-child/past-life/ancestral trauma. So even when we want to speak up and be seen, we just can't – we are essentially hijacked by the parts of us that feel unsafe.

The fear of not being seen in our imperfection affects the Sweet One's finances in the following ways:

- **Stagnant income:** The Sweet Ones energetically turn down career, business and media opportunities because they fear being criticised and judged, and steer away from trying new things in case they fail. They are scared that others will see them failing, which scares them, and can lead to procrastination or taking a long time to make

decisions, which in turn leads to delays in business and thus stagnate their income.
- **Increased debt:** The drive to attain a certain image of perfection – whether in terms of material possessions, lifestyle, or appearance – can be so strong that they are willing to incur debt to achieve it.
- The fear of being seen as being imperfect leads to them spending money they don't have to win people's approval and be seen to be doing the right thing, which can lead to living beyond their means or impulsive financial decisions.
- **Decreased savings:** Stagnant income and increased debt lead to a decrease in savings, because the Sweet One often needs to delve into their savings to cover expenses.
- **Repressed anger stored in the womb:** In their book, *Womb Awakening*, Bertrand & Bertrand (2017) call the womb 'a hologram of God' and explain that the womb has the power to birth and rebirth our reality. They explain that individuals with wombs, when connected to their wombs, have the ability to birth whole new worlds and manifest their wants, needs and desires from the womb.

The Sweet One, especially if a woman (it is more common for women to adopt the archetype of the Sweet One to survive this patriarchal world), often struggles with repressed anger. This stands in contrast to the widespread belief of the feminine that the woman is at peace and has it together, only radiating love. The archetype never feels anger or expresses anger violently; she responds to everything with calm because she is soft and feminine. She never shouts or screams or fights because she embodies love and makes everyone comfortable.

We rarely talk about the fact that sometimes, in order to keep our softness and stay loving, we need to find our voice and protect our peace by setting fierce boundaries. A woman who is fully in her feminine can make people deeply uncomfortable because she is, in fact, wild, fierce and free. Maybe she's that aunt who comes to family gatherings dressed to kill and leaves everyone unsettled because she refuses to hide her greatness to make others comfortable. But no one wants her around because she triggers their wounds around money, power and visibility.

Sometimes embracing the fullness of our femininity means saying, 'I am feeling my feelings and I give myself permission to feel what I feel.' Sometimes, to sink into our softness, we have to say: 'Enough' or 'I choose me'.

Even the Divine has boundaries and a tipping point.

Even the ancient orishas, like Oshun, get angry and cause droughts or floods.

Even goddesses, like Kali, go to battle and kill monsters, drink blood, and go crazy.

Women have been taught to be 'nice' girls and to please people, so most women tend to bury their anger in their womb (where we tend to bury our most uncomfortable feelings and emotions). In return, our wombs rebel against us because we have stored anger in them, and they get sick because the anger is too heavy for them to hold.

When we are people pleasers, we essentially give up our power in return for validation from others, especially in intimate relationships. As a result, our wombs learn that they cannot trust us because we will always betray them in favour of the opinions or love of others; our wombs then protect themselves by becoming hypervigilant or they scream for our attention.

If we betray our wombs in intimate situations, they may rebel by making it harder to reach sexual pleasure; the yoni/vagina may find ways to make sex impossible (we may get our period the day we know we are going to have sex or we get ill or we get thrush, for example). This is when the womb takes control in an effort to protect itself because we are refusing to do so. Basically, our womb armours up. And they armour up because of the world in which we live – wombs have always been attacked and made to feel unsafe.

Even if we have not experienced sexual violence in this lifetime, our wombs hold the collective female memories, ancestral memories of the women who came before us and in our past lives, and will armour up to protect us from re-experiencing that pain. If the situation persists and we don't listen and honour the anger carried in the womb, our wombs may go to extreme lengths to get our attention and things may get worse.

On the other hand, when we give ourselves permission to stand fully in our power, create boundaries, choose ourselves and honour our deepest needs and desires, we start to build a relationship with ourselves, our inner child/teen and our wombs. Our wombs begin to feel safe and can start to relax, feel calm and stand down from their hypervigilance stance because they can trust us to protect them and ourselves.

The following are ways in which repressed anger stored in the womb impact the Sweet One's finances:

- **Decreased income due to anger or being disconnected from the womb:** Anger can make us behave irrationally to make a point; we may refuse great income opportunities out of anger (Makwakwa, 2013). Anger can also lead to damaged interpersonal relationships, which can lead to reduced income.
- **Increased income due to anger:** Anger is an emotion that can mobilise us to demand better treatment, even in our finances (Makwakwa, 2013). In fact, it has often been used to mobilise the disenfranchised and the oppressed to seek better work conditions, wages and salaries. In the same way, anger can drive us to make drastic changes in our lives and to seek better income.
- **Increased debt:** Anger can lead to impulsive spending, using money to feel better and to distract us from feeling (Makwakwa, 2013). Sometimes we can refuse to pay our

bills in order to teach people a lesson, which can impact our credit scores and debt.
- **Decreased savings:** Anger can lead to poor financial decisions, such as impulsive spending and refusing income opportunities, which can lead to decreased savings.

If you are feeling disconnected from your womb and that your womb is armouring up, ask your womb:

- Where am I not standing in my own power and not protecting myself?
- Where am I not fully expressing myself?
- How am I making myself small in order to make others feel bigger than they are?

Of course, this is not a one-off exercise – these questions are mainly to start the conversation with your womb – but it needs to be work that is done consistently and often, allowing the conversation to deepen over time. As the relationship between you and your womb deepens, you will start to see your need to people please also start to shift.

CASE STUDY

The Sweet One

VANGILE: Thank you for doing the interview, Lindiwe. Please can you tell us where you're from?

LINDIWE: I'm from South Africa. I was born in a town called Brakpan. I'm now residing in Johannesburg.

VANGILE: What would you say is your relationship with your family like when it comes to money?

LINDIWE: I don't know. At some point I was a breadwinner, but then my mother managed to get a job. We're now assisting each other. I'm a single mother of two kids, ages 14 and five. As a single parent, I'm the one who's financially taking care of everything at home, paying for the school fees, rent and food. Everything is dependent on me. And sometimes it gets a bit heavy, but we need to survive.

VANGILE: What is your role regarding money when it comes to extended family? Beyond your kids and your mom.

LINDIWE: I have a brother who's 42 years old, who's currently unemployed. I'm helping him financially here and there where I can. I have a sister who just graduated. She's currently looking for a job; she's also staying with me now. I'm also assisting her. Those are the only people I can say I'm helping, except for cousins who occasionally ask for cash here and there, but it's not as hectic as the responsibilities I have at home.

VANGILE: Who would you say has affected your money story the most?

LINDIWE: My mother. When I got a job, I wasn't working for some time and I already had one child. As soon as I got a job – my mother was not working at that time) – I was pressured into taking personal loans so that we can renovate the house. After three years, I had to relocate and leave my child with my mother because my workplace wasn't good, but then I had to pay rent, and send money home. But I tried to manage that by taking my child with me two years later, thinking that it will cut the cost. I thought, if my child is with me, then I'll be sending less money home. But it went on for years and years; until I drowned in debt, because at some point I was taking loans for just my personal survival.

VANGILE: Did you try to have a conversation with your mother or your siblings about taking care of them?

LINDIWE: No. To my mother, I'm the firstborn. My brother is from my father's side. So you know that responsibility: you're the eldest – it is your job. You are supposed to be taking care of the family. I couldn't. I still can't. Sometimes I feel that I should be doing more. Even in a competition, you know how parents are ... they'll be telling you about somebody else's child. How they did this and that for their parents. And you feel guilty and, you know what, I wish I had the opportunity or the ability to do the same for my parents as well. So, yeah, it's something that I can't raise. I don't know. I don't feel comfortable talking about it with them.

VANGILE: How do you feel talking about money in general? Because you're saying it's something you can't raise with them.

LINDIWE: I have so much anxiety around money. Even when I have money, I don't feel comfortable. I just have that anxiety that it will finish now because I have a lot of things to do and so little income. Talking about money, it's a topic that I like to avoid. I like to avoid the topic even when I'm sitting with friends; when they talk about money, I don't say much. I'll just listen because I feel like I'll be exposing myself. I'll be feeling like, you know what, maybe there's something wrong I'm doing. How can people have so much money? I'll be just having those internal conversations and wondering how they are surviving when they're going on vacations and I can't afford; I'll just come up with excuses. But I would sit and ask myself: How are people surviving? Where are they getting the money? So, yeah, I don't feel comfortable that much talking about it.

VANGILE: What is so scary about bringing up the topic of money with your mother and even your siblings?

LINDIWE: I don't know how to put it. I already feel like I'm failing in terms of finances. I feel like if I bring it up, I will be exposing myself that I am failing because I'm not supposed to be where I am today. With my siblings, I act like I've got it all together. When they ask me for money, I'm even scared to say I don't have; I would rather borrow from someone so that I can give them because I feel like it's my responsibility. I feel like I can't tell them how I'm drowning in debt. I feel like I'm that role model. They are supposed to be looking up to me. And then, if I'm failing already, what example am I setting for them? And with my mother, it's complicated.

VANGILE: Do you feel that if you had to tell your mother it would hurt her?

LINDIWE: It would hurt her. And it's like mothers – they are a bit manipulative. If you say no or say this is the situation, they will make you feel sorry for them. I don't know. They'll just make you feel guilty for not helping.

VANGILE: How do you think your relationship with your family has affected the way you make money and earn money?

LINDIWE: It affects me in a negative way because there would be times where I would just ... Maybe I'm trying to save for capital for something. And the fact that they're not going to be supportive, and they'll be asking: So what about this? How are we going to manage with this? We're still busy with this project of getting a tombstone for your father.

So then you end up concentrating on things that are problems of today instead of planning ahead for the future. You get carried away on those immediate things and you end up not being able to invest for the future and not being able to invest in the business that you want because the money always has things it has to sort out. Already, before my salary comes, someone is planning what to do with it. This month we have to do this, next month that. Sometimes they'll even tell you two days before and you already have your budget.

And another thing: I don't know if maybe it's something that can be affecting me and my family. It was very hard growing up. My mother struggled, so I feel like there's an opportunity for me to take care of her. She suffered for a very long time, and she shouldn't be suffering any more because I'm supposed to be helping her. So if I come up with stories that I can't do this, I can't do that, after seeing her suffering for a long time, I feel like I'm disappointing her. When is she going to get a break? I forget about myself – when am I getting a break?

VANGILE: That is the loyalty to the struggle that our mothers have endured. When we have seen our mothers endure that struggle as children, we feel this wounding that our mothers have been forgotten by the Divine or by society. And we make this unconscious decision in a vow that we will either be like our mothers or we will mother our mothers. So, as life starts to happen and we become more grown, we may find ourselves mothering our mothers from a very young age to try to protect them.

How do you think the need to mother your mother affects your ability to save money?

LINDIWE: I can't save. I don't ever have enough money to save. But, yeah, it's ... yeah. I don't have money for rainy days. When it's rainy days, I have to borrow. I even got to a point where I had to go on debt review. The loans that I can manage now are through the loan sharks; I can't get a personal loan any more because it's just overwhelming.

At some point, I was even thinking of resigning and using some of the money to pay off everything and start afresh. But it has been ongoing because I've been employed for 11 years, from 2011, so 12 years now, same company. I haven't really seen much progress in my life except for all the responsibilities from home. It has been there for a long time and, so far, it's not changing. I feel like, because of my mental state now, I'm even attracting more of these situations that will require me to take up money instead of working on bringing in money.

VANGILE: I am sorry. What advice would you give to someone, say, in this situation, or what would you like someone in this situation to know?

LINDIWE: I think the biggest thing is to set boundaries from the get go. Don't let it prolong because it will get to a point where you won't be able to go back on your word and say, 'You know what ... I'm actually not managing.'

That is one thing I wish I did when I started working – that I should have set boundaries. I should have learnt to take care of myself before I can take care of the external members. Deal with it as you start. Have a plan. What is it that you want to achieve? Set goals. As you start, don't wait 10 years, because it gets difficult as time goes by. It gets more difficult. So if now I want to go back and tell them, 'Okay, this is the problem.' It will be an issue because this has been how we've been doing things for all these years right now.

VANGILE: What do you think is stopping you from setting those boundaries right now?

LINDIWE: I think it's mostly fear. Fear of hurting them, fear of disappointing them. They're comfortable now, so for me to bring them out of that comfort is just going to be difficult for me.

VANGILE: Thank you, Lindiwe, for your honesty and vulnerability.

Ask yourself ...

1. What was the most striking aspect of the Sweet One profile for you?
2. Which of the traits of the Sweet One do you identify with and why? Conversely, which traits do you not resonate with and why?
3. Who do you believe embodies the Sweet One profile in your family, and what is their role in your family dynamic?
4. How does the Sweet One typically fit into the financial landscape of your family?
5. What are three actionable steps you can take to provide

support for the Sweet One in your family or for yourself if you identify as a Sweet One?

Take action

1. **Give yourself permission to set boundaries:** As a Sweet One, you may find it difficult to say no to others and prioritise your own needs. When someone asks for your time or help, take a moment to breathe and ask yourself if you truly want to say yes. If you're unsure, give yourself 24 to 72 hours to think it over and then respond with a clear yes or no. If you're feeling anxious or guilty about saying no, take a few deep breaths and check in with your body.
2. **Be clear about what you truly want:** As a Sweet One, you may have a tendency to prioritise others' needs and desires over your own. It's important to take the time to get clear about what you truly want and practice communicating your desires to others in a clear and direct way.
3. **Meditate on self-acceptance:** As a Sweet One, you may struggle with self-doubt and feeling like you're not good enough. Take time to meditate on the question, 'What if I gave myself permission to be imperfect and to be fully seen in my imperfection?' Allow yourself to sit with this question and notice any feelings that arise. Remember that it's okay to make mistakes and be imperfect – that is what makes us human. Practice accepting yourself exactly as you are, flaws and all.

CHAPTER 8

The Destroyer

The Destroyer reveals (and may actually display) all the hidden toxic behaviour in the family, often in a violent and unpleasant manner. Where the Sweet One tries to be perfect in order to get love, the Destroyer will rebel and force their parents to see themselves and to see them. They will not allow their parents to check out and will behave in a way that forces them to pay attention.

I was this shadow archetype as a teen and, when threatened and in my shadow as an adult, I can default to this role. The Destroyer is my Primary archetype, my Secondary being the RunAway. I relied on my shadow Destroyer to survive my tumultuous and violent household and that served me well until my early twenties.

The Destroyers are the ones people perceive as angry or the outcasts in the family. They are that family member who will bring up uncomfortable conversations and air the dirty laundry in the middle of a peaceful dinner. They seem to have no peace and can ruin the family get-togethers with *truth*. They will call out the family paedophile without a second thought and hold everyone accountable for any other hidden secrets.

They fail to fit into the mould and, as a result, have been forced to go find their own path. And because they are the rebels and have long given up on doing what's expected, they tend to make money in various ways. They contribute financially only when they want and will let you know where to get off.

Their role in the family

Think of that aunt or uncle everyone dreads having at an event – the one the family calls private meetings about because they're scared of what they will say and do should they be present. Everyone knows they will be coming to a function, no doubt about it, but they're nervous about it. When they do see them, family members are immediately defensive because they never know what drama they will bring with them. They know it will be uncomfortable and their drama will inevitably play out in full view of 'the people'. They have their own money and assets and they use the truth as their weapon. That's the Destroyer.

The role of the Destroyer is to shine the light on the family's skeletons in the closet and bring these to the fore so they can be healed and dealt with. When the Destroyer's role is not honoured in a family and they come to be considered the black sheep of the family, the family keeps repeating the same financial and other behavioural patterns for generations. If, however, a Destroyer's role is indeed honoured, the family can experience new patterns, which leads to expansion and financial growth. The Destroyer is here to awaken us to the pain and trauma we are refusing to deal with and which is now keeping everyone stagnant. They are here to help us deal with trauma so we can tap into our ancestral wisdom and start building healthy relationships.

Because of this role, the Destroyer tends to air all the family's dirty laundry in very unsettling ways. And because most family members will try to shut them down and label them the villains, they often have to fight to have their voice heard and get people to do the deep, dark healing work that's required. Destroyers are energetically strong because getting people, especially adults, to face themselves can be scary.

A family without a Destroyer runs the risk of having many RunAways and Eternal Children because no one in the family knows how to process trauma or has the courage to process trauma so it will just keep getting passed down from one generation to the next. Nobody actually wants a Destroyer in the family, but without the black sheep, a family never experiences friction and thus the catalyst to change the things they need to change. If a family doesn't have a Destroyer, but has a Fixer, there may be times when the Fixer steps into that role.

I don't think we talk enough about the generational trauma of hiding dirty linen, keeping secrets and burying truths to 'protect the children' or the other family members. How many families have been and still are being torn apart by secrets and hiding truths that should indeed be aired in public? How many women carry the resentment, pain and hurt that they've hidden deep within their bellies and wombs because of these secrets? How are these manifesting as digestive ailments and womb issues because we choose to protect others rather than heal ourselves? How do these secrets weigh on our souls and stop us from going home, or make us feel guilty because we don't want to feel the pain or experience the triggers?

Here's what I know and have seen from a young age: family secrets have a way of coming out.

One day an 'inconvenient' soul (the Destroyer, or black sheep) is born into that bloodline, and they feel everything and say, 'No more'. In my maternal line, my mom is that soul. She shared everything – and I mean *everything*. She made it all public and that tore the very fabric of the family. Growing up, I hated it; I wished she would just keep quiet – until I started reacting to my family trauma in the same way.

I now realise that my mom freed my sister and me. We have no secrets to protect or laundry to be aired. But I also understand that the blowback that comes from being this soul is hard, lonely and painful, which is also why most Destroyers sometimes struggle with a deep fear of rejection even as they constantly reject people and systems.

As a child

These are the rebel children, the ones who really push the boundaries. When you say A, they say B, and no one can convince them otherwise, except themselves.

Many adults find these kids difficult or exhausting, not because of their propensity for rebellion but because of their uncanny way of pointing out the truth and calling the adults out on it. They are smart and well read, but may not always apply this smartness to schoolbooks because their role in society is to question the system. These kids are often misunderstood as being rebellious for the sake of rebellion or to find their individuality, but that's not true – a Destroyer child is trying to show up the erroneous beliefs, stories and systems in our societies and our families.

While the Sweet One decides to survive the trauma in the family by numbing themselves and pleasing everyone, the Destroyer decides to feel it all (they are highly emotional) and fight the trauma by shining their light in order to reveal the lies.

Destroyer energy tends to be intense and extremely violent because they are warriors and respond to any sense of unsafety by defaulting to fight mode, so they tend to be hypervigilant and ready for war, and because of this constant hypervigilance, their nervous system is always on alert, which occasionally leads to struggles with anxiety and depression. If a Destroyer is silenced and not allowed to let their warrior spirit out, they will suppress that anger and turn it on themselves and go to war with themselves, which can lead to depression and self-harm.

Unfortunately, children and teens seldom have the resources to fully process every experience and then act diplomatically, so they often end up being very direct, fighting many battles – often on their own.

Because they often have the gift of foresight and sense or see things many others may not see, I have noticed that a lot of Destroyers are also the healers in their family. Which makes a lot of sense, because to truly heal a wound you have to see it and understand its root cause and Destroyer children tend to (but not always) understand the root cause of their family trauma, often more than the adults around them.

Their role is to be critical because they act as a catalyst for change and expansion; they are the ones who are not afraid to unearth the skeletons not just in the closet, but also buried deep underground. They force the family to confront their trauma so they can start to heal it and change what needs to be changed and, because of this role in their family, they tend to have a very strong energy and can't be easily ignored at home or in society. They were, after all, born to be the catalyst and to shake things up. But getting people to see and face the things they are not ready to see isn't always fun, so most Destroyers, even as children, feel misunderstood and are not always well liked and can often be loners.

A family without a Destroyer archetype (or a weak one) can remain emotionally and financially stagnant for years or even generations. A lot will be swept under the rug and never brought to the surface for cleaning and examination. Think about how societies change and start doing things differently ... Destroyers arrive and point out all the things that are wrong and unfair and then march or fight for change. They are the ones who start revolutions, go into workplaces and start rebelling against the rules and challenging the laws.

A family with a strong Fixer may move forward financially, but will still struggle to get to the core of the wounds and trauma because there is no archetype that makes them uncomfortable enough to do that. The issue, though, is if a family has a strong Destroyer and not a strong Fixer archetype to hold or absorb the destructive energy of the Destroyer. If you have a strong Fixer energy but no real Destroyer, the Fixer may play both roles, but make sure you don't upset them to a point where they stay in the Destroyer archetype. For example, my mom was a strong Fixer energy until she went nuclear and defaulted to her Secondary archetype, the Destroyer, and in the absence of a strong Fixer energy, the family started fragmenting.

As a parent

As a parent, the Destroyer can have unique and truly innovative ways of parenting, which can lead to innovative and creative children who also choose a different path. In their Shadow archetype, the Destroyer can be challenging because they can end up battling with their own kids and bullying them. They get so used to fighting their family and the world that even as parents they go into warrior mode, no matter how deeply they love their children.

This constant fighting can be jarring to a child's nervous system and make them fearful of their parents and keen to escape them for some peace. To cope with a Destroyer as a parent, a child may adopt the following archetypes:

- **The Sweet One:** In this case, the child rebels by being everything their mother is not, agreeable, sweet and one who fits in.
- **The RunAway:** The child runs away to escape the parent and their intensity.
- **The Destroyer:** The child decides to fight fire with fire, and so take a first stand for themselves and go to war with the parent.

Managing life and finances

Adults with the Destroyer archetype may often find themselves trapped in a perpetual warrior mode, an exhausting state where they are constantly battling against people and various challenges. They learnt to fight to survive in childhood, which trained their nervous systems to react to situations by being confrontational and, as a result, struggle to stay calm. Fighting takes a lot of energy, yet they manifest challenges for themselves because this is what they have normalised.

The great thing about this response from Destroyers is that they have stamina to keep going in the face of adversity, their childhood and teen years having taught them resilience and given them grit. On the flipside, they have a hard time knowing when to let go of the fight, rest and ask for support. In fact, they don't know who they are outside the rebellion or the fight. And at some point in adulthood, they may be so exhausted from being disliked that they choose to assume the role of the Sweet One, which, if it's not their Primary or Secondary archetype, may leave them depressed because this is not who they are at heart.

Blocks to wealth and expansion

Most Destroyers are capable of building great wealth in creative and distinctive ways, especially when they are in their healed state. The Destroyer is here to teach us to do things differently, so they are likely to seek out a non-traditional path with money. It is ironic, however, that it's often Destroyers who invent things that will hurt humanity in some ways, but it's also Destroyers who come in and fix things.

Unlike the Sweet One, they are not trying to do things the right way – mainly because they don't know what the 'right way' is or even how to do things the right way, so they tend to find their own path and follow their own callings. They are not scared of challenges and because they learnt resilience at a young age; they are able to do what seems otherwise impossible. In fact, the Destroyer is not here just to change things but to show us what is possible when things do change.

The Destroyer is the most likely of the archetypes to build several fortunes and lose said fortunes often in their lifetime. One of their greatest blocks to lasting wealth creation is their tendency to destroy and burn things to the ground, so they often find themselves leaving jobs and having to live off their savings and/or investments and are forced to start from scratch every time. They may shut down businesses or just walk away because a business is not working (this is often their rebellious streak). This delays their ability to build lasting wealth and to grow the wealth they have already built.

An unhealed Destroyer tends to manifest chaos and then has to use their money to fix that, which again delays wealth creation. One of the key lessons for the Destroyer is to learn how to build and use diplomacy so they can preserve what they have built.

A huge part of their boom-and-bust periods is due to their vows of loyalty and rebellion. The Destroyer is a rebel at their core, but their inner child also has an intense longing to belong and to be accepted so, amid their rebellion or world changing, they find themselves being hijacked by the inner child who has strong vows of loyalty to family and desires nothing but to be loved and accepted.

Blocks to increasing income

As Destroyers have an intense energy, when focused, they can use this energy to start or even reinvent companies and even industries. They have the capacity to make (and lose) large amounts of money in their lifetime.

Destroyers do well when involved in income-generating activities that show us another way of being because this is their passion. It doesn't have to have a lofty mission, but it must change things in some way.

One of the challenges of the Destroyer is learning how systems work and working within a structured environment, such as a corporate system or established industry, which can work to their benefit at times but can also stall their growth. As a rebel, their first instinct is to resist all systems and point out their flaws (which is important to the very make-up of the Destroyer), but understanding the system can be helpful when there is a need or desire to either break it down or make money.

The Destroyer is also most likely to be conflicted with the idea of making money because they feel as though they are buying into the financial system rather than fighting against it (to rebel against systems is an instinct for them). While the Sweet One, for example, struggles to charge for their products and services for fear of what others will say and be criticised, the Destroyer struggles to charge because they feel too much and are oftentimes scared of perpetuating systems of oppression. And because of this conflict, they are most likely to start non-profits (in support of some cause) or work for non-profits or even for free.

It's important to note that because they have a large amount of resilience, Destroyers have a high likelihood of building successful companies and thus generational wealth. All that rejection and being the black sheep of the family has taught them to overcome hurdles, a skill they may exercise in business.

Blocks to getting out of debt

The Destroyer is very independent and can often feel alone in the world. They feel as though they are the only one they can rely on, which makes it hard for them to ask for help and often leads to them resorting to debt to support themselves.

Their recurring cycles of boom and bust pose the most significant obstacle to their journey toward debt freedom.

They may, for instance, have to go into debt in order to survive during their seriously destructive periods, which can keep them in a cycle of debt and negatively affect their credit scores.

Their fear of rejection can also affect their creativity and quick thinking, which can also impact their income and lead them to walk away from income-earning opportunities, further creating the need to rely on debt to live.

Destroyers are also most likely to find themselves stuck with fighting the system rather than learning about it, so they may not understand or care about things like credit scores and overdraft facilities, and so find themselves caught in a cycle and resist conformity even when it comes to their finances.

Family dynamics around money

Destroyers are often the ones who either sever ties with family members or are cut off by other family members. They have experienced rejection often and can often respond to pain with their own rejection.

While the Sweet One lacks boundaries, the Destroyer has firm boundaries in place and is used to being the misfit of the family and, when they are in their true shadow, will give to family members as and when they feel like it. However, although the Destroyer takes full financial responsibility for themselves, they don't willingly take on extra responsibilities in the family. One thing we need to understand about the Destroyer is that they give when they see a need or when they feel like it – and may do so generously without expecting anything – but it is often a decision they make on their own and because they care about their families.

Most people may mistake the rebellion of a Destroyer as a sign that they are uncaring, but nothing could be further from the truth – they care deeply, therefore they choose to fight for what they believe is right and true.

When a Destroyer is trying to get validation and be liked, because it's draining being an inconvenient soul, they will override their own boundaries and give more than they should in an effort to buy their way into the family unit, but rest assured, when they get over this phase, they will go back to telling people off.

The core wounds

Let's take a look at the wounds of the Destroyer and how these influence financial behaviour.

The wound of not belonging

A study by Torgerson et al. (2018) found that a sense of belonging leads to resiliency and protects us from the negative effects of childhood trauma later in life. The study also found a link between the trauma of not belonging and risky behaviour when it comes to alcohol.

A 2013 study by Pearce & Pickard found a direct correlation between a sense of belonging and improved self-esteem and overall wellbeing. The authors also argue that belonging is a 'fundamental human motivation' and requires constant contact over time as well as positive and mutual concern.

A core need for every child is to feel that they belong and are part of a tribe. As children, we fully accept our parents and family, but as we grow older we start to question what we have learnt from our families. We start to see all the ways in which our family is not perfect and may decide to rebel against what they have taught us and all they stand for. And when, as young children, we start questioning our family (even our society) we may be silenced or scolded or even punished, which leaves us feeling like our way of seeing the world is wrong and so don't belong.

In his Hierarchy of Needs triangle, American psychologist Abraham Maslow listed the need to belong as the third basic need after safety and physiological needs (McLeod, 2023). As a result, being the black sheep of the family and seeing things differently from the rest of the tribe can leave a Destroyer feeling alienated. Baker (2018) states that it's difficult for a person to hold onto their creativity and soul calling if they don't feel like they belong. Baker further states that when we feel that we don't belong in our families we craft our identities out of 'consumerist ambitions' and so, to be accepted by everyone, abandon our identities. This self-abandonment then leads to suffering. If we take Baker's research into account, we can conclude that not belonging can lead to one using money and consumer goods to fill the gap, which can lead to increased debt.

I saw first-hand how breadwinners who were making more money than anyone else in the family were resented or shunned, which taught me that people are only loved and accepted if they don't stand out from the crowd. In fact, my own constant desire for expansion and innovation often conflicts with my fear of coming across as too overwhelming, which plays out as a deep desire to get rid of money and shrink because my inner child believes this is the only way to get love.

Almost every idea and belief we have about money, success and relationships comes from childhood; these ideas and beliefs then impact our entire view of money and success as adults. We walk around thinking we're adulting, being all grown up and making our own decisions around money, when it's really the four-year-old version of ourselves who's making those decisions. Every time we have to deal with money, we're triggered and our childhood memories and decisions about money rise to the surface at a subconscious level. Our inner child or teen takes over and starts managing our finances, which is why it can feel like we're having an out-of-body experience when we manage money.

If that's not bad enough, kids and teens make decisions based on their need to belong and receive love, which means that most of our financial behaviour won't always be rational and will be geared to give results that keep us within the tribe. This is why we find ourselves repeating our mother's or father's financial mistakes – because we're trying to get love by being embraced by the tribe.

When the Destroyer heals their childhood wounds of not belonging, they give themselves permission to redefine what belonging means and looks like and break free of the boom-and-bust cycle. But the truth is that we don't need to replay our family's dysfunctional relationship with money or with other people in order to belong. It's possible to be loyal without repeating cycles and giving ourselves permission to have a wildly different life to that of our families. When we give ourselves permission to feel the pain of not belonging, we allow ourselves to see the ways in which we willingly keep ourselves apart from the tribe – and that is true freedom. This way, we get to choose who we truly want to be rather than simply rebelling, and that ability to choose is what leads to uncharted roads and innovation.

The following is how the wound of not belonging in your family of origin may impact financial behaviour:

- **Decreased income and investments:** Feeling that we don't belong has a negative impact on our self-esteem (Leary & Baumeister, 2000). We can therefore conclude that when a Destroyer feels as though they don't belong with their family of origin, that can lower their self-esteem, and individuals with low self-esteem or self-confidence underestimate their own abilities and value, leading them to accept jobs or promotions that pay them less than their counterparts (Rouault et al., 2022).

    People with low self-esteem are also the least likely to negotiate for higher salaries or charge fair market prices in their businesses because they underestimate their own value. They may also lack the confidence to take calculated risks, such as starting their own business or investing in opportunities, which further lowers their income and investments.
- **Increased debt:** When a person doesn't feel as though they belong, they are unlikely to ask for help and support and may feel lonely and have a hard time asking for help. This is especially true of the Destroyer. Because they don't feel that they belong, they often resort to debt to look

after themselves and not ask for assistance from family members, even if their family is indeed able to help.

People respond to rejection by seeking inclusion elsewhere and will in all likelihood make themselves more likable to a new group so that they can fit in (Weir, 2012), which suggests that there are times when the Destroyer may use money to buy love and also get into debt by giving too much simply because they want to feel connected. In fact, they are more likely to spend money on friends they feel deeply connected to because this may be their first experience of feeling as though they belong, and so – out of fear of losing this connection – tend to give more than they should just to be accepted.

A study by Lejoyeux et al. (2011) argues that compulsive buyers purchase items (self-gifts that they rarely use) in the hope of restoring their self-esteem, which suggests that low self-esteem may also lead to Destroyers buying items to make themselves feel better, which in turn leads to increased debt.

- **Decreased savings:** The wound of not belonging can result in a Destroyer earning less money than their counterparts and yet they spend more money on self-gifts that they never use in an effort to make themselves feel better, thus eating into their savings.

Self-doubt and the fear of being 'too much'

While the Sweet One is scared of being seen as imperfect, the Destroyer – because of their childhood experience of not being accepted for who they are and being constantly asked to change – is scared of being too much: too emotional, too sensitive, too loud, too rich, too much to handle.

On her blog, My Meadow Report, Fishman (2018) says that when you believe you're too much, too overwhelming to those around you, you shut off a part of yourself and start to hide yourself and downplay your strengths (intelligence and perceptions) so others feel more comfortable. Lo (2018) argues that the wounds of fearing you are 'too much' can lead to feelings of shame and loneliness.

Children who go against family norms and question the way things are done in the family are often shut down and labelled troublemakers, or seen as being 'too much'. They're considered the rebels and may even be called 'difficult' or 'the problem child', especially if they refuse to follow the norm or butt into 'grown-ups' business'. As a result, some may learn to just keep their thoughts to themselves and suppress their own voices so that they can be seen as agreeable. This is how they learn how to survive within their families of origin.

I'd always thought of myself as outspoken until an incident in my MBA programme – my Management Accounting lecturer gave me an A-minus for the course; I was really confused because I'd generally get 100% on almost all my tests and exams and I was always speaking up in class.

When I went to her and asked her why she'd given me an A-minus instead of an A or an A-plus, she said it'd been because I'd withheld information through my class participation. She said I would answer just enough questions to get by and get a good grade. And it was only later, when she looked at my paper, that she realised I'd known the answers or had a different approach all along, but had decided to keep quiet.

I tried to explain to her that I didn't want to come across as being 'too much' because how would it look if I constantly raised my hand to answer questions? By this point, I had made an art form of doing enough to be considered outspoken and a bit controversial, but not annoying.

She told me that when I did that, I was withholding information from my peers and limiting their growth as well as my own. This was an Aha! moment for me. As a child and in my teen years, I'd been told to keep quiet, to stop disturbing the adults, to stop talking back and to learn to be quiet.

I'm still not sure if all of this warranted a lower grade, but it did change my perspective and make me aware of the ways in which I learnt to silence myself out of fear of being too much. It had never occurred to me that my different way of seeing the world could help others move forward. That when I questioned my teachers and my classmates and debated with them, I was actually helping move the conversation forward, and this difference in opinion was important for progression and growth.

A lot of Destroyers are taught that they are causing trouble and making everyone in the family uncomfortable with their observations. As a result, most Destroyer children get the message that they're doing something wrong rather than bringing things to light and using their voice in order to get those around them to question the norm and, in so doing, fostering a different way of doing things.

As they get older, this fear of being too much starts to spill into their finances because they learn that it is that, in order to belong and to be loved, they have to tone it down and so they start to dim their light and focus on being agreeable.

But the world really needs Destroyers to be themselves, to question why things are the way they are, even if it means upsetting everyone, even if it means making everyone doubt themselves. Destroyers are the ones who urge us to innovate, to look at things differently, to face different parts of ourselves we're unwilling to face so that we can do things differently and try something new.

How the wound of being 'too much' influences financial behaviour:

- **Decreased income:** It can be argued that if you harbour a fear of being too much, you spend a lot of energy hiding yourself, your skills and your brilliance, which limits your career progression and business opportunities, thus decreasing income. Because of that fear of coming across as being 'too much', Destroyers struggle with self-doubt, which affects their ability to negotiate for themselves, and thus affects their ability to negotiate a fair salary or fair prices for their products and services.

- **Increased debt:** Those who struggle with self-doubt are most likely to spend impulsively and to buy items in an effort to feel better and more confident about themselves, which could lead to increased debt.

  I would also argue that someone who is scared of being too much would have a deep desire to fit in so that they are not seen as 'too weird' or 'too poor', and it is this fear that drives them to spend money in order to be more readily accepted by others.

- **Decreased savings:** Someone who is scared of being – or seen as being – too much may feel unsafe having a lot of money and it would overwhelm their nervous system, especially if they believe that having a lot of money will lead to them suddenly being seen as too rich. The parts of them that feel unsafe being too much will thus find a way to get rid of money, leading to an increase in spending and a decrease in savings.

The fear of rejection

The fear of rejection is born from the wound of not belonging; being shunned and othered as a child by their family breeds a fear of being shunned by others in the same way as an adult (Leary, 2015). The Destroyer is afraid of rejection because they reckon that if their own family couldn't accept them, why would anyone else? Rejection – especially parental rejection, whether real or perceived – is thus associated with negative self-belief and self-worth, as well as a distorted view of the world (Smith, 2016).

Being rejected can feel like death, because in the Stone Age, being rejected from the tribe often meant you had to fight the elements alone and that often led to death, so the reptilian brain (which has not evolved much) registers rejection as death. It is thus very human to seek connection and acceptance because we associate that with survival and staying alive, so being rejected – or witnessing someone being rejected – can be very traumatic. In fact, according to Leary (2015), rejection from family or friends (be that subtly by being ignored or more overtly by intentionally excluding someone) is one of the most distressing and defining events in a person's life and much of human behaviour revolves around avoiding it.

The Destroyer archetype is fascinating because, as much as they are the rebels, they've also felt the effects of being rejected simply for being different or making people face dark, scary truths. They know what it feels like to stand alone in the face of lies, secrets and oppression, so they fear rejection more deeply than the other archetypes simply because they've experienced it so often. This fear of rejection may make it scary for them to own their full power and embrace their role as a change-maker, which means they tend to minimise themselves.

I would also argue that treating family members who have money differently from anyone else is a way of rejecting them as it creates a sense that you are othering them. They feel they are different simply because others, for example, talk to them in English (if that's not their home language), serve them from the good plates and glasses, put on a show for them so that they feel like guests rather than family.

When The Destroyer is scared, they may believe they have only one option: to buy their way into the tribe with money and make themselves useful to the family by making themselves financially indispensable. Or, worse, they learn to protect themselves by rejecting others before those people reject them – and then, in turn, apply the same logic to their own family, rejecting their family before the family can reject them.

My parents (both Fixers) don't like debt – in fact, they love paying for things in cash and believe in having a financial plan and life goals. When I was growing up we didn't have store cards and never saw either of them buy clothes on a store card and yet, when I was in my twenties, I bought everything with credit and managed to accumulate US$60,000 in debt before my 28th birthday. I was in full rebellion against everything I had learnt as a child.

I struggled to save and stay out of debt, until I began healing my mother wound, father wound and family trauma. My inner child and teen felt like they didn't belong anywhere so, as an adult, I was terrified of not fitting in with those around me and used debt to keep up with the Joneses.

My soul craved to be a writer and share my journey and truth with the world but I abandoned that and instead followed the safe path of looking for jobs in investment banking.

I rebelled against my parents' creativity and business acumen. My mom is great at sales and marketing, but for years I couldn't sell or market anything in my business until I healed my wound of belonging and gave myself permission to go back to what I had seen her doing in business when we were growing up. My dad, on the other hand, is great at operations and systems, and yet it never crossed my mind to create systems in my business until I started working through my father wound. And when I did, my business started making money in my sleep.

Most of us grew up watching this dynamic and we learnt that, in order to stay in the tribe, be accepted and avoid rejection, we had to be *like* the tribe and that meant either emulating the tribe's financial behaviour or rejecting them outright.

Fear of rejection is one of the biggest blocks to following our dreams and making our vision a reality. We are all born believing we can do the impossible and that the world is open to us, but somewhere along the way we encounter rejection and convince ourselves that we're not good enough. This small loss of faith in ourselves then leads us giving up on our dreams. Unfortunately, this is most common in the creative fields where we tend to face a lot of criticism and rejection.

My fear of rejection led to years of writers' block. Writing has always been my escape from reality (my Secondary archetype is the RunAway, so I need my escapes from reality). Poetry and writing kept me sane in my teen years when I ran away from home, worked three jobs to survive and paid my way through varsity. I'd slip on my headphones, put pen to paper and start crafting stories or poems from the ether. It was all so easy and effortless.

It seemed natural to me that I'd graduate from business school and start a writing agency but when I told my entrepreneurship lecturer my plans, she told me I'd never make it in the publishing industry. She gave me all the stats about 'failed' and starving writers and suddenly this fear of rejection set in, and I struggled with writers' block for three years. I essentially rejected my own writing before I had even got started.

How the fear of rejection plays out in the Destroyer's finances:

- **Decrease in income:** The Destroyer withdraws and makes themselves invisible to make others comfortable and avoid experiencing rejection again. As a result, they may block job promotions or hamper marketing efforts in their business.

    Fear of rejection also makes it hard for people, such as the Destroyer, to take advantage of opportunities or to sell themselves and their products and services (Verbeke & Bagozzi, 2000).
- **Increased debt:** A study by Smith (2016) found that people who have experienced maternal rejection have a maladaptive attitude towards money, which means that those who were rejected by their mothers are more likely to have a dysfunctional or unstable relationship with money. This may then lead to increased spending or a cycle

of booms and busts when it comes to money, which would lead to an increase in impulsive spending, which could lead to an increase in debt.
- **Decreased savings:** The fear of rejection leads to decreased income and increased debt, which in turn leads to the Destroyer using more of their savings to pay for day-to-day activities.

CASE STUDY

The Destroyer

VANGILE: Thank you for doing this, Mpho. Can you please tell us where you are from?

MPHO: I am from Johannesburg, South Africa, born and bred.

VANGILE: What would you say your relationship is with money when it comes to your family or your relationship with family when it comes to money?

MPHO: My relationship with my family when it comes to money is tricky, I guess. There's always been a lack of panic or stress around money from the time we were small. I would say that it brings up anxiety, maybe some resentment, pain, maybe some anger as well. My earliest childhood memory with regards to money was at the end of the school term [when] they would give us letters for school fees and stuff. Our letters stated that we owe school fees and would be read out loud. My dad just didn't bother paying our school fees. And my mother only earned so much and she could only maintain the things that she needed to maintain, like making sure we had proper school shoes, clothes, and that we were fed. And it wasn't that my dad couldn't afford to pay – it was just not a priority. I hear a lot even now: my mom and her view of money and the lack of it and just a continuous complaint and not so positive feelings around money. Money is not shared; it's not ours. What's mine is mine. And I think that then spilled over into my twin sister as well. And I remember when we were living together, it was, like, she made more money than I did and we didn't make decisions together.

VANGILE: What do you think your emotional and financial roles have been in your family?

MPHO: I'm still trying to understand what that is for me because, for the first time, I had to step out of my own patterns of behaviour with my family. And that's why you're helping me with that, realising that, oh, this is the role I assumed in this family. Yes, you might not have money, but you give in different ways. And the people that do have money don't know how to even be generous, not even just with their money, but generous in being able to appreciate and value that they are given. I think it's a bit layered and it's still a thing I'm unpacking as I'm standing more in my power and giving myself permission to not be small and to not be angry at money or hate money because of the way it's being used.

I started working when I was quite young. From early on, I was quite generous because I think the situation we were in when my parents got divorced and, just with my father, I tried to use money as the source of joy for us. So I would either take us out for dinner or do things where I was trying to make my mother happy and my siblings happy as well. And it wasn't just my money for sharing. And then that evolved into I don't like to hold on to money because I've now learnt that I resented it.

So when I do get it, I share it and I splurge it and then it's gone. What happened last year, or the year before last, is that I took out an insurance policy for my uncle who was very sick for a long time, and he passed away and I was able to contribute to a successful and beautiful funeral. And it felt like it was the first time that I was able to do something big. I thought that my mom would see me for the first time. I thought it would mean something. But my sister had to chip in at some point and my mom was just praising her. And I realised that I was looking for validation because I felt rejected and invisible as this so-called black sheep most of my life. And it was the first time that, after all these years with sharing what I have emotionally and financially, that I realised that I was trying to get approval. I was trying to be celebrated and to be seen. And I think, yeah, emotionally, I was very gifted. I am still gifted.

I was very active at school. As a child, I got full colours and awards and I invited my parents to come and watch my plays and all of those things. And it never really felt like it was an important thing. But there was a celebration if my sister got 80%. So I think I don't know if I'm answering your question, but emotionally, my role has been to try and ease people's wounds, to save people maybe, to make sure that people don't feel unsupported or don't feel alone. I've been the one to hold space emotionally and physically.

VANGILE: I have noticed that the black sheep comes into the family to help them see themselves. You have been the one that has unearthed the trauma in your family. Can you talk about that?

MPHO: Yeah, sure. I think the most obvious way that that has manifested itself was when I tried to take my own life. I think that was the first time that there was this confrontation because there's been this silence within the family for years. Even after my parents' divorce, no one really spoke about anything. Well, my dad took us to McDonald's one time and told us the reason why this was, at the beginning of the divorce. But we were just a family that didn't talk about anything. And then this thing happened. Although I did try and reach out, I sent them an email. That's how distant we are from each other. I sent them an email saying, 'This is where I am at.'

My sister was aware because I lived with her. But I don't think she told my parents the state that I'd been in for some years. So I wrote the email to make them aware of what was happening. And nothing really came from that. So about, I think, two years or a year and a half later, I then tried to transition myself and ended up in a mental-health facility. And then in that situation, in that space, we had to have sessions with a therapist for the first time and had conversations.

But that was the beginning of my, I guess, stepping into this role of the genetic path cutter of showing the wounds of the family and the patterns we were in. In fact, in one of those sessions I remember the therapist, an old and mature lady, was, like, 'Okay, wait, but can you hear what you guys are doing?'

We were like, 'Huh?'

She then pointed out that my sister and my mother were talking as a 'we'. When they referred to themselves, they'd say 'we' but when they referred to me they would say 'she'.

When she does, we don't know, we, we, we.

And, obviously, my nervous system had clocked this in, but I hadn't even noticed that. At that moment, the therapist was, like, 'You guys are a unit and it's like you guys against her.'

So that was the first. Then we started unpacking these things over years. And, yeah, it's been for both sides.

VANGILE: How has this role that you've played in your family over the years affected your relationship with money and how you make money?

MPHO: I think my working career, I have always been underpaid. I worked for billionaires. I've always had to scrape through each month, which I think speaks to how I feel about myself. I subconsciously believed that I don't deserve to be valued, to be seen, to be compensated appropriately because that's the pattern in the home.

And then when I stepped into the space of making more

money, making money on my own, which I mean, even for a long time, I couldn't even say I'm an entrepreneur because I didn't think I was worthy of that, or that I could even ... But it is what it is, even if it is within the healing space. But I couldn't reconcile all those parts.

And it took coming home and looking at all these things to see that this is because of the way that I feel about myself. I'm good at manifesting things, but it's been hard for me to hold the things I manifest for a long time. And I realised it's because of the words, the feeling worthy. I didn't see my own self. My light brings magnetising things to me, but my internal – the way that I felt about myself – then repels it away. I reject it and it goes away.

VANGILE: So you can manifest the money and call it in, but the challenge is still holding on to it because part of you don't feel worthy and deserving. But the other thing is, as you're talking about this, and for the first time, I'm hearing just what you said about the 'we' language. Your sister felt worthy, she felt deserving, she felt celebrated. So, obviously, she has no problems believing that she can make that amount of money, that it's okay for her to make that amount of money because she's been affirmed her whole life. So suddenly when people pay her, she feels like, yes, people are supposed to pay me. But when people pay you and you've been told that you've been made to feel like it's not worth it.

How do you think the messaging and the feeling of being the black sheep in the family have affected the way that you respond to financial challenges?

MPHO: I think I just get frozen. I'm numb in financial situations. And I don't know. I think I can't even say I'm afraid. I'm sure there are all those feelings, but to me, it's a state that I'm so used to that I think I'm just numb. I can't even feel. I don't panic. I mean, I panic because I want to be able to pay Vangile the money I owe her.

I'm thinking about these scenarios that are coming up in my mind that I've never really spoken about; I would go to dinner with my family, and then I would talk about politics or whatever the case might be. My dad always thought somehow, he even [said] this to me as a child, 'You are stupid, your sister is the smart one.'

When we were at dinner and I spoke on things, no one ever believed me. I think my sister also had the same ideas about me because I've always been a little bit quirky but I am an intelligent woman. It's just maybe the way that I express myself or because of my interest, people didn't really feel like I needed to be listened to. I would just be spoken over. And I remember I used to get so angry. Sometimes I would go to the toilet and cry because no one took me seriously. But, you know, the thing about this was you have to be exiled from your family sometimes to go and find your gift somewhere else before they can take you seriously.

The reason why I'm bringing that up is that I feel like that's how it feels when I'm in a financial crisis. I feel like I am at that dinner table.

VANGILE: Maybe the nervous system response is the same as that? Maybe there's a parallel that can be worked on and explored?

MPHO: I think that's it. Also some of these things I'm only seeing as I'm talking to you now. For instance, my sister is a golden child. I wouldn't let myself believe certain things or allow myself to feel what I truly felt. One of the reasons why it's coming up, I think, is because I was watching you and [your sister] Honey and just the way that you guys flow with each other. Before we started, you told me you guys were speaking until 3am and I was, like, 'Whoa, that's crazy. It's so beautiful because we don't do that.'

When we were young, my sister would ask me to go to the salon or some place with her and I would go, but when I asked her she would say no, very nicely. I would be so sad and so angry because I would do anything for her, Mama and Papa.

And then she would ask me again and I wouldn't be able to say no just because she'd said no to me. Now, as I'm talking to you, I'm thinking that it's that same messaging that was consistent in different ways from different family members and this is the money block here. That's what has affirmed my lack, deep lack, self-belief, all that I don't deserve.

I'm no longer extending myself. And that energy that I've put so deeply into everyone else is going into me now.

VANGILE: How do you think your relationship with your family has affected the way you spend and save money?

MPHO: It's like holding my breath because I can't really fly because there's this expectation – maybe it's resentment. From when I was young, I was almost like my mother's mom. And then there were these aspects that were like I was the husband. I was very masculine and I would be the one protecting if there's noise in the house, even as a little girl or teen girl. I'm the one fixing things. I'm the one climbing on ladders and whatever. And I realised that I've been subconsciously feeling like I owe my mother something, but it's also something that she said, like, 'And you get it together so that we can fix the house ...'

I remember I came back from Cape Town last year and she said, 'I'm tired. When are you going to save me? When are you going to show up for me now?'

I remember feeling really bad when I heard that. I remember feeling so bad. It was only much later that I realised it's not my responsibility to save anyone. I was brought into this world and that was the responsibility she had – to look after me, so it's not like a trade exchange.

There's been the element of my sister being the one that intervenes financially. And so that's her place. I can't take her place. I'm the one who puts my hands in and my whole energy into funerals and family functions. I'm always there – my sister doesn't even come. That's my position. Her position is to be the one that's financially able, who can sometimes pay for dinners for the whole bunch of us. I've never really been the person who's always consistently able to do that.

Now our relationship is a little bit weird because I'm no longer – for lack of a better word – the victim. She doesn't have to fix me or anything. Now it's hard to then have a sustainable relationship because my lack sustained it; there wasn't really a deep care.

VANGILE: How have things changed between you and your family over the years as you've gone on your healing journey and become a healer yourself?

MPHO: There's been a lot of resentment from different family members at different times. A rejection of me. But there is more respect and reverence. But I think there's also still a struggle because of the role that I played for so long.

Maybe others feel disempowered that they can't control me in the ways that they did. Because I'm so sensitive. I think there was a manipulation that used to happen that I didn't even notice, I know what I want, I know what I deserve.

In the last while, my mom and I have become closer as well because I think, for the first time, I was able to reflect so clearly herself back to her and I am no longer allowing her to scapegoat me and she is seeing all of her children as they are. I am also allowing people to look at themselves.

VANGILE: What are some of the key things that you've had to heal and how has that changed your relationship with yourself?

MPHO: I'm sure you're aware of kinesiology? I went to a kinesiology session with some powerful people in Cape Town, some French woman. The first thing she said to me was that the energy that's stuck in my body and that I'm here to resolve is the energy of subjugation and that goes with abandonment and betrayal. Right?

So I think the biggest wound that I had to heal, and some of these things are just becoming more highlighted as I'm speaking to you, is the violation of sisterhood. I've never really let myself accept it and let it sink in. But, as you know, there should be a certain kind of way of showing up for each other. And there're these core experiences and memories that are so etched in my mind. So, for instance, I was quite sickly as a child. And of course, because I'm the sponge spiritually, I was taking all of this madness in – the emotional stuff of the family.

I remember I was asthmatic, I would wheeze at night and it would be quite loud and my sister would hit me with the pillow and tell me to, 'Just shut up.'

So I always felt so bad. I remember I was so convinced that she didn't like me. I used to put on perfume because I thought I smelled or something.

But you don't see these things as traumas, right?

But then when I went au pairing in Holland and I remember that my very good friend at the time was just acting funny the whole year. She was not really responding to me. I found out later that she thought I'd never come back or something, but, anyway, she and my sister became very close when I was gone. When I got back from Holland I thought my sister would be so excited to have me back. She had bought herself a car and I thought she was going to be excited and offer to fetch me from the airport after being away for one year. My sister didn't fetch me. She was at a party with this friend of mine. I took a cab home. No one fetched me.

I had to realise that there was deep loneliness, abandonment, aloneness, rejection – there were constant experiences, even with friends, of bullying and stuff. I had to deal with being laughed at because I'm weird and things like that. My sister would lead other people to disrespect me, or she's abandoned me for other people in other ways many times, but I didn't see it.

I also had to heal sexual trauma – how I broke my virginity. I was violated by a guy I really liked. I thought I was in love with this guy. I had to heal being abandoned from my own body, being violated, in my first home.

VANGILE: Thank you, Mpho. This has been a powerful and insightful interview.

MPHO: I needed this. I thank you for asking me to do it because it has helped me to unblock some things. These are our stories and it's okay for us to tell them.

Ask yourself ...

1. In what ways did the Destroyer profile stand out to you?
2. Which characteristics of the Destroyer profile do you relate to, and how have those shown up in your life?
3. Have you identified anyone in your family who embodies the Destroyer profile, and how do they contribute to the family dynamic?
4. How does the Destroyer profile impact your family's financial dynamics?
5. What are three effective strategies that can be implemented to improve communication and relationships with a Destroyer archetype, either within yourself or in your family?

Take action

1. **Feel your anger and release it:** As a Destroyer, it's important to acknowledge and give yourself permission to feel your anger. However, it's equally important to let it move through you so that you can address the underlying pain of abandonment and rejection it's masking. A simple but effective way to do this is by screaming into a pillow

for five minutes a day. This can help release the built-up tension and allow you to process your emotions in a healthy way.
2. **Inner-child and inner-teen affirmation:** Write letters to your inner child and inner teen every week. This can be a powerful tool in healing your wounds as a Destroyer. Take the time to explain to them why they are so incredible, despite feeling their feelings of being different or rejected. Acknowledge their strengths and remind them that being different is their superpower. By doing this, you can help heal your own wounds and reconnect with the parts of yourself that may have been suppressed for years.
3. **Release the fear of rejection:** You can release your fear in the following ways:
    - **Acknowledge your fear:** Until you acknowledge your fear, you can't release it. The best course of action is to simply breathe and acknowledge that you're feeling scared. Acknowledging your fears out loud releases their hold over you.
    - **Understand the root of your fear:** Your mind is like an onion so be open to exploring its depths. Understanding the source of your fear allows you to release it at its deepest roots. Two writers can have a fear of rejection stemming from two very different incidents that lead to two different behavioural tendencies. Events in our past plant seeds for negative emotions and behaviours in the present; to change our behaviour and emotions, we have to destroy these seeds at the root.
    - **Surrender to the fear:** It's okay to be scared of rejection. It takes a lot of courage to put yourself out there and follow your heart, so take the time to question the beliefs, stories and memories that gave birth to

The Destroyer

that fear and then celebrate every time you step out of your comfort zone and allow yourself to risk rejection. Celebrate the courage it takes for you to write something and share it with the world.

CHAPTER 9

The RunAway

This is my Secondary archetype. RunAways are adults who have learnt how to escape from situations. They are probably scared of confrontation and easily overwhelmed by their emotions or anything that requires them to fully drop into their bodies.

They appear to be inconsistent because they don't have a lot of staying power and will quickly leave challenging situations and relationships. One of their biggest life lessons is developing resilience and sticking to it through the hard times.

They have learnt to run away by dissociating from their bodies; they run away either physically, through books or other fantasy outlets, addiction (as a form of self-medicating) or by completely numbing out and not allowing themselves to feel anything emotionally.

As adults, they have checked out of the family structure. They seldom show up for family events. They are out there looking after their immediate family and have minimal contact with extended family. Being around their family can be triggering because they sense everything so they rather stay away.

They may always be travelling, partying, with friends, doing drugs/drinking, involved in a new relationship – any distraction that means they are not with themselves, at home and/or within their bodies. In fact, they are seldom around to resolve any issues. And even if they do show up for a wedding or a funeral, they're just there for a minute and then escape. They have learnt to cope with the trauma and all the emotions they feel within the family by avoiding them. Often, they will establish their own family unit elsewhere, outside of the family unit.

They also very rarely contribute financially; they attend family functions when they feel like it and don't call or keep in touch with most family members. Because of this, they are not bothered with financial issues at home.

Their role in the family

When I think of the RunAway archetype I think of myself (and others like me in many Black families). I left home at 17 to go to university. But I wasn't thinking of studying; I was leaving because university provided an escape for me – an escape from family drama and the trauma I saw playing out. All I could think about was how freeing it would be to fall asleep not having to sense everyone's anxiety or be overwhelmed by my family's emotions, or to stick my head in a novel just so I could escape my family. (Book nerds are often obsessed with books not because they are studious, but because books offer an opportunity to leave their bodies and stay in their minds.) I knew I was never going to return home to live there permanently, which is why I purposefully chose to move 2 000 kilometres away, to get an apartment and live off campus and find myself a job as soon as I got to university. I knew I was not going home, even for holidays. I was finally free and I could stop running away from home; I was going to have my own home and finally do me. And that's exactly what I did for years: I never went home, even for Christmas, because home was just too scary. If I did go home to visit, I would go with a plan and a set time of when to leave.

When I graduated I went travelling and used travels as my excuse to not return home; I rarely came home for funerals or weddings and was seldom involved in anything family-oriented. There was a period when my family didn't see me or hear from me for four years; my paternal grandmother was the only one I spoke to on a regular basis (she was the only one I was concerned about) while I was off seeing the world. To be honest, I was very selfish – I only called home when I needed something. This was normal to me and it was amazing! I think I could have gone on like this my entire adult life, but then I discovered vipassana meditation and ancestral trauma and started my healing journey. Within a year something strange happened – I moved back home for a while and I got involved in family stuff. Even though I travel constantly and am a dedicated nomad, I am always in touch with my family and always come home now.

The role of the RunAway is to metabolise the unseen and unprocessed trauma in the family. RunAways absorb the trauma and try to energetically process it for everyone so that it doesn't weigh family members down. They are extremely empathic because, as children, they simply did not have the resources to process the trauma they felt and absorbed and were easily overwhelmed by it all, carrying too much in their bodies. Unless they have a Destroyer or Fixer Secondary or Primary archetype, the RunAway is often overwhelmed by the complexity of this trauma and has to leave their bodies in order to cope.

Often there's this misconception that RunAways flee from the issues within the family because they are uninterested, but that's not true. They run away because they are overwhelmed and unable to handle any more of the trauma because they lack the means to process it. RunAways actually feel too much. So they feel almost everything happening within the family and they don't have the resources to process what they are feeling and sensing within their unit. As a result, they tend to escape and completely dissociate from their bodies.

Dealing with the RunAway can be very frustrating for many because you're only likely to see a RunAway at family gatherings; the rest of the time they are never around.

When I started doing my healing work I was taken aback by the number of the memories I had to process concerning other people's emotions experienced in my teens. I sensed so many of the adults' fears and anxieties and so co-dysregulated to a lot of their nervous systems, because at that age I had no resources or tools to set energetic or nervous-system boundaries.

As a romantic partner, the RunAway may often check out of the relationship when things get bad – they may withdraw emotionally or escape into new relationships.

As a child

As a child, the RunAway learnt to deal with trauma in the family by shutting down emotionally and dissociating from their body. The deeper the trauma or the more dysfunctional the family, the more trauma the RunAway child was required to metabolise within the unit, which lead to the nervous system being overwhelmed. Some RunAway children shut down and dissociate because they reach capacity (referred to as allostatic load) at a young age.

The allostatic load refers to the wear and tear of the body and its ability to handle day-to-day stresses; the more stress a person is exposed to, the more the body is affected (Guidi et al., 2021). This is why the role of the Destroyer is so important – the Destroyer forces all the members in a family to do their own healing work, which alleviates the burden on the RunAway.

When things got very hard for me at home in my teens and I could no longer take all the emotions I was sensing because I am also an empath, I would just check out and I run away, head to the streets or just disappear for a few days. To the adults around me I was just a rude and troublesome child, but the truth was that I was just overwhelmed by everything I was sensing in my family and the adults' inability to process and integrate their trauma.

Most people tend to think that the RunAway child just couldn't be unbothered, or is self-absorbed, doesn't care, isn't invested in anything within the family, and yet nothing could be further from the truth. The RunAway is a child whose nervous system is overtaxed so they have no idea how to process all that they are feeling. The only way they can feel safe enough to process anything is to escape so they can get a break from feeling too much.

As a parent

The RunAway as a parent is interesting – they can either be an ostensibly present but essentially absent parent or completely absent, depending on their Secondary archetype.

The RunAway parent and the Eternal Child archetypes are the most likely to disappear and very rarely, if ever, see their children or even support them financially or emotionally, because they just don't have the emotional capacity to parent since they are so often overwhelmed by their own trauma. This is especially true if these archetypes are primary profiles.

If the RunAway parent does choose to stay and be present, they may struggle with being fully present; they will thus avoid dealing with the uncomfortable situations of raising a child or having anything to do with child rearing. The child seldom sees them and barely has any relationship with them, because they have checked out. The parent may escape through their work – the workaholic parent – or as a result of alcohol or other addictions so that they are never emotionally available. They have simply never learnt how to deal with emotions, how to sit with them and how to process them in their nervous systems and in their body.

The RunAway parent can also be fantastical – they don't know how to deal with the everyday realities of parenting; they are always living in a fantasy and easily make and break promises to their children. In fact, their children may trigger their own childhood wounds, which forces them to deal with their childhood needs and, when they are triggered, they run even further. Essentially, they don't know how to show up for their children, how to parent them and how to deal with realities of child-rearing or any of the discomfort their children may bring up, so they tend to leave all child-rearing to the other parent. And, of course, if both parents are RunAways, the child may be left to parent themselves.

To cope with the RunAway as a parent, a child may adopt the following archetypes:

- **The Sweet One:** The child believes they have to be good and do everything right to get their parent's attention and to keep their parents in their lives. They become the 'perfect child' who is overly sweet and agreeable.
- **The Fixer:** The child now has to learn how to parent themselves or to be the sidekick to the present parent and may end up helping with other kids.
- **The Eternal Child:** Because the parent is never available to parent, the child never learns how to be an adult and has no resources to guide them into adulthood. As a result, they remain an Eternal Child, unable to grow up because they have just never been parented.

Managing life and finances

One of the biggest blocks to the RunAway's wealth creation and expansion is their inconsistency. Of all the archetypes, the RunAway is most likely to start projects – especially wealth, investment and entrepreneurial ventures – and abandon them when the going gets tough.

They often have fantastic ideas, but have a hard time bringing any of those visions to life and may find themselves jumping from project to project. This makes it challenging to work with them to build generational wealth in a family or even in a romantic relationship, because challenges are part of our journey.

On the flip side, the RunAway may run away to work and business and use money-making as an escape, a substitute for feeling safe in their bodies. But when this happens, they may equally have a hard time spending money (because having money means being safe); the belief that money keeps them safe will also lead to them fixating on making money and growing wealth, to the detriment of everything else.

Interestingly, because they spend a lot of time in their heads, this archetype is blessed with the ability to manifest a lot of their desires. The challenge arises when they must bring about really ambitious goals, particularly financial ones, that challenge their sense of security. In this case, they will reach a ceiling and then ensure that they stay there in an effort to remain safe.

Blocks to wealth and expansion

The RunAway has a difficult time increasing income because of their inconsistency and lack of resilience.

This lack of consistency can work against them when it comes to entrepreneurial ventures and building wealth – they may never hang around long enough to see any business through and build generational wealth. Although they do well when the business or venture is succeeding, they will jump ship as soon as things start going bad.

They may also have a hard time advancing in their careers because they don't want to have to deal with the stress and conflict in workplaces or, worse, they may get sucked into their work and work politics to escape feeling their emotions or interacting with their families. Ironically, they make great academics because studying and research provide an escape to a less emotionally messy world.

Blocks to increasing income

The RunAway's most significant block to increasing income is their inability to remain consistent. They always quit when faced with difficulties and move onto the next exciting venture when they are challenged. This means that they tend to quit entrepreneurial ventures when they don't get the results they want or jump from job to job and never really build a career. They may look like free spirits, but there's also an element of escapism at play, and this can lead to reduced productivity and efficiency, potentially affecting their ability to perform well in their job or business.

RunAways also have a hard time feeling safe in their bodies, which can affect their self-esteem and confidence. This may make it harder for them to pursue opportunities, or present their skills and abilities to others. Confidence plays a significant role in professional success, because it affects how you market yourself, negotiate, and take risks.

Blocks to getting out of debt

The RunAway often uses money to accumulate possessions or buy experiences to avoid dealing with their feelings or simply to stay out of their bodies. Because they have no connection to their family of origin, they can also use money to buy their way into social circles and become part of a tribe. To satisfy their desire to belong, they may be social butterflies, but are also reluctant to fully commit to any social tribe too deeply (unless that tribe is into escapism with alcohol or parties) because commitment means getting emotionally involved and they don't have the capacity for that.

Their downfall is that they choose the easiest path. So, if it's easier to buy things on credit, that's the path they will choose; and if getting out of debt seems too challenging, they will stay in debt and keep recreating the cycle of debt. They tend to have a bad credit score and will avoid looking at their bills and debt statements because that's too uncomfortable for them, so they struggle to pay bills on time.

Because of their resistance to face reality, the RunAway's family dynamics when it comes to money can be challenging, and others often have to step in to try to save or help the RunAway.

Family dynamics around money

A RunAway may step back from a family project (or business partnership) when things get challenging, leaving everyone hanging. They never ever see an investment through, and may even give up on savings goals at the first hiccup and remain in debt if repayment is too challenging.

If your partner is a RunAway, you may end up shouldering the bulk of the responsibility for their finances (savings, investments and budget) because they prefer getting help from their significant other rather than their family of origin – especially if approaching the family means being dragged back into the trauma.

Core wounds

Let us take a look at the core wounds of the RunAway and how they affect financial behaviour.

Wounds around safety

Trauma affects our ability to regulate our nervous systems and to feel safe in our bodies. Porges (2022) argues that health and wellbeing strategies fail us by not acknowledging that feelings of safety are directly connected to our physiological state and regulated by the nervous system.

A regulated nervous system isn't one that is in perpetual calm, but one that can experience stress and integrate trauma and emotions and then go back to normal when the threat has passed (MHS Journals, 2020). In other words, a regulated nervous system can go from fight or flight to rest relatively easy and doesn't get stuck in hypervigilance.

When the brain cannot differentiate between real and imagined danger it will stay stuck in hypervigilance, because that is the mind's way of protecting the body from danger. However, most of us are already carrying ancestral trauma and in a constant state of hypervigilance or we have been avoiding our feelings for a long time, forcing ourselves to feel happy or grateful, so when hectic events unfold around us, they tend to overwhelm our nervous systems, and it becomes difficult to process these events. As a result, we get stuck in hypervigilance, or just dissociate and pretend things aren't happening.

When we are in a state of hypervigilance, we are anxious, unable to sleep, unable to focus, tend to overanalyse situations and are overwhelmed by crowded and noisy environments (Burgess & Legg, 2017). And when we dissociate we can feel detached from our experiences, become numb, experience a blurred sense of reality or completely blank out to such a degree that we are unable to remember anything for a period of time (Tull, 2022).

Often, individuals who have almost no memories of their childhood or find it hard to access these memories have dealt with the trauma by dissociating. For the longest while, I had no clue why I couldn't remember my childhood and teens; those memories only started coming back when I began to connect with my body.

We can also become frozen in the trauma, resulting in us feeling exhausted and stuck and feeling like we cannot breathe deeply enough. As RunAways, we have learnt to deal with trauma by running away and/or dissociating from the body, which means either physically fleeing situations, or escaping (emotionally and/or spiritually) through imagination, zoning out or self-medicating.

RunAways struggle to stay in their body and feel everything, so they must find a way to distract themselves. They, more than any of the other archetypes, need to practice self-care in order to keep processing and integrating past and present trauma so that their body can once more feel like a home for them.

How does feeling unsafe affect the financial behaviour of RunAways?

- **Decreased income:** According to Burgess & Legg (2017, being in a state of hypervigilance can lead to physical and mental exhaustion, difficulty with relationships, problems in the workplace and social anxiety. Anxiety, in turn, leads to avoidance behaviour (particularly when it comes to money), which leads to us running away from our finances by refusing to make money, which leads to a decrease in income (Makwakwa, 2013).

    Physical and mental exhaustion, of course, affect our ability to think clearly and take action and so lead to procrastination, which leads to a decrease in income. Problems in the workplace, on the other hand, diminish our chances of promotion or career progression, which further decreases income. Difficulty in relationships and social anxiety make it difficult for entrepreneurs to build a team and connect with clients effectively, which affects business performance and also leads to a decrease in income.

- **Increased debt:** When we are in a state of hypervigilance and feel unsafe, we are likely to feel anxious; anxiety then leads to impulsive spending, which means that we tend to get rid of money by spending it as quickly as possible, which leads to increased debt (Makwakwa, 2013).

    Physical and mental exhaustion also lead to a lack of mental clarity, which may lead to us feeling overwhelmed by our finances, making it even more difficult to make good

financial decisions, which leads to increased debt.
- **Decreased savings:** Anxiety due to our continued state of hypervigilance can lead to extreme panic and depression (Makwakwa, 2013), which can lead to the RunAway completely avoiding all matters of finance (including their bank account), which leads to decreased savings.

It should also be noted that if the RunAway feels unsafe with money or associates money with unsafety, they may create emergencies in order to get rid of money or savings until they return to their money set point, because that set point gives them a sense of safety, even if it means always being in overdraft or zero in their bank account.

Feeling powerless

A study by Booth et al. (2012) explored the link between neighbourhood safety and mental distress and found that the more unsafe a person felt in their neighbourhood, the more powerless, distrusting and alone they felt. So, if we grew up feeling unsafe in our environment – either because the environment was unsafe or because our caregivers' nervous systems were dysregulated – there's a high probability that we learnt to feel powerless and that our inner child still carries that sense of powerlessness. In fact, one of the reasons the RunAway is inconsistent with their finances is because their inner child believes they are powerless and, as a result, they tend to be easily overwhelmed by certain activities. They struggle to feel at home within their own bodies, or feel the power that their wombs or solar plexus hold, which then impacts on their ability to bring their vision to life (Lynch, 2011).

If RunAways grew up in an environment where there was a lot happening and they were constantly processing events, their nervous systems in a constant state of hypervigilance, they may have reached their capacity to deal with complex (or even basic) life events and experiences at a young age and may have been labelled as someone who gives up easily, which would have affected the way they see themselves as well as their identity. This sense of powerlessness, the inability to bring their visions to life and/or lack of follow through, can then impact their sense of self and leave them feeling inadequate.

Most people think the feeling of 'not good enough' is a mental issue, but it's also a nervous system issue. We have to delve into the body to heal this and tap into our power to feel safe in the body and start feeling powerful again.

One of the things I had to do as a RunAway (Secondary archetype) was to learn to be in my body, and the most transformative tool for me was vipassana, because for 10 days I could no longer run away. I could no longer overspend. I could no longer use money and credit cards to pretend that I wasn't feeling the things I was feeling. I couldn't go out to movies and restaurants. I had to sit and be in my body and get to really, really understand what was going on within my body.

That's when I started incorporating (and developing) a lot of somatic healing exercises into my healing journey. I worked with my body to start integrating the trauma I had stored in it. And the more I was able to do that, the safer it felt for me to be in my body. And the safer it felt for me to be in my body, the more I was able to start reclaiming my power. The reason for that I was also starting to integrate a lot of the trauma, which meant that my allostatic load started to lower and I was able to actually start processing events in my day-to-day life and integrating childhood trauma.

The more trauma I started integrating, the less overwhelmed my nervous system felt and the more capacity I had to process events in the present, as they arose, which meant that I could eventually find my own power, build my resilience and persistence muscles, be more consistent and start making my visions a reality.

The more I healed, the more compassion I was able to find for myself and my family, and to see that I was capable and more than enough. I had, in fact, always been enough – I just didn't have the tools to process all I was feeling and experiencing at a very young age.

How feeling powerless affects the RunAway's financial behaviour:

- **Decreased income:** Research by Van der Toorn et al. (2015) found that US workers who were powerless and most financially dependent on their supervisors were most likely to describe themselves as fairly paid. They concluded that those who are powerless want to make sense of the world by justifying their unfair treatment and are most reluctant to change their situation, no matter how bad it is.

    Based on this research, it can be argued that employees (RunAways) who feel powerless are thus most likely to accept unfair treatment and a lower income than their peers, and even price their products and services at a lower price, which would lead to decreased income.

- **Increased debt:** Research by Rucker & Galinsky (2008) found that people who feel powerless have a strong desire to purchase products that convey a high status, because they believe that this will make them feel powerful. Those who participated in the study were willing to pay above market rate for items when they felt powerless.

    The RunAway often feels powerless, which can prompt them to purchase luxury products and spend more on products and services to regain their sense of power, leading to increased debt.

- **Decreased savings:** Considering the above arguments, the RunAway is likely to have limited income and increased debt, which will lead to decreased savings.

CASE STUDY

The RunAway

VANGILE: Hello, Laila. Please tell us where you are from.

LAILA: I'm from Morocco.

VANGILE: What would you say is your relationship with your family when it comes to money?

LAILA: When it comes to family, it's a little complex in a sense that I am not taking up that role of provider. I'm the eldest, so I'm expected to be providing or helping or bringing something to the household, either through my own income or my husband's income. But right now, I'm not taking any roles in the conventional structure.

VANGILE: And how has that been received?

LAILA: It's hard to tell because I don't live with family. I'm not taken seriously. I'm seen as the lost kid. I'm pitied. I'm asked if I need help. So the conversations with my mother are going to always revert back to 'I know that you can't provide for yourself, so how can I help you?' It's a way to regain control.

The fact that I don't give means that there is something wrong. Since she's not receiving from me, the only way to justify that is that I don't have enough in the first place to be giving because they can't even imagine a scenario where there is an alternative. They can't imagine a scenario where I am saving for something for myself.

VANGILE: How did you free yourself from these family expectations?

LAILA: I physically left the family unit. That was the first thing I did after I started working. The decision was to not even be in the same city but to leave. That's the only way I can justify moving out of the house, otherwise I'm expected to stay in the household until I get married. The only way I can justify my independence is by saying there is a better opportunity elsewhere with a better salary. Even that was not reason enough; I received resistance and they stopped talking to me for a while. But I had to remove myself physically to another city and then completely out of the country to do what I wanted to do, but also to never disclose how much I was making.

VANGILE: How do they imagine you are able to travel as vastly as you do and live the life that you do in foreign countries?

LAILA: I don't know. They never get curious. I can only make assumptions. I share sometimes that I get help when I'm in between jobs because there is that worry of, 'Do you need something?' No, I don't need anything. I can provide for myself and I have a plan. And I over explain so that my mother gets it. With freelancing, it's not always secure, but I have learnt to have some savings for when things get hard. I have friends around; I am resourceful. I make sure that I tell my mother what's happening. But at the same time, there were times when I was doing well, but instead of sending money home, I would just downplay what I was making. I have that pressure to not have anyone ask me for anything. I don't know even how to express it, but there's a lot of hiding.

VANGILE: Would you say you're hiding so that you don't have to take part in the family unit and some of the stuff? Are you only hiding because of financial obligations or are there other factors within the family that make you want to hide so that you don't have to participate in the family unit?

LAILA: Yeah. It's both – there is guilt associated with the lifestyle I'm leading when it's seen as luxury. I'm travelling, I'm living abroad, I move a lot. There are extra expenses for visas, for example, to stay in places. Moving can be expensive. I'm not living lavishly, but there is extra cost that can be seen as unnecessary.

My family can't wrap their head around this life choice,

instead of sitting at home and getting by the way they're getting by. I could pick up any job back home and sit at home and be okay with whatever salary I'm making; I can provide little things. I can be close to them and gift them instead of living the way I'm living because my need for travel or need to see the world is seen as being spoiled or a luxury and we are not allowed to have those luxuries if the family is in a different status.

VANGILE: It's almost like you've had to make a decision to choose yourself or choose the family?

LAILA: Exactly. There is always an underlying shame or guilt linked to my way of living. There is always this thought that I have that I'm not supposed to have nice things when I left my parents who don't allow themselves to have nice things. I'm happy for myself. I'm happy. I chose to live this way at a conscious level. I'm intentionally doing this for myself. But, subconsciously, there is this fear at the back of my mind that this might end soon. I'm not supposed to have this. There's this anxiety, which is why sometimes there's some hiding because I'm scared of judgement. Because a part of me still believes that I'm betraying my family in a sense.

VANGILE: I think this feeling of betrayal will often be there for those of us who come from very collective families, especially within Africa, because we have been taught to do for the collective, not just ourselves. How do you think your relationship with your family and this internal conflict impact your income in the way that you earn money or make money?

LAILA: There's a lot of internal conflict. This is just my theory. But my father doesn't talk to me for different reasons. For one, it's this whole choosing and leaving home. I think I triggered him; it's betrayal or it's threatening his social life. Maybe he can't face society whenever people ask about me, and maybe it was too much for him to handle. I can only just make excuses because he's not talking to me, so I don't know the reasons because no one is telling me why. I am just left to make assumptions and left to justify this. But if I make a guess, my guess is that I threatened his social survival as the man of the house, not living by his rule. I defied him. I betrayed him. I'm being ostracised in a way. He refuses to talk to me. Mind you, I was close to my father, but now I'm closer to my mother.

I realised, though, that because I don't have that relationship with my father, I am vulnerable in workplaces, in negotiations. I don't know why [but] in my head I keep thinking that money is a masculine energy, or at least that the spaces I navigated to negotiate for myself or to work are masculine.

In recent years, working with men and working in those environments has been hard for me because of the wounds related to my relationship with my father. So I feel like it affected me in a way that I don't know how to trust myself. I am not pricing properly ... I'm not valuing what I do. I don't price well. I have an unstable source of income. I'm still navigating that. I'm still trying to understand. I'm still trying to see if it's true, if it's real, if these two are linked – my relationship with a father and money.

My mother's side ... I'm not sure yet, but it has affected me in ways that I don't feel supported. And if I feel supported, I don't trust myself. And if I don't trust myself, then I'm not confident and I always have this low self-esteem and I'm not valuing my work and I am vulnerable. My position is a bit vulnerable when it comes to navigating work or even daring to do business.

VANGILE: Yes, that makes a lot of sense. I won't go deep into just the specifics of the mother and father wound, but life without family support is challenging. Imagine a chair. When you lean back, you're not often aware that the chair has a back, but when you lean back, that back support is there. When it's not there, you're so aware of it. I think that sometimes it becomes harder to take risks when we don't have that support because who will hold us when we fall apart?

How do you think your relationship with your family and your decision to leave the family have affected the way you spend and save money?

LAILA: I think the way I spend money is affected by what I learnt growing up. The way I earn is fuelled by anxieties, like you said, because I know I'm not supported, because I know there's no way I can go back to seek refuge in case things don't go well.

If I take a big risk and it doesn't work, I can't go back home. I can't go back to that dynamic. So I'm always going to go for scraps or for enough to get by. I would rather do that than risk going back. So even when there is an opportunity for me to go after something that I really want, I wouldn't do it because I know that I would rather just survive out of that house, out of that dynamic, out of the family unit than to go back and have to need them. My fear or my nightmare is to need them.

It's really hard to accept that. That's how it affected the way I make money. The way I spend money is a contradiction – I spend a lot. The minute I get money, I feel like this force of just wanting to get rid of it because I'm not used to it. I'm not used to having enough. I'm not used to saving. I'm not used to looking at my bank account. I've gotten used to being in survivor mode and seeing numbers in my bank account is just temporary before it's a zero. I just know that I have the bills and if there's anything left, it's unsettling. So I find ways to spend it. And I always come up with things that I need to spend it on.

I see a big portion goes to food and it's not even things that I can see. It's things that can finish. But I also understand that it's just that part of me that's not getting the nurturing. I wouldn't say it's expensive dinners, but I'm always after food experiences because that's what's homely to me. That's what's familiar. That's what's nurturing. Whenever I was back home, my mom would make me a nice meal. Or when we're fighting, there will always be food outside my room.

They won't say they love you, but they will always want to feed you. Even my relationship with food is that way. I think that's how it affected my spending.

VANGILE: So why do you say you're very scared to ever need your family?

LAILA: I feel like it would come with a price. I feel like if I need them, I will have to give up something. It feels like it comes at a cost and the cost would be my freedom and independence. It feels like money is control. It feels like it wouldn't feel okay for me to keep living the way I live. If I needed them it would just be affirming what they already know about me or what they already think of me as a child and incapable of providing for herself.

VANGILE: I'm fascinated. Do you feel like resilience is something you've had to learn, or do you feel naturally resilient – that you can stay when things get tough? Or do you find yourself leaving situations, relationships, etc., when things get tough?

LAILA: I think I leave. I think I've always left when things got tough. I'm always ready to pack. I'm on my guard. But it takes a lot for me to reach that point. When I reach that point, I'm breaking. I feel like I need to just save myself. It's also because it's triggering because of all the times where that's the only thing that I wanted to do but couldn't do when I was a child. I was in a situation where there was violence, there was physical violence, and I couldn't escape. So all those times when I was trapped and unable to leave was a build-up, a force that I can tap into every time that part of me is triggered. I can remember I'm not trapped. I give myself that out and I just leave. It feels like every time I do that I release my past self or the child I was that couldn't leave those situations.

VANGILE: That's interesting because I resonate with that so much. It's also making me reflect, as you talk about getting rid of money ... I wonder if maybe, because you can't run from the money, you help money run from you by giving it away and getting rid of it as fast as possible?

LAILA: Yeah.

VANGILE: I'm just wondering, what money advice would you give to someone in your position who barely goes home?

LAILA: I had to observe without judgement. I was writing in your *Next Level You* money journal once and I found myself apologising to money over and over again. Then one day I just wrote, 'I will stop apologising', and I need to acknowledge that I have started unpacking this only two years ago and packing over 27 years of my existence. I'm expecting to all of a sudden, in two years, to do better – it's not going to be possible. And then I just wrote that it's going to be a learning experience. For now, I need to forgive myself for all the mistakes that I will be making. And I accept that I'm making a lot of those same mistakes. And, for me, I think that was one of my breakthroughs – to just give myself grace and to relax. I feel like every time there's money coming in, I'm learning. And I celebrate the fact that I'm just watching myself getting rid of it. I'm fascinated that I can see it. I've never seen it. I seriously think that it's part of my healing to just watch myself without judgement and try my best to not judge myself.

It's a complex, difficult, vulnerable, hard thing to do. And it gets easier if I just watch myself and see the consequences, too. I accept the consequences and keep writing about it. And the change is very incremental. I start to see how, if I hide a little bit in another account, it stays there. If I don't see it, it's not there. I experiment from time to time and see what works for me.

VANGILE: I love this. I love this. And it is a journey. It takes time. And I think that when we do have triggers, we sometimes go back to the old habits, but then the new habits will kick in after a few months. So it is quite a journey. Thank you so much for your time, Laila.

Ask yourself ...

1. What struck you the most about the characteristics of the RunAway profile?
2. Do you find yourself identifying with some of the traits of the RunAway profile? Can you reflect on how these traits have affected your relationships and your finances?
3. Have you noticed any family members who display the RunAway profile? How does their behaviour affect the family dynamics?
4. In what way does the RunAway profile affect your family's financial situation? Are there any patterns of behaviour that lead to financial instability or insecurity?
5. What practical steps can be taken to create a more supportive and welcoming environment for the RunAway profile within the family?

Take action

1. **Movement:** Fitness of any kind helps. Yoga a few times a week is important. Yoga helps the parasympathetic nervous system, which helps us relax, especially yin and tantra yoga. Vinyasa, bikram and ashtanga yoga help activate the sympathetic nervous system and release tension. Actually, all exercise helps release tension.
2. **Breathwork:** Breath is connected to our emotional state; if we can breathe deeply, we can calm the nervous system. Adding sound to the breathing process helps move energy and unlock trauma so that it can be processed.
3. **Meditation:** All meditation is important and beneficial. I prefer vipassana meditation and my own guided meditations in my online course – vipassana because it

focuses on the body, and my course meditations because they focus on integrating ('healing') trauma and being in the body.

4. **Pranayama:** This is also a form of breathwork. I am not good with it, but it did help me in the past when I had a lung infection. It helped me heal in a matter of days. You can find more information on YouTube.
5. **Sleep and rest:** Research shows that our nervous systems are constantly interacting with other nervous systems, so just going out to a shop or work affects us in some way because our nervous systems automatically tune into other nervous systems, so if everyone around us is panicking it takes a toll on our nervous systems to remain calm.
6. **Take breaks and focus on pleasure:** Do this for at least one hour a day. Be intentional with pleasure so that your nervous system knows it is safe to relax and feel pleasure rather than always being hypervigilant.
7. **Get body work done:** I love massages.
8. **Use herbs and herbal products:** There are lots of herbs that we can drink to support our mental health and the nervous system.
9. **Avoid caffeine and sugar:** Coffee is linked to anxiety and simply adds fuel to the fire. Substitute with herbal teas and water.
10. **Talk to an expert:** Consult with a therapist or a trauma-informed coach if things become overwhelming. Remember: self-care means looking after our mental health.

CHAPTER 10

The Fixer

As a child, the Fixer is a mini adult: they either co-parent or play mother or father to their siblings, and so can be bossy and tend to be high achievers from a young age. This is also the big difference between the Sweet One and the Fixer; the bossy Fixer isn't always 'nice' or likable. In order to organise everyone, they have to be driven and sure of themselves, and are not scared to show their true emotions and ruffle feathers and be confrontational. They are outspoken.

Their role in the family

The Fixer, together with the Eternal Child, is the most likely to stay at home in adulthood, but each has different reasons for doing so. The role of the Fixer is to move the family forward financially and materially. In fact, a strong Fixer archetype can move an entire family from abject poverty to true wealth or financial freedom in a single generation.

Fixers are the most energetically strong in the family; they are the ones who often make the hard decisions and the hard calls, sacrificing their dreams for the collective (the family) and taking on the breadwinner role in a family.

They are practical and decisive because it's their job to keep the family from falling apart and they often do this financially because they have the capacity to move their family to the next financial category. Sometimes this can backfire, however, because the Fixer has a vision and a strategy that they came up with on their own (and they are often right), but don't get buy-in of the family, so end up helping – and imposing their help on – those who either didn't ask for it or need or want a different kind of help. The Fixer can then come across as controlling.

Fixers are determined to fix things and get everyone on board, so they can be rather overwhelming because they want to take everyone on their financial vision. If a Fixer starts a company, they want the whole family involved. Their fear of losing love makes it hard for them to just do things alone and because they have such a strong energy, they can move people in the direction they want. However, this may backfire on them and lead to resentment, because they often override other family members' soul choices in favour of what they (the Fixer) deem financially viable. They are the family members who can get the family artist to give up art to study engineering simply because it makes financial sense.

They are focused on building and so often fix what the Destroyer is demolishing – which is very important because someone needs to build what is being broken down. Where the Destroyer wants the truth to come out, even if it tears the family apart, the Fixer is determined to keep the family together even if it means doing so on a shaky foundation.

As adults, Fixers sometimes struggle to set boundaries with family and friends, not because they want to be liked and loved, but because they believe it is their duty to help everyone and take on this role wholeheartedly; they are driven by family responsibility, which adds a lot of pressure and leaves them overwhelmed. They then deal with this by being focused and controlled.

Having started co-parenting their siblings in childhood, they can be very controlling and are scared to lose control in any way, so often come across as having it altogether and perfect. And because they seem to have it altogether, they are saddled with the family's problems and issues, which can be financially overpowering and are thus the ones who feel the impact of Black Tax more than any of the other archetypes. The issue is that deep down they want the perfect family and, at times, they want that at any cost, working themselves to the bone to maintain the family and keep this image of the perfect family.

My own deep money scars come from having seen my mom in this role. I saw how she was willing to sacrifice herself and her children (my sister and me) to keep the family together. But, as sometimes happens with Fixers, people can get frustrated and feel controlled by them and so rebel and turn on them.

To all the Fixers I say, heal your fear of losing love. Don't set yourself on fire for those who will only rejoice when they see you in flames. Walk alone if you must. Just heal. I promise you, the universe will respond to your efforts to heal.

As a child

When I reflect on the Fixer archetype in the family, I see breadwinners, like my mom and my dad, who started shouldering the bulk of the emotional and financial responsibility in their families at a young age and continued to do so into their adult lives. They know Black Tax – they would look after their siblings and siblings' kids and were always loyal to the family. But I have also seen how this responsibility has taken its toll on them as they got older and went through their own financial ups and downs. I have seen the love they have for their families, but I have also seen how emotional they get when they reflect on how much they have given to others and how they feel that may have impacted how much they actually gave to their own kids.

At a self-development workshop a few years ago, I met a 24-year-old who was a recent graduate. As often happens when people meet me, we started talking about money. She told me that she was the first in both her mom and her dad's families to graduate from university and that she was overwhelmed by the responsibilities that come with this degree. She shared how she was expected to attend every family meeting and how all the elders (uncles and aunts) in the family turn to her for advice – how she's now the one that makes decisions about funerals and weddings. And how her mom leans on her and expects her to take over running the house. She felt like her mom was treating her like a husband and the other members of the family were treating her like an adult. And yet, at the age of just 24, she was the one who needed *their* advice and support, but the roles were now reversed.

I keep hearing this from so many young women, who feel like they are taking on a father role in the family. Some of us come from broken families with no father figure, so we struggle with the 'absent father syndrome'. We all know about the daughter who will try to replace her father through romantic relationships and dating older men, but we don't talk about the daughter or son who feels obligated to help their mother carry the financial load. Often, it will be the firstborn who steps into the role of the father, be super responsible and become their mom's wingman. They are the ones who look after the kids and even get a job early so that they are able to pull their weight financially. And, suddenly, their siblings are not just their siblings – they become their kids.

So how does a Fixer deal with life?

These kids are amazing in all they do (no one can argue that). The challenge that they face, in this case, is that they never get to be kids and have no clue how to put themselves first. They have been forced to make decisions a parent should make and learnt to compromise themselves in the way a parent would compromise.

They derive a lot of their value from being everyone's rock and strength, but fear being disappointed, so they have learnt to take control of situations to avoid dealing with disappointment. And, just like a parent, they can't stop themselves from supporting their siblings and eventually even other extended family.

They won't ever say it out loud, but they tend to feel alone; they are seen as the strong ones, the one that everyone leans on, and their strength is thus their downfall. Added to that, their moms or dads have relied on them for a long time, so they have a gaping mother and/or father wound because they have had no parent(s) to speak of.

The financial implications of this is not knowing how to say no to family members, feeling responsible for everyone (especially siblings), trying to do it all alone and not being able to trust the universe to provide and support their dreams. This makes life bittersweet and more difficult than it should be. And when we don't have faith in the universe or we don't feel supported, we block miracles and manifestations.

The Fixer daughter-and-mother relationship

I talked about how the Fixer has the capacity to drive their family to wealth and financial freedom, but the parent-child relationship can sometimes make this challenging, especially the mother-daughter relationship and the father-son relationship.

I focus here on the Fixer daughter-and-mother relationship because that's what I experienced growing up in my maternal family. My dad is also a Fixer, but his dynamic was different with his mom because society has normalised men succeeding on their own terms and providing.

Seldom is the Fixer daughter asked to take on financial responsibility for the family. Instead, they take it on themselves and that is usually linked to their mothers and the mother wound, especially if they grew up in a single-parent household or a two-parent household where the mom parented alone.

The Fixer daughter can sometimes find themselves feeling guilty the more successful they get, and with no way to handle that guilt, they find themselves giving more than they can afford to give to their mothers. They are then confused because they want to remain their mother's sidekick, but they're experiencing so much more than their mothers ever experienced. In fact, very often their adult lives are nothing like that of their mother. They don't want to outshine their mothers or make them question who they are. They may even be scared that their mothers may disapprove of their success or envy them that success and freedom because ... patriarchy!

They understand that they enjoy privileges never available to their mothers, simply because they're living in a different time. And so they feel obligated to give more than they should in an effort to make up for the unfairness of patriarchy and all their mothers gave up for them so they can have this life. They may even feel some resentment for having to give more than they really want to, which makes them feel even guiltier, so they give even more out of guilt and shame. Because how dare they feel that way about their mothers?

The Fixer daughter may even move back home so they can be closer to their mothers (and they don't like it – nor do most other family members) or they leave their kids with their mothers so that their mothers always have someone with them. Of course, they continue to support their children, but then also support their mothers; Fixers are fiscally responsible and always take financial responsibility.

And the more they give financially and emotionally, the more complex their feelings become and they find themselves mothering their mothers out of obligation, love, guilt, shame, gratitude, resentment. Very often these emotions can be extremely overwhelming, which makes it hard for them to be honest as their emotions fester and affect their finances and their relationship with their mothers. This is what makes the Fixer mother-daughter relationship so intense.

So, what is the impact of the Fixer daughter-and-mother relationship on finances?

Guilt and shame are two of the most complex emotions when it comes to money. Anxiety and fear are easy to recognise, but guilt and shame are more subtle and layered, which makes them more challenging to identify or even understand, especially in relation to our mothers.

One way to recognise guilt and/or shame around the mother wound is to observe what happens to your relationship with money when you're around your mom. How do you use money? Are you overspending? Are you taking care of all household expenses? Are you suddenly faced with emergencies out of the blue when you're around your mom or when you have to leave your mom? Or maybe your finances just get stuck and the flow of money slows down dramatically when you're around your mom?

Why do I ask this?

Because guilt and shame are emotional responses to a deep belief that we're doing something wrong, when we feel like this we have to correct this wrong by getting rid of money or blocking money altogether (Makwakwa, 2013).

As a parent

As a parent, the Fixer is goal-oriented and focused on giving their children the very best of everything. They understand the importance of having a solid financial foundation and building generational wealth for everyone in the family and can pass this down to their children. In their shadow archetype, the Fixer can be one of the most domineering and controlling parents, focused on money and overly critical, putting a lot of pressure on their children. This can make kids anxious, and take on a feeling of not being good enough, leading them to deal with that trauma by commonly adopting the following archetypes:

- **The RunAway:** To escape the criticism or the pressure of

the Fixer parent, the child physically removes themselves from the environment by leaving home or they self-medicate or spend their time in daydreams, thus escaping mentally.
- **The Fixer:** To gain their parents' approval, the child becomes a Fixer themselves and so adds to their own pressure, becoming the hyper-focused mini-adult.
- **The Destroyer:** The child says, 'Enough!', and refuses to be controlled and to live up to the parents' standards, so they rebel and start to question their need to hold the family together.

Managing life and finances

Let's take a look at what prevents the Fixer from attaining success.

Blocks to wealth and expansion

One of the key things that may prevent Fixers from fully expanding is their need to control both the process and the journey, thus missing out on great opportunities because they simply don't align with their plans. They may have a hard time learning to stay open to the magic of the universe and receiving with ease. For the most part, though, they do tend to build a wealth portfolio with some assets.

The Fixer is the most financially responsible of the archetypes. They take their responsibility to the family seriously and often start making financial decisions and taking constructive financial action from a very young age. They are also most likely to build lasting wealth in their lifetime, but the challenge for the rest of the family comes after the Fixer has gone.

On the flip side of all this is the Fixers' fear of losing money; losing money can be extremely traumatic for them and can take years to get over, because they have tied financial success and money to a lot of their personal and family goals. One of the lessons they must learn is to give themselves permission to make financial mistakes.

The Fixers are often the ones who manage and control all the finances and do everything without considering a succession plan. They can sometimes take over many of the family's expenses and bills and even force other family members onto a wealth-creation path, even if that means that they are the sole propeller of that path. As a result, when they pass on or anything happens to them, the wealth tends not to stay in the family. How many times have families in African communities gone from wealth to extreme poverty after the breadwinner (the Fixer) passes on?

This is also because the energy of a Fixer is extremely strong and overrides everyone else in the family and so, without a strong Destroyer, they run the show and have everyone going along with whatever is suggested, which is not always beneficial in the long run.

Blocks to increasing income

The biggest block to increasing income for a Fixer is the pressure they put on themselves. Due to their vows of loyalty, they may struggle with boundaries and self-care and end up taking on too much, especially in their younger days, which could then delay their growth and the wealth they plan to create for their family.

Out of anger and resentment, a Fixer can give up all their plans to grow and quit their job and leave their business in an effort to protect themselves and alleviate the pressure they feel. They may even energetically block money in order to do so.

Another block to increasing income is in allowing themselves to step fully into their power because they fear being seen as 'too much' and so hold themselves back to accommodate the feelings of the rest of the family or their friends. In this case, they may subconsciously block themselves from 'thinking big' and committing to their big goals, allowing the universe to support them in their dreams. Ironically, many Fixers understand the power of the magical because sometimes there's no other explanation for their incredible achievements and success.

But Fixers also tend to be very practical because they don't like to be disappointed, so to avoid being disappointed, they may limit themselves to what they believe is indeed possible and work towards that before setting the next goal and going on to achieve it.

Their fear of disappointment and the need to stay in control can also stop them from asking for help and getting the support they need for their careers and businesses. Allowing themselves to be open to support can help them reach their financial goals in a shorter timeframe. Typically, Fixers naturally create magic and can accomplish the impossible, so imagine what they can do when they have support in their business and personal lives and can focus on what Gay Hendricks (2010) calls the 'zone of genius'? The things they could achieve.

A true Fixer will work on finding a solution to their income problems and work to make it happen, no matter what, but they do need to simply accept that disappointment is part of life.

Another thing that can block a Fixer from increasing their income is the pressure they place on themselves to reach certain goals at a certain time. That pressure can leave them feeling overwhelmed, which can lead to procrastination or depression, and in turn delay their expansion process.

A Fixer who allows themselves to think big and to have faith that they have support outside of this earthly plane (Divine and ancestral support) can radically increase their income within a short space of time.

Blocks to getting out of debt

Most Fixers tend to be over-indebted. Much like the Sweet One, a Fixer will go into debt to help family members, but they will often also have a strategy on how to get out of that debt.

A Fixer may go into debt to grow their income or business, but it will be for practical reasons. They do the math and, if it makes sense, they will take on debt. If, however, they go into debt without a strategy in place, they can end up feeling deep resentment and anger towards their family, and the shame of being in debt could cripple them and lead to depression and to them staying in debt. However, the role of the Fixer in the family is to build, so if going into debt will lead to destruction or interfere with their plans of moving the family forward, they will avoid debt.

When I was in my teens my mom (a Fixer) would always complain that my uncle (a Sweet One) was barely able to look after the family for five years before his finances fell apart and she looked after them for 16 years before quitting. She didn't get into debt – she quit.

This is because the Fixer has a lot of energy. A huge part of a Sweet One's energy is spent on suppressing their emotions and desires and playing a role, so the Sweet One doesn't have the boundless energy of the Fixer to constantly go out and take action. Contraction robs us of energy in other areas of our lives.

Family dynamics around money

The Fixer is the consistent giver in the family, except their giving often feels like control and never feels fully free. And they do tend to use money to control others. The only other archetypes a Fixer can't control through money are the RunAway and Destroyer.

Fixers struggle to give to themselves and they struggle to have fun with money (unless they are able to rationalise it and attach a goal to it) but tend to give (unprovoked and unasked) to others. They are so intent on fixing that they give money to fix issues and it almost never works – in fact, they may face push-back at times. People seem not to appreciate their efforts and that hurts them.

They are not the same as the Sweet One because their money

comes with conditions – their money is for fixing what they see as problems, so they complain and make a big deal if the money is not used in the way they see fit.

In their focus and need to control and build the family, most Fixers, especially in Black families, tend to rescue and save the family financially, which is amazing, but in doing so, they tend to deny other family members the opportunity to make financial mistakes and learn from those mistakes, which actually disempowers others and leaves them constantly reliant on them, which can leave many resenting the Fixer. This resentment and dislike can leave the Fixer confused, feeling betrayed and unappreciated because they often see themselves as helping others. But when we help others in a way that leaves them disempowered or at our mercy, those individuals end up resenting us.

The Fixer's need to control and the way they disempower people is why they often find themselves at the centre of family fights and feeling very alone and misunderstood. Just like the Destroyer, the Fixer is confrontational (they may not see this, though) and are often the source of the confrontation.

One point that needs to be emphasised here is that families should beware of upsetting a Fixer, especially one with a Secondary Destroyer archetype. When a Fixer feels unappreciated and betrayed, they can feel deeply hurt and resentful and, as a result, turn all the loyalty and sacrifices they made against the family; they can go nuclear and switch into Destroyer mode and destroy everything. And when that happens, the family will almost certainly fall apart, because a Fixer understands the core foundation of what they have built and so knows how to tear the foundations apart. Sometimes all it takes is for them to step back, leave (if they have a Secondary Run-Away archetype) and stop contributing in any way.

While Fixers can be challenging and exhausting to most of the family, their role is significant and it's important that their efforts be acknowledged and deeply appreciated.

Core wounds

Let's take a look at some of the wounds that may plague the Fixer.

The God wound

The God wound in the Fixer manifests as an inability to surrender and the need to always be in control of everything and everyone. According to an article by Dibdin (2022), the need to maintain control is rooted in a history of trauma and hypervigilance, which keeps us scanning our environment for danger, so we try to control everything to protect ourselves from the trauma. Dibdin explains that someone's need for control will be greater if they grew up in an environment with unstable family dynamics or with emotionally unavailable caregivers.

The Fixer is obsessed with control because they believe that if they let go, things will simply fall apart. They believe that they have to be the one to fix everything for everyone or to fix everyone because if they don't do it, no one else will – or at least do it right, which is something they learnt in childhood (part of the reason they became an adult too soon). They, therefore, have a hard time letting go, surrendering and trusting the process.

They may also have a hard time trusting people, even those who know what is best for themselves, so Fixers may interfere with people's soul callings or purposes, which can cause deep harm and lead to people sometimes cutting them off.

Interestingly, a study by Burger (1985) found that individuals who have a high desire to be in control have higher aspirations, more determination, higher resilience and higher levels of success. This study explains why Fixers are able to achieve such high levels of financial success for themselves and their families.

There is a wound that I call the God wound (a body of work I created) to encapsulate the relationship we have with our own Divinity and how this impacts our ability to ask for and receive money and support.

The God wound has nothing to do with the church or organised religion; rather, it's a wound that originates because of us forgetting our own power and that we are Divinity in human form. It's also a wound that develops when we encounter constant disappointment and are left feeling betrayed or unfairly treated by God/Source/the Universe. This is very real and can cause deep wounds and block manifestations.

When I started understanding how trauma affects our relationship with Divinity, I googled 'Divine wound and God wound' and came up with nothing, so I created a body of work (I created journal prompts, guided meditations, breathwork and EFT tapping exercises with specific scripts) to help people heal this wound, and tested the work with hundreds of clients. The results have been astounding.

When we experience trauma in childhood, we don't just develop issues with family – we also develop issues with the Divine and how we experience our own Divinity in this life. As children, we see our families experience all they experience and so sense the pain and financial frustrations. As a result, we feel powerless and have no idea how to help them overcome that pain. We may start to feel that we don't have the power to change these situations. We see the adults around us struggling to change unpleasant situations and so feel alone and at the mercy of these events and we forget our magic and start to lose faith in miracles. We then start to minimise the Divine and start asking/praying for things we think are indeed possible so that we avoid disappointment.

In the process, however, we forget not just our own bigness, but the bigness of the Divine.

The Fixer child may have an opposite reaction: they may decide to take control and do whatever they can in that moment to start working towards a change and to regain their sense of control. But they will only work with earthly tools, and so they learn to rely on themselves. Even if they are 'prayer warriors', they will pray only about those things they know they can do or that they deem possible and then go out and do those things.

There's nothing wrong with this, of course, because Fixers will always achieve what they put their mind to, but research by Watanabe et al. (2002) found that individuals with a high desire for control tend to adopt a problem-solving strategy even when they have no control and so their blood pressure and levels of depression increase drastically. So the need for control, while valuable, can also be stressful and a health risk.

As we get older, we learn to be more realistic and rarely tap into the full spectrum of our power and Divinity. This is a deep hurt for the soul. We pray and believe and, when things don't change, we feel betrayal. It's a deep betrayal, but we are taught never to question God and to have faith. We live with these feelings and emotions. Even worse, as we learn about money and start to establish our own relationship with God/Source, we are taught that Divinity isn't to be mixed with money and yet money is often the reason our families are in pain, or we are in pain. So there's even more confusion and shame that we would be angry at God/Source about our financial pain, which further affects our ability to co-create. As a result, we actively block expansion or even stop asking for Divine help so we can be the truth of how God/Source really doesn't show up for us.

What I have found interesting with the God wound is that the most religious and spiritual people have it on deeper levels. A part of them is stuck in the trauma and angry at God/Source for the constant financial disappointments, but because they've been told that it's wrong to express anger towards the Divine, they choose to go to war with the Divine and make a decision to never break through in order to show that God/Source doesn't really respond to prayers or asks. In doing so, they can get enough people to question the role of faith in our lives and plant seeds of doubt about people's faith. At a subconscious level, our inner child decides that God has abandoned them and, in that state of pain, they separate from the Divine.

This wound will often manifest as deep anger and frustration about life, a sense that no matter what you do, nothing ever works out for you and, as a result, you feel unsupported and alone on this life journey. The trauma of the God wound is thus mixed into our belief of struggle and is played out in our prayers.

Because we have been taught to believe that life is seldom easy – 'Easy come, easy go,' we are told – even our understanding of the Divine is a struggle. We see miracles and quantum leaps as impossible or we attach a price tag to our desires, either through prayer and tithing, or by calling God the King of everything and offering a string of compliments before we even dare ask. This is one of the biggest God wounds and is one of the things that stop us from asking and receiving. After all, who are *we* to ask and receive without going through the song and dance we think Source requires to give us? Consequently, we block our own gifts and miracles until we have done all we can possibly do to be worthy of the Divine.

This also has to do with feeling good enough, but it goes even deeper than that. It's about ease!

I have a feeling that sometimes we delay our breakthroughs until we are thinking positively enough and feeling good or grateful enough. Until we have affirmed enough or healed enough. It's as if we are saying we'll only be granted our desires/dreams once we are perfect or deserving enough. Or, worse yet, we delay the manifestation of our dreams until one day in the future. But let's not fall into that trap. It is still the God wound at play.

Who taught us that businesses take years to grow and turn a profit?

Who taught us that we need to take vacations once or twice a year?

Who taught us that we need to work around the clock to build or grow our businesses? Why can't we work two hours a day or even a week?

Who taught us that it's easier to save the little money we have than to expand and give ourselves permission to make more money?

Who taught us that to receive more money and make more money, we need to do extra, work twice as hard and do all we can?

Why do we believe these teachings?

And I think we do this in church as well – we delay the breakthrough and our receiving until we have prayed hard enough and long enough. Until we feel deserving enough! This is a not-good-enough wound, but it is also a God wound. We assume we have to prove our 'enoughness' to the Divine so that we can be deserving enough to receive the support and make the impossible dream a reality.

To heal our finances and open up to Divine and earthly support we may have to heal this wound and confront our own perception of self and what we have been taught about being in our power, receiving and Divinity. When the Fixer allows themselves to heal this wound, they give themselves permission to do things differently and to seek support, build teams and start to grow in innovative ways. If we believe we are capable of manifesting and shaping our own reality, then we also accept that we are the gods of our own lives. If we are made in the image of the Divine, then we are Source/God in human form; we are also Divinity and responsible for our own reality.

And how do you go to war with yourself?

So, how does the God wound (that need for control) affect the Fixer's finances?

- **Increased income and investments:** As mentioned earlier, the study by Burger (1985) found that those who have a need for control have higher aspirations and higher chances of financial success. The Fixer's need for control leads them to set lofty goals for themselves and their families, and to achieve these goals in the time period they decided on.
- **Decreased debt:** A study by Fernandez-Lopez et al. (2023) found that people with self-control issues have more debt

and are more likely to take personal loans, loans from family and friends and credit card debt, and are also more likely to ask those in their social circles for a loan. However, as already, discussed, Fixers tend to have high levels of self-control and are unlikely to get into debt due to impulsive or reckless spending or even from borrowing money from their social circles, which leads to decreased debt.
- **Increased savings:** Due to the Fixer's need for control and their high levels of self-control, they usually have high income and good spending habits, which leads to an increase in their savings.

A low pleasure and fun/play set point

An article by Dietrich (2017) suggests that we may deny ourselves pleasure as a way to protest against the pain we have experienced in our life, and yet pleasure builds resilience and gives us the capacity to overcome challenging and difficult situations.

The Fixer is the child who became an adult too soon and so they tend to be high achievers. Their inner child may, however, carry deep resentment about being forced to grow up too soon. This child is starved for fun and attention and this starvation can show up as procrastination and self-sabotage.

For a Fixer, procrastination can be a sign that the inner child has had enough of adulting, simply because they've done it their whole life. In this case, the child needs attention and fun. If a Fixer keeps ignoring these emotional signs, though, they will end up sick and burnt out. The issue, however, is that a Fixer often has no idea how to play because they have always been the responsible one, which means they were always on guard and on duty. As adults, they struggle to have fun – especially with money – and have a difficult time understanding how other people can be carefree.

Left unchecked, the Fixer will move the family to the next

income bracket, but may choke the life and energy out of other family members as they impose stringent restrictions on their activities and the way they use money, which may contract and limit financial growth after a certain point.

They may also have a hard time spending money, especially on themselves, which could make it difficult for them to pay for much-needed support in their financial affairs and to look after themselves, both emotionally and physically. Spending money on themselves, especially for self-care, is, however, important for their personal growth and the family's development since they manage so much emotionally and financially within the family. If the Fixer doesn't replenish or look after themselves, they compromise their health and the wellbeing of the family they have worked so hard to support and build up.

When we deny ourselves pleasure and are thus pleasure starved, we may look for pleasure in unhealthy spaces or activities, which can derail our focus. When we are pleasure-full, we can let go of the hypervigilance, trust and allow things in more freely and get quicker results.

As practical as the Fixer may be, they need to start giving themselves permission to go inward and learn how to sit with feelings and sensations of joy and pleasure as much as we learn to sit with feelings and sensations of pain and sadness. We must become as comfortable with joy and pleasure as we are with suffering. A huge part of the work the Fixer thus needs to do is allow themselves to feel safe enough to receive and enjoy pleasure.

I have seen how the more I create safety for myself and allow myself to deepen into expansion, the scarier it becomes for my nervous system because I have spent my whole life learning how to stay safe and protected by playing small and being hypervigilant, so feeling safe by allowing myself to feel relaxed in my body is a constant journey on which I hit my set point often.

One of the first things I learnt in tantra yoga is that the yoni will fully open when we feel safe and relaxed. Our teachers always stressed that heightened sexual pleasure – and orgasms that last for hours and connect us to other realms – rarely come from sexual positions and multiple rounds, but rather from feeling safe and relaxed in our bodies, and that the practice of tantra yoga is to learn to truly relax in our bodies.

I learnt in my practice that if I want to experience great pleasure I need to relax, but in order to relax I need to feel safe, and that safety has many facets – both physical and emotional. Feeling emotionally unsafe means that we contract the body and this can lead to physical pain, which can make expansion challenging.

So how does a low pleasure and low fun/play set point affect financial behaviour?

- **Decreased income:** The Fixer is most likely to make a lot more money than most others in their social circle or family, but allowing themselves to play and experience pleasure would actually lead to an increase in income in their lives. An article by Camille (2021) explains that people who limit pleasure struggle to channel their creative energy and so experience blockages in their sacral (second) chakra, which is the sexual chakra. Sexual energy or excitement is attractive energy and can lead us to attract more money in our lives, which can lead to an increase in income (Makwakwa, 2013).
- **Increased impulsive spending and debt:** Camille (2021) states that if we have a poor relationship with pleasure, we are likely to go to the extreme – we are likely to over consume. This seems counter intuitive, but it makes sense when you think about diet culture and why it never works, how when we restrict food and deny ourselves the pleasure of eating, we end up binge eating and now have a culture of yo-yo dieters. The Fixer may, for example, be hijacked by

their inner child who desires pleasure and fun and so will end up spending more on things they didn't plan for, which may lead to more debt.
- **Decreased savings:** If the Fixer is denying their need for pleasure and fun, they may find themselves on impulsive spending sprees, which may lead to a decrease in savings.

The abandonment wound

The abandonment wound refers to the fear of losing loved ones or having them leave a relationship. This often stems from trauma or anxiety – in fact, a person with abandonment issues may experience chronic anxiety (Villines, 2023).

The fear of losing love manifests as over-giving to – and control of – family and loved ones in the Fixer. On a subconscious level, the Fixer not only gives too much, but is overly involved in their family's lives to make sure that their family needs them and is so reliant on them that they never leave.

Love, together with belonging, is the third need on Maslow's Hierarchy of Needs (Mcleod, 2023), and so the fear of losing love makes sense from an evolutionary standpoint. During the Stone Age, people would die from hunger or the elements if they were cast out from their tribe or were different or disloyal to them in any way. Our ancestors needed each other in order to survive, so they learnt to do things that made them accepted or liked. And being accepted or liked usually meant being like other people and doing what others were doing.

Even though we've evolved, the amygdala – the emotional part of our brain – is still very primitive and hasn't really evolved much, so doing anything that will make us lose love feels like death (Makwakwa, 2017). This is why we have this need to be liked and to be accepted; it's why we obsess about what people will say or think about us, because to our ancestors that information was important to keep them in the tribe.

We learn a lot of our survival mechanisms from our caregivers and families because they are the first people we connect with as children. We learn our money patterns from them, for instance. When we find ourselves going against these money patterns and going against our tribe, we panic, which leaves us with only three viable options:

1. Sabotaging and limiting our growth and expansion so we can be loved and fit in with our family;
2. Continuing to grow and risking making everyone uncomfortable and so losing our family and friends; and
3. Continuing to grow and expand and take the family with us on our financial journey so that we don't lose their love.

Fixers choose the third option: they choose to keep growing and expanding, but also insist on forcing their family and friends to come on the journey with them, which, as already mentioned, can cause problems of its own because Fixers take on a lot of financial responsibility and end up violating the boundaries of a lot of boundaries in the name of expansion and financial growth.

A lot of my clients are Fixers and they often come to me angry and hurt because they've spent years as the breadwinners and have given up so much for their families and then one day, out of frustration, they tell their families just how much they have done for them, expecting gratitude and praise. But, instead of being met with the validation and praise they desire, they receive only resentment and a painful question: 'But who asked you to do all this, to make all these sacrifices and to dictate what's best for my life?'

I understand the Fixer's pain, because this is the same question my mom was asked by one of her siblings when she listed all the ways in which she had helped the family. I can, however, see the hurt and pain from both sides: the Fixer is trying to do good, to not lose their family and make sure everyone grows, but in so doing, they can be dictatorial. Other family members are hurt because they feel as though they have been forced to take a particular path in order to ensure the family's financial growth.

On social media, I also observe Fixers who try to inspire people with business ideas and motivate them to pursue success, only to become frustrated when their ideas are rejected. They see so much potential in others and firmly believe that we all possess the same boundless energy and drive that they do.

How does the fear of losing love impact financial behaviour?

- **Decreased income:** People who are scared of losing love may experience chronic anxiety (Villines, 2023), which could lead to avoidance behaviour and self-sabotage when it comes to money, leading to a decrease in income (Makwakwa, 2013). A study by Mannor et al. (2016) also found that CEOs that struggled with anxiety took fewer strategic risks simply to avoid losses, which affected productivity and led to a reduction in income. And so a Fixer scared of losing love – and experiencing chronic anxiety because of it – may end up taking fewer strategic risks, which could lead to decreased income.
- **Increased debt:** Individuals who are anxious and scared of losing love may give too much to get and keep love, and may even go into debt to help those they love, which could lead to an increase in debt. This is what often happens with the Fixer when they are scared of losing love and are being driven by this fear.
- **Decreased savings:** The Fixer's fear of losing love may lead to a decrease in income and an increase in debt, which can lead to a decrease in savings.

CASE STUDY

The Fixer

VANGILE: Hello, Sipho, where are you from?

SIPHO: I am from the Eastern Cape, but I'm now currently based in Johannesburg, where I am running multiple businesses.

VANGILE: What would you say your relationship with your family is when it comes to money? And what is your role in the family when you think about it?

SIPHO: When I think about my relationship with my family in relation to money, I think of myself as being almost like a mini parent because I'm the firstborn and because I have found myself to have been the most financially literate in the family. I see myself almost, not like the main breadwinner, but a parent for the family where my role is to guide the family financially as I come across more financial information. I then pass it on to the family and I try to implement it. I also see myself as someone to organise the family financially because I found that the family's finances have been all over the place. My role is to try to organise the family's finances so that everything is well packaged and well organised so that my parents and my siblings can have a bird's-eye view of the finances.

VANGILE: Would you also say that you have been working with your family to help grow the financial legacy of the family?

SIPHO: Yes, absolutely. As I come across certain investment opportunities, I take those to the family and encourage them to get into those opportunities after I've assessed them because one would obviously not want the family to invest in something that will lose money. So, yes, I see that part of my role is to also grow the family legacy financially besides just organising it. I also see myself almost like being a hunter for the family but, at the same time, almost like a gatherer.

VANGILE: How has your family received this?

SIPHO: In terms of my efforts to organise and really just package everything properly, I feel that I've not been as appreciated by the family as one would have expected because there have been a few interventions that have, in a way, protected the family because I encourage the family to implement a certain intervention, for example, to establish a trust. Then I found that just by doing that assisted the family in protecting its assets. But I have not really felt that there has been appreciation from the family, particularly from my dad, who's seen as the main breadwinner in the family. He seems to try to almost credit himself for things that may have been suggested by me or implemented by me. Or he will try to quickly move past things that have been suggested by me and have been implemented and been good for the family. It's almost like he wants the credit to go mostly to him. I've also not seen my mom appreciating or showing appreciation for it. Then, with the siblings themselves, I've noticed a bit more appreciation from them in terms of what they say to me verbally, where they express it verbally.

I think for somebody like me who was maybe seeking validation from the parents, I feel underappreciated. I've often felt that my suggestions with the family have been mostly undermined or overlooked, particularly by my father.

VANGILE: Would you say that your relationship with your siblings is more parental than it is a sibling relationship?

SIPHO: Yes, correct. Because, from my teenage years, I have often been indoctrinated by our parents that you must be an example. Your younger siblings are looking up to you. I have then noticed that my siblings were not expected to be an example and I noticed them not doing things according to the textbook. I then found myself trying to parent them and to say to them that they also need to do certain things for their lives to go in a certain direction. I found that this was strenuous on me in terms of my mental health because I've actually been very caring about their lives and where they are going, almost like father-son relationships.

VANGILE: How has this affected your relationship with your siblings?

SIPHO: I will start with the negative sides. What I found is that they often, whenever I'm calling them or trying to talk to them about their careers or their financial lives, I found that they really disregard what I say, almost as if I am being stressful to them, almost like I'm trying to disrupt the carefree lives that they are living according to their own standards. I've also found that if I make certain suggestions to them, they also disregard them. When one is speaking to them, either face to face or telephonically, they will want to quickly change the subject because the things that might matter to do not really matter to them as much. Also, whenever we are hanging out together, because they know me, they don't want me to bring up serious issues like finances or careers.

I get the sense that they may feel that I'm a bit of a control freak in terms of how I want their finances to be. But then, on my side also, there is a feeling of frustration because they often ask me for financial assistance. My motivation to get their finances in order is so that they ask me less for financial assistance because there's the old saying: rather teach them how to fish for themselves instead of you always giving them fish. Now my frustration, when it comes to them and their financial lives or even their careers, is that I want them to get to a position where they fish for themselves.

But the fact is my parents gave me the responsibility, where they said that I mustn't forget my siblings. I must always be caring towards them. I found that to be an extra burden on me, which then motivates me to really want them to be totally independent so that there is no need for me to take care of them. That has been quite strenuous on me, having to always either take care of them or to be like a parent and to control them.

But then on the positive side, I would say that, they have shown more appreciation when it comes to certain interventions that I have suggested for their lives. They might not take it seriously initially, but whenever I try to emphasise it, and I persist, and eventually they do it. Unlike the parents, they do come back and show appreciation later. There was one instance where I suggested to the family that they needed to have properties that would help them to earn an income because both siblings have been unemployed for some time. I thought that a property business for each of them would be a good solution. They have both come back to me and shown gratitude and appreciation.

VANGILE: How do you handle financial challenges? Do you feel that you have a support system, or do you find that you are usually the one giving support to others?

SIPHO: I would say it's the latter, where I feel that I'm the one giving financial support to others. For example, in my immediate family, the parents and the siblings, I find that when it comes to knowledge, information and investment opportunities, I'm the one that is always giving the support. When there is a negative financial issue in the family, I'm the one that often comes up with a solution because of the financial education that I've also invested in myself. There are certain situations where the parents have asked all three of us as siblings to come up with a solution, [and] I found that my two siblings simply just continued as usual without really caring about coming up with a solution because I think they knew at the back of their minds that I will be the one to come up with the solution. In terms of the extended family, I do give actual financial support, maybe not voluntarily, but I find that whenever there is a cousin, an uncle, or an aunt who needs financial support, I often find it a bit difficult to reject their request, almost like coming from a feeling of guilt.

VANGILE: How do you think this has shaped how you make money and handle financial challenges along the way for yourself?

SIPHO: The realisation that there may be many people who need financial support from me has motivated me to build, or to strive to build multiple streams of income, whereby I will know that at a certain stage money doesn't become an issue because there will be such an inflow of it so that whenever a family member is asking for financial assistance, I will be able to assist them. But, on the negative side, I would say it has also made me to, oftentimes, give money, even if I may not want to give it. In other words, it may be difficult for me to say no when somebody is asking for money. But it has motivated me to really try to make more money. But it has also made me really be almost more conscious of my expenses because my mind is always expecting certain financial emergencies.

VANGILE: How do you think your relationship with your family has affected the way you spend and save money?

SIPHO: In terms of the saving habits, it has made me really strive to build up a large amount of savings and investments because my subconscious mind is always thinking that I need to be the saver of the family and I must always have financial resources. In terms of the spending, it has made me a bit more frugal, where sometimes I find myself looking for the cheapest price without looking at the quality. In a way, it creates a scarcity mindset instead of abundance, where my focus shouldn't be on trying to limit the spending on expenses, but my focus should be on increasing the income. I find that the provider role has made me to be a bit more conscious of expenses and wanting to limit expenses.

VANGILE: What do you think has been the impact of this provider role in your life outside of finances, in your personal life?

SIPHO: Because my mind has focused more on the short term, where

I want to spend less now in the short term instead of focusing on the quality because, with quality, then one may spend more now, but you may spend less in the long term. Also, in terms of other relationships outside the family, I've also found that it has made me almost paranoid when it comes to people. My mind will think that a person is approaching me because they want to benefit from me financially. I will also be a bit more conscious of what I'm spending when it comes to my travelling and the time that I spend with friends outside the family.

VANGILE: What would you say to someone who is in a situation such as yours where they feel so much of what they do is about putting the family first?

SIPHO: The advice I would give this person is to really try to strive towards a situation or a life whereby you will be totally independent, or you will be independent of family. In other words, you create a situation where you actually say no, or you reject more requests from family, so much so that it creates a situation where the family finances collapse, especially for the people who are always asking financial assistance.

You want to get to a point where your family realises that they must make their own money, get their own jobs or start their own businesses, instead of one person, or a few people, assisting the rest of the family. In other words, even though you will always remain family and you will continue to love each other, but when then family comes together, they can either assist each other or also coordinate better together.

I would encourage and advise someone to create a life that is independent and doesn't rely on their family, and does not always consider how this can benefit the family, but rather focus first on themselves.

VANGILE: Thank you for your time, Sipho.

SIPHO: Thank you.

Ask yourself ...

1. What inspired you about the Fixer profile and how they approach money matters?
2. Can you identify with any of the Fixer's traits when it comes to managing finances? If so, what resonates with you and why?
3. Have you observed anyone in your family who displays the Fixer profile, and how do their financial habits impact the family's dynamics and money conversations?
4. Reflecting on the Fixer profile's influence, what are the positive and negative effects on your family's financial situation?
5. If you recognise the Fixer profile in yourself or someone in your family, what are three financial strengths that can be harnessed to benefit the whole family's financial wellbeing?

Take action

1. **Reparent your inner child:** The Fixer's inner child needs attention and must be given permission to have fun. When you do the inner child meditation, talk to your inner child, play with them, hug them and tell them that you are giving them permission to have fun and be a child. Ask them what they need the adult-you to do to make them feel better and to just have fun, and then do it. As you do this, you'll notice a shift in your waking life and productivity.
2. **Focus on increasing your pleasure set point:** Make a list of 10 things you like to do for pleasure, like eating, walking on the beach, or taking naps, for example. Then focus on doing at least one of those things every day.
3. **Meditate on the following questions:** What would it feel

like to surrender to uncertainty and changes in my life? What becomes possible for me if I surrender to life? What identities have I constructed about myself? What version of me becomes possible to birth if I strip myself of all my identities?

CHAPTER 11

The Eternal Child

The Eternal Child is the one who never grows and who is always financially supported and looked after. They never achieve financial independence and are cooked for, have their clothes washed, and don't really hold down a job – and even when they do, they always run out of money and need money mid-month. Essentially, their inner child is simply asking to be parented and will force their parents to parent them right in adulthood. This frustrates everyone.

This archetype is different to any of the others in that they don't contribute financially to the family; instead, everyone else usually contributes to them and parents them. In fact, unless they fully heal, they may be parented up until old age. Some may not even move out of home, or live so close to home that they 'shop' for groceries at home. When I reflect on the Eternal Child, I think of the Black man or woman who never leaves home and lives with – and are supported by – their parents or grandparents for most of their lives.

They are parented even in their marriages, so the Eternal Child can be a father/mother or a husband/wife, exerting power even in their powerlessness and forcing everyone to take care of them.

The Eternal Child, like the RunAway, is also prone to addiction and 'running away', having 'sleepovers' at different homes.

Their role in the family

The role of the Eternal Child is to mirror to everyone in the family the parts of them that were denied love, parenting and compassion. This may be because a parent has left, wasn't able to parent, didn't have parenting skills or has passed on, so the Eternal Child feels the lack of parenting the most. As a result, they are the entire family's inner-child and inner-teen wounds and trauma made manifest.

This is a challenging shadow archetype, and often the most triggering, because they represent the trauma of the whole family, forcing everyone to deal with their own parenting wounds. They thus reflect the trauma that family members carry from not being parented or nurtured and their role is to help us acknowledge this so that we can change it and do better with the next generation. This call to acknowledge our inner-child and inner-teen wounds can be triggering for almost all the archetypes.

The Eternal Child can hold everyone in the family hostage, stuck in a pattern. They sabotage their own financial success to force their parents to parent them. Occasionally, this may be a conscious decision, where, for example, as adults they refuse to work and insist a parent pay for things. At other times, it's a subconscious decision, and they block their own expansion because becoming financially free would mean giving up being supported financially.

Across cities, towns and villages around the world, we encounter adults having the same arguments with their parent(s) as though they were teenagers. They still argue about curfew and food being cooked for them and not being bought clothes or their rooms not being cleaned. Much the same is true with lovers and spouses who are being parented in relationships and marriages and refuse to pull their weight.

The child/teen demands love by refusing to grow up or allowing the adult in them to take over the psyche. They need their parents (I'm not even sure whether siblings would suffice) to sit them down, listen to them unpack their wounds, apologise, and affirm their pain, simply to hold them and tell them they are loved. They must do this often until the Eternal Child feels satisfied. It is difficult to say how long that process will take, and my fear is that, in this instance, the Eternal Child may become enabled, simply prolonging the process. So, if a parent decides to take on this role, they have to re-parent with strong boundaries and teach them to be adults.

The issue is that when the Eternal Child goes on to get married and have kids, it can be taxing on their spouse and kids.

As a child

As a child, the Eternal Child never needed to take responsibility for their actions because others in the family always took care of them. They were popular, funny and charming, which allowed them to get away with things. Lacking the parental support they desired, they looked to their friends for guidance and tried to fit in. This led them to adopt a charming and carefree persona to hide their fears, insecurities and trauma.

Unfortunately, as they enter adulthood, it becomes evident that they haven't fully matured. They may struggle with trauma, using it as a way to manipulate others and guilt their parents into giving them what they want. Instead of facing their trauma and healing, they rely on manipulation to meet their needs, hindering their personal growth and work ethic.

It's thus important for the Eternal Child to recognise and address their trauma, heal, and develop healthier ways of relating to others. This will help them break free from the cycle of manipulation and embrace personal responsibility and maturity.

As a parent

If any of the parents is an Eternal Child, it creates deep issues within the family and will most likely lead to an Eternal Child or a Fixer child. As a parent, the Eternal Child, as well as the RunAway archetype, is the most likely to leave their children with their parents or other relatives, fleeing any type of parenting responsibility. They may also become the extra child in their marriage and, because their spouse also has to parent them and look after them, they end up taking resources from their own kids.

The Eternal Child is stuck in the state in which they experienced trauma, so their growth is stunted and the adult self is constantly hijacked by their younger self as the latter tries to protect the Eternal Child from re-experiencing that trauma. Because, in essence, they are children or teens, they either can't fully parent, or are incapable of parenting their kids, and will often leave that to someone else – their partner or other family members. Although they developed physically as they got older, they did not mature emotionally so they are unable to look after themselves let alone someone else. As a result, an Eternal Child won't (or is unable to) pull their weight financially or emotionally in a marriage so they partner well with a Fixer or a Sweet One.

As a parent, they can be tiring, forcing their children to step into the parental role and look after them financially and emotionally. To cope with the Eternal Child as a parent, a child may adopt one of the following archetypes:

- **The Fixer:** In the absence of a parent, the child sees that they need to step in and be a sidekick to the other parent or take over parental duties altogether, and so they turn into a mini adult and start to take care of the Eternal Child parent. They also become a deputy parent to their siblings, picking up the slack of the parents.

- **The Sweet One:** The child longs to be parented and yearns for the parents' love, but does not understand that the parent cannot parent due to trauma. As a result, they try to win their love and validation by doing everything right and by being super sweet.
- **The Eternal Child:** This child has seen adulting and parenting as being little more than a child, so part of them remains loyal to the parent and they choose to mirror their behaviour by remaining the child. Or they struggle to grow up and integrate their own trauma because they don't have the tools or a parent to show them how, so they remain an Eternal Child.

Managing life and finances

Let's look at what prevents the Eternal Child from attaining success.

Blocks to wealth and expansion

The Eternal Child is constantly at war with themselves – an internal war between the adult self and the inner child and inner teen. They are constantly, or often, hijacked by their inner child and inner teen and these sub-personalities now run the show.

The issue is that children don't know a lot about the complexities of wealth creation and often spend money recklessly, living in the moment, with little regard for the future, so it is quite common for the Eternal Child to never accumulate any assets or ever buy property. Some Eternal Children can even go years without a bank account because they have no financial responsibility.

Because children generally have minimal financial responsibilities, part of them believes that they will always be taken care of and show almost no interest in planning for the future or building generational wealth, not even for their children or spouse.

Blocks to increasing income

The Eternal Child is not proactive in making money, content to just chill at home doing nothing. They may receive income from other family members, which is often the only way that they are able to survive.

They struggle to create consistent income and find it challenging to keep a job or a business running. They don't like routine, consistency, or responsibility because they are like children or teenagers who are easily bored and need constant entertainment. And even if they do have a job or a business, they may do only the bare minimum, often leaving others to do the work for them, yet tend to take credit for the work, which makes them extremely challenging to work with, because they want all the fun but none of the responsibility.

And when they do have jobs or start a business, they may struggle to use that money wisely or to keep growing the business or working towards a promotion in the job because, to children, any amount of money looks like a lot of money.

Blocks to getting out of debt

Having money may overwhelm the Eternal Child, leaving them worse off than before. I feel like South Africans see this playing out on the TV show, *I Blew It*. The Eternal Child is essentially a child in an adult's body. They reason like a child and, just like children, don't care about credit reports and credit scores.

The subconscious of the traumatised inner child or inner teen is overwhelmed because they have no clue what to do with all that money and try to find ways to make themselves feel safe. Having money (or more money than they're used to) can feel unsettling and unsafe for the Eternal Child's nervous system and so, to protect themselves, the parts of them that feel scared, unsafe, guilty or ashamed of having more money, block money or get rid of money in an effort to feel safe again.

To make themselves feel safe, they tend to spend recklessly until they have almost nothing left, and may even buy extravagant gifts for others. They enjoy spending their income with friends. Think about it: kids tend to be all about sharing and having fun, so the Eternal Child loves spending money on having fun with friends.

When they make money, they don't think about family, responsibilities, budgeting, or bills. They also tend to give away money to family and friends (kids can be very generous). Because of this behaviour, the Eternal Child either has no debt (especially if they have no bank account) or an insurmountable amount of debt.

Family dynamics around money

The Eternal Child can be one of the most selfish family members because they require constant looking after – emotionally and financially – yet give very little back to the family unit. At their worst, the Eternal Child may seem to be a Destroyer because they also have the capacity to destroy a household, especially if the family has limited resources and their constant taking energetically and financially depletes a family. They will take and take – in marriage and in their family of origin – in the same way children and teenagers do.

They may stay at home and never pay for food, rent or household expenses; like children, they assume that these will just appear, which can be frustrating and can lead to those around them trying to get them to change, to give them purpose, a vision, a job, anything to make them take responsibility so that the burden is lifted. So, although the Eternal Child doesn't start conflict, they are often the source of the conflict because at some point everyone (except the Sweet One) starts to feel the burden of parenting them.

Family members will exhaust themselves trying to force the Eternal Child to be responsible, but dealing with the Eternal Child is like dealing with a child or teenager and you need to work on helping them heal that child or teen so the adult can step up and start to adult.

If the Eternal Child has a Sweet One as a parent, they may never feel a need to heal because the Sweet One will enable their behaviour, support them financially, be overly understanding and constantly parent them, which creates an element of co-dependency.

Core wounds

Let's look at the core wounds of the Eternal Child and how they affect their financial behaviour.

The wounded inner child or teen

Our mind and our nervous system are hardwired to keep us safe, so when the mind perceives danger (real and imagined), the amygdala is activated. This then lets the body know that danger is near and the motor functions that control fight or flight are activated, which then triggers the release of stress hormones and the sympathetic nervous system (Javanbakht & Saab, 2017). As a result, the body gets ready to either flee or fight – blood flows to the muscles, the brain becomes hyper alert and digestion slows down (since blood goes to the muscles) (Javanbakht & Saab, 2017). When the stressful situation abates, the mind will register that the threat has gone and the amygdala will let the body know that all is well and bodily functions will return to normal.

The problem comes, however, when we are exposed to highly stressful situations or psychologically, energetically, emotionally and physically unsafe situations (in either childhood or adulthood) for long periods. In these cases, the amygdala constantly registers danger and consistently sends signals to the body that we are unsafe, which means our fight-or-flight response is always activated. This keeps us in a state of hypervigilance and can overload the nervous system, making it harder for the nervous system to process trauma, which leads to nervous system dysregulation and can eventually make it very difficult for us to differentiate between non-threatening and threatening situations (Weinreb, 2019). In fact, the research by Weinreb (2019) also states that people who are hypervigilant are more likely to register threats than non-threats.

Tanasugarn (2020) argues that people who struggle to let go of past pain and regret tend to struggle to move forward in their lives, which may lead to stagnation, adding that past trauma can prevent individuals from living in the present and so keep us living in the past.

In their own study, Firman & Russell (1994) explain that our early wounding causes a split in the personality, which causes our inner 'childlikeness' to go into hiding and so split off from our everyday lives and emerge only during times of crisis. They argue that we don't leave childhood behind just because we have grown physically – the inner child and teen are always in the immediate present, influencing us and how we respond as adults. So it's possible to get physically older and still have your wounded inner child running your life (Diamond, 2008). This helps explain what's happening with the Eternal Child archetype and why they struggle with day-to-day activities in the present moment – their trauma keeps them in the past, replaying past pain.

If a child is constantly exposed to trauma or experiences a trauma that is too great for them to process (trauma is relative so what may be insignificant to one person can be huge to another) that can overload the entire nervous system and make it harder for the nervous system to get back to baseline functioning. It puts them on edge (hypervigilance), their nervous systems always on alert, which affects them physically because they are constantly trying to process and integrate events, thus overwhelming their entire system, exhausting them and making it hard to think ahead.

Over time, the nervous system gets too burdened and may even stop processing traumatic events. Imagine a machine that's always working at high speed and is never given downtime or ever serviced –

at some point, it will crash and burn and stop working. The same can happen with humans when our nervous system is constantly on and never gets a break.

The sad thing is that most children don't have the resources to process complex trauma and adults don't understand that this is happening (or has happened) to a child, so the child is frozen in time and constantly 'glitching'; they get older, but their psyche is constantly being hijacked by the inner child or teen version of themselves, constantly reacting to the past and the trauma of the past as though it's happening today.

As a result, many of the Eternal Child's emotions stem from events in the past, rather than what is happening in the moment. They learnt how to react in a particular way when it comes to money and other things in childhood, and most of the events in their adulthood just trigger those emotions. Their childhood beliefs and emotions are thus basically recreating life events in the moment to keep proving those past emotions and beliefs right.

Their inner child or teen has not learnt how to process the earlier trauma and is still hurting, because the subconscious is not rational and the child part of them doesn't have the reasoning capability to process these emotions, so they need to *feel* them, be with them and allow them to pass through their system before their adult self can start running the show.

How does a wounded inner-child or inner-teen sub-personality influence our financial behaviour?

- **Decreased income:** When the wounded inner child runs our lives, we may exhibit destructive behaviour and subtle sabotage because we don't know how to run a business, have a relationship or a career (Diamond, 2008). When that inner child runs our lives, our finances tend to be chaotic and it can be difficult for us to grow our income because children don't know enough about business or career

growth and may actually be daunted by it, which may lead to self-sabotage or procrastination, and ultimately a decrease in income.
- **Increased debt:** Children love bright, shiny things and they love spending – in other words, most haven't mastered delayed gratification. So when the wounded inner child is running our lives, we may have a hard time with self-control and impulse buying, which would lead to an increase in debt.
- **Decrease in savings:** Children don't know enough about budgeting, delayed gratification or saving, so the Eternal Child rarely has any savings or investments.

The key to re-parenting this inner child is to acknowledge their pain and anger and then work with the inner child. Once your inner child trusts you, they will show you the ways in which they subconsciously sabotage you so that you remain dependent on your parents and punish them by forcing them to look after you.

You can then ask that inner child what they need from you to move beyond this and either try to give them that or support them in finding that resource within themselves.

The Vengeful Child

Sometimes the Eternal Child has a sub-archetype: the Vengeful Child. This is an inner child or teen who is angry and resentful and wants to punish their caregivers for not protecting them from whatever trauma they endured.

One of the symptoms a child displays when they experience psychological neglect (name-calling, insults, ridicule, threats, gaslighting, self-criticism) is deep seated and low self-esteem (Davis, 2020). When the Eternal Child was hurt and had their power taken from them, they had no way to fight back and so they plotted on how to get their caregivers back, either consciously or unconsciously, so that they can make them feel the same kind of pain. In some cases, these children will use money to avenge themselves – they *choose* to be financially unstable to show their parents just how they messed us up.

A study by Goldner et al. (2019) found that experiencing humiliation and unjust hurt at the hands of another increases our desire for revenge and revenge fantasies and that the desire is related to traumatic experiences. The desire for revenge is a universal personal response across all cultures.

To quote a study by Bloom (2001), 'Child emotional abuse is seen to be a possible cause of damage to brain organization and failure in ability to modulate emotional control. Extreme feelings of shame resulting from child abuse, physical, sexual, and emotional are seen to underlie violent, retaliatory behaviour.'

For example, if the Eternal Child grew up in an abusive household and their mother exposed them to that, their inner child may be angry because they may feel like it was her duty to protect them and so, to punish her (instead of empathising with her), they choose to remain dependent on her in adulthood, so she is compelled to step into the role of protector or nurturer. Or they choose to self-sabotage, forcing their parents to be parents, boxing them into a corner, especially their mothers. Their reasoning is that, if they are successful, the world may think their parents were good parents and may ask: So where are your scars to prove that they hurt you?

By remaining dependent on their parents when they are older, they thus force them to take on the role they didn't play when they were younger. They subconsciously choose to remain hurt to remind their parents what they did and force their parents to acknowledge how they messed up as parents – even if they don't say this out loud (in fact, they may not even be aware of it).

So, how does the Vengeful Child (the sub-archetype of the Eternal Child) influence our financial behaviour?

- **Decreased income:** We have all seen movies where someone loses everything in their quest for revenge; they refuse to be rational or to focus, and are thus destroyed by their desire for vengeance.

    Vengeance is an emotion that drives us to use money to punish those who have wronged us by playing small, undercharging for our services and self-sabotaging so that they (our parents, for example) give up their lives or finances to look after us (Makwakwa, 2013). When the Eternal Child makes the subconscious decision to punish their parents by making them look after them financially, they sabotage themselves and prevent themselves from moving forward financially.
- **Increased debt:** According to McDermott et al. (2017), revenge is not motivated by the desire to stop the wrongdoer from committing further wrong acts in future; instead, it is motivated by the pleasure of paying back a wrong. Although this may be what makes it so psychologically satisfying, there's also a high probability that the quest for revenge can destroy us – in effect, leading to *mutual* destruction.

    The Eternal Child's inner child takes pleasure from punishing their caregivers for the trauma they endured because of them (directly or indirectly), this desire to punish their caregivers keeps the Eternal Child in a cycle of giving away money, spending recklessly and recreating debt to keep exacting revenge. They do this even when it harms them too.
- **Decreased savings:** The Eternal Child rarely, if ever, has any savings or investments, and if they have a Vengeful Child archetype they may even create emergencies in order to get rid of money. Much like the RunAway they do this in order to feel safe but, unlike the RunAway, they also do

this to punish their caregivers by forcing them to step in to rescue them.

So, how do we heal the Vengeful Child?

- One sign that your inner child is vengeful is to look at your inner talk:
  - Do you blame your parents for your circumstances?
  - Are you angry about your childhood?
  - Do you make your parents feel guilty for the things you endured as a child or teen?
- Start communicating with your inner child or teen (through inner-child or inner-teen meditation) as much as possible, and re-parent them by listening to them and holding them as they talk.
- Scream into a pillow as you reflect on your childhood and your teens or even specific memories.

The God wound

Who do you blame for the unfairness of life and how unfair things have been for you and your family? Who do we scream at when we get the short end of the stick and no human is at fault? What do we do with all those feelings of unfairness?

Studies have shown that when humans see others experiencing unfairness, the amygdala is activated and we get angry; humans don't get angry only when *they* are being unfairly treated – they also get angry when they see others being treated badly. And that causes us to punish those who have committed the transgression even if we aren't the victims; we will even pay a personal cost to have others treated fairly (Smith, 2020).

My theory is that the God wound shows up as an inability to trust and surrender in the Fixer and it shows up as blame, anger and a refusal to breakthrough, heal and/or expand financially in the Eternal Child.

The Eternal Child refuses to break through to show the unfairness of God for subjecting them to the trauma they experienced, or they decide to prove that the Divine doesn't exist or care.

Very often, the Eternal Child openly blames the Divine, their parents, their teachers, their family, or their circumstances for their situation and their inability to move forward, because the only way they can process their emotions about the unfairness of life as children is to blame others. Unfortunately, as adults, their inner child is still controlling them and running the show, and that inner child hasn't learnt how to deal with complex emotions, so they keep resorting to blame. According to Cooper (2021), we play the blame game to avoid dealing with difficult feelings that accompany 'negative' events; positive 'events' trigger feelings that are easier to handle.

As children, we see our families experience trauma from life events that sometimes feel out of their control (money struggles, systemic oppression, or the death of a loved one, for instance) and see and sense the pain that comes from those experiences. This, in turn, causes us pain, and we have no clue how to define that pain and who to blame, so we blame something outside ourselves (some kids may even blame themselves). We thus get angry with these outside sources and subconsciously wage a war with them to prove their unfairness or non-existence.

Some studies have found that when people have strong faith or are spiritual before they experience a trauma, they are less shaken by the event. But if someone experiences a traumatic event and they're not spiritual or don't have a strong relationship with their God, the event will either make them spiritual or lead them to believe that there's no God or that God had abandoned them (Thomas & Savoy, 2014).

The reason I've called this the God wound is because I believe that the outside sources with which we wage war is the Divine or whatever our view of the Divine is. For some, the Divine is God in the traditional sense; for some it is their higher self, while for others it's nature and for still others it's the universe. It really doesn't matter.

As children, blaming this source and being angry with it helps us deal with the pain we see life inflicting on our family, but because we live in a world where it's often considered taboo to feel anything but love towards Divinity and to question the Divine, this anger is buried deep down and shows up as a passive-aggressive vow to prove the unfairness of the Divine.

As children, we know that we can't vocalise that we're angry at the Divine for letting us suffer and for subjecting our families to suffering, so we subconsciously decide that when we grow up we'll stand in solidarity with our families and show people just how unfair the Divine is by upholding our family's struggles for others to see; we vow on a soul level that, no matter what happens, we will be very good people and do everything right, but we will not allow ourselves to surpass our families in love, money, or business, for example.

In this way, we get people to question the fairness of the Divine and Divinity itself. Over time, as we enter adulthood, this vow (because it's subconscious) leaves us angry and feeling powerless, like nothing ever works out for us no matter what we do, and we lose our faith, not just in the Divine, but ourselves as well. We start to believe that Divinity has favourites and that we have to work harder than others to make money, that we have to sacrifice ourselves to receive love and pray longer and harder than others to find a breakthrough.

In our anger and sadness, we forgot that we are Divinity and that to wage a war against the Divine is to wage a war against ourselves and that it's not just the Divine that keeps us stuck, it is ourselves. So the Eternal Child doesn't just feel anger towards their parents and family, but also towards the Divine about the unfairness of life.

Because of the God wound, the Eternal Child may find themselves accepting and simultaneously rejecting help and support from family. Their wounded and vengeful child may want family support (and even demand it), but the God wound makes it difficult for them to accept and receive that help. This tends to be very confusing for family, friends and spouses.

I have done the God wound healing with hundreds of individuals who felt as though they were doing everything they could, but were still struggling to break through or move forward. I have seen how scared they were to do the work, because they were convinced that the Divine/Universe would punish them, and I have seen how, when they start healing the God wound and give themselves permission to feel the anger and accept blame for how unfair life can be at times, their lives shift radically.

How does the God wound and the desire to show the unfairness of the Divine affect our finances?

- **Decreased income:** The best way to prove the unfairness of the Divine is to keep ourselves financially stagnant or to sabotage any breakthroughs with any of the challenges we are facing, which stops us from moving forward and experiencing a shift.

    The Eternal Child's desire to prove the unfairness of God keeps them financially stuck and they may find themselves sabotaging their financial breakthrough, leading to decreased income and feeling financially stagnant, no matter what actions they take.
- **Increased debt:** Being divorced from or at war with parts of ourselves can be extremely painful and leaves us feeling lost, like something is missing. We will often use material possessions to make ourselves feel better, which leads to increased spending and increased debt.

    The Eternal Child, just like the Destroyer, may feel alone, but their loneliness is a little more complex because it's not just related to family dynamics – it's also related to the spiritual and their relationship with the Divine. They may feel as though the Divine has forgotten them, which may lead to impulsive spending and even stealing.

- **Decreased savings:** Part of the vow of proving the unfairness of God is to show how the Divine never shows up for us or supports us. Having savings and other resources means that we are supported and protected, which disproves this vow and, as a result, the Eternal Child very rarely has savings, and if they do have savings and a God wound, they then create 'emergencies' to justify getting rid of their savings in order to honour the vow to prove the unfairness of God.

CASE STUDY

The Eternal Child

VANGILE: Hello, Precious, where are you from?

PRECIOUS: I am from the Eastern Cape.

VANGILE: So far, everyone I have interviewed has been someone who has identified with one of the archetypes, but it's been challenging for me to find an Eternal Child who is willing to be interviewed, so I am interviewing you as someone who has dealt with this archetype most of your life. What would you say is your relationship with your family when it comes to money?

PRECIOUS: A very complex one. I think because, like many other South Africans, I grew up with my uncles and aunts at my grandmother's house. There are personalities of people and how they spend money. My mother knew how to make money. She was always trying to make money in some way. I didn't stay with her, but I noticed that when I went to her house we had different cereals and things like that. And with my grandparents, it was totally different when it came to money. I thought my grandmother was the breadwinner because my grandfather was a truck driver, and I saw him driving, but I didn't know he was working. My grandmother had a stroke when I was 10 years old. My uncle, who was staying with us at the time, also had a small business. He was a mechanic engineer. And he had a lot of money. He had power. I don't know if it was because he was an elder brother or maybe because he had money, but I felt like the whole community respected him for it. I only see money as something that gets you respect.

But, at the same time, money was the reason I didn't have a relationship with my mother because she had to stay far away to make money. I resented that because why would you not stay with me if you love me? I had money growing up, but I never knew what to do with it. I was brought up in the village; I had everything I wanted at home, so I never really knew what to do with money.

VANGILE: What role did you start to take on in your family as you started making money?

PRECIOUS: We all had similar roles in the family, like my uncle took care of not only his siblings, but his cousins. There were always people coming in and out of our house. My grandmother was the same. What I learnt is that if you have money, you need to take care of everybody. That's one thing that I think they had in common because, although it happened at different stages in their lives, it's like everyone who had money had to somehow take care of the rest of the family.

I remember my mother had to send her siblings to college. My aunt was a teacher and this uncle was an engineer. So I know that she had to assist with paying for their college fees. When I was 10, my grandfather retired to take care of my grandmother who had a stroke at the time. My mother did the same. She left the business with the other younger brother to take care of my grandmother. Now, here's the thing – my other uncle came into power and earned more than everybody, so he had to carry the weight of my mother, grandmother and grandfather. So my uncle couldn't move out to stay at his own place because now the responsibility of the family was entirely up to him. When my aunt found a job as a teacher, he actually moved then and the role reverted to my aunt.

The other aunt started to work as well. We had four uncles. Everybody started to work again. Only then could they move out. But now the responsibility was entirely on my aunt. The idea that when you have money, you need to take care of the family, I think that's what happened with me. I had adopted that mentality that once I have money, I need to take care of people. Because what's the use of money if you're not taking care of people?

VANGILE: You talk about taking care of people in the family, but who have you felt like you need to take care of the most and how has that affected your relationship?

PRECIOUS: My sister. I call her my sister. I'm the only child my mother had. I was brought up by my aunt (who was like a twin to my mom) because my mother had to go work. My aunt's daughter and I grew up as sisters; we have always been identified as sisters because of the relationship between our parents. When my sister first came home, my God, I have never felt like that about anybody in my life. That was the first time I fell in love. I was 10. She came home and I was so excited and so happy. I've got this beautiful human being coming into my life. I've got a sister. My aunt also had a baby boy, who I consider my brother.

Then, when I was 22, my aunt passed away first; she was more of a mother to me. Two weeks later, my mother passed away and then my uncle. They had three weeks in between. And my entire life changed. I was in Cape Town; I went back to PE, where my aunt had bought a house, and I had these two kids (my brother and sister) to look after. My aunt left everything to me, even when she passed before her own sister. There was no way she could know my mother was going to pass.

She had a book, some papers written down what she wanted done and how she wanted it done, who was supposed to do it. And the person to do it was me. I decided to look after my sister who was 12 and asked my uncle to take care of my little brother, who was three at the time, because I couldn't handle both kids.

So I guess, instead of being a sister, I stepped in as a parent. Now my life was at a standstill. I didn't want to move too far away. I had plans to go to the US. And I always say, I don't know what happened because if it had happened five days later, I could have been gone. Everything was done deal. I had applied for au pairing and I had found the family. I was busy with my licence. I was just going to get my licence and be gone. Everything came to a standstill because I had these kids to take care of.

I felt like I got all the love from my aunt, like everything. That woman gave me everything. I can't even say 'aunt' when I talk about her – she was my mother. She gave me everything. She was gentle with my upbringing; she was a listener and someone I could rely on her. I felt guilty that I got everything. How do I now give my sister everything that her mother gave me?

Not knowing what to do, I started to pour into her financially. She acted out, of course. She was a teenager. She'd just lost both her mothers (her mom and my mom) and she was in a new environment. Unlike me, she didn't grow up with my uncle. Unlike me, she didn't know him like that. I was a mess. The whole family was a mess from the losses; my uncle started drinking because he was very close to my mom and my aunt.

My uncle and I didn't know what to do so we showered them with everything that money could buy. I think that, to an extent, I disempowered [my sister] because my love language was: 'What do you want? How can I make it better? Can I buy you this? Would you like to have that?' It was the best schools, best anything. I was not emotionally available, only financially available because this lifestyle needed me to work two jobs.

And, mind you, my aunt was not materialistic. I always had a choice to do things, and my voice was heard with my aunt. Whether it was rage, whether it was anything, she would just let me be.

VANGILE: You were really young to have to take care of a kid at that age. How do you think your behaviour has affected your younger sister's relationship with money?

PRECIOUS: I would say that has been such an emotional training process for both of us. I never really gave her a choice to grow up and make decisions on her own. So even now she's still 12 years old. Instead of getting emotional support and that, I think now she doesn't value money so much because even now she is the only person I know in our entire family who still depends on others for money. I think she feels, 'You didn't care about me. All you care about is working for money.'

There's some sense of resentment, but also the entitlement of 'Continue with what you were doing. Keep on doing everything for me because I don't know how to'. I feel this is exactly what she would say if she was able to express herself; her actions are saying that to me because my sister can find work at any given time anyway. She just refuses to work.

Most of the time, I must pay her rent, do all of that. I've done all of these things all these years. I remember finding her a job at my work. I had to make sure that she's got transportation. We were working in trans parties; we would camp for the weekend and work. She would rock up in just her clothes and nothing else, no bag, nothing. And people were like, 'Why are you coming out like this?'

And she would respond, 'My sister will take care of it.'

VANGILE: So would you say, after reading the summary of the profiles, that your sister is an Eternal Child or just a spoiled brat?

PRECIOUS: Definitely. Definitely. One, I'm telling you, there's nothing she wants to do. Even if she had a million rand in her hand, she would still want to be taken care of financially. I don't know if it's a cry for emotional help or what, but she absolutely doesn't want to work. She's got a son and his grandmother is taking care of him. But my family helps financially because we can't let them do all the work themselves. She will just rock up here and tell me, 'I don't have money for rent.' It's month end. I'm like, 'So what am I to do with that?'

When she got her inheritance at 18, she packed her bags and disappeared for the entire year. When she came back, she didn't have anything. I had to start from scratch, buy her underwear, clothes, get her back to school, do all those things. Everything from scratch with no question asked.

We were all freaking out, wondering where she could be? She had found a boyfriend at the time and she was staying at his place and it was just a mess.

We were like, 'You need to come home.'

She was like, 'No, I'm having the time of my life.'

Mind you, when my aunt passed on, she left us equal amounts of money. I took my portion and halved it between my brother and sister, because I was like, 'I'm working. When they're 18, I need to pay for university and things like that. This money better go to them, then I know that I don't have to worry about things like that. All I have to worry about is for them until they are 18.'

I remember the Creating Money Magic course; I said to you, the first thing I want to heal, one thing I want to heal, I want to learn how to set boundaries. I didn't want to heal my money story. I just needed to have a better relationship with myself and a better relationship with my sister. We couldn't go on the way we were.

VANGILE: How do you think your sister's refusal to grow up and be an adult has affected your family and their relationship with money?

PRECIOUS: I will start with my uncle. That dude is broken, probably for life.

My brother recently said, 'I don't want to have a conversation with our sister. She asked me for money. It's my inheritance. She blew hers. I'm done.'

My other cousin, when I first moved here, said to me, 'I need to sit you down because I need you to understand this. I had a conversation with your sister and I said to her, "Listen, if you come to my house, it's because I invited you to my house. We're going to do what I'm inviting you for and that's it."'

My sister keeps on depending on people for anything and everything, even when she is working. It started with lies, the instigation and then manipulation. She told people my uncle was eating her inheritance money when in truth he only used it to buy her clothes twice a year – everything else was coming from my uncle and I: the food, transport, school fees. She would go from one family member to the other telling stories and it caused such a big issue between the family because she would get money from everyone and other family members thought badly of my uncle and he started to drink.

She's been playing us like that for years. We eventually moved to Cape Town, only to find out later that she would take my card and take my daughter so they could eat out every single day. My card stayed at home just in case something happened, and they needed bread or anything like that. She would eat out with her friends and I never checked my account. I didn't know until she told me years later.

I was taken aback – I didn't even know. So it's super draining. It makes you really depressed when you think about it. I don't want anyone depending on me. I hate having money because I feel like, if I have this money, then she will want it.

She does it with the little brother. Demands money from him, lies to him and makes him lie to my aunt so she can give him money to give to her.

VANGILE: Do you feel that this relationship with your sister has affected the way you save money and your ability to save money?

PRECIOUS: Not just me, my daughter as well. My daughter is so scared to save money. She saved money here at home but it's, like, what's the point if her aunt is just going to come and take it?

It breaks me because we are saving people. Even when I worked at the restaurant we had a big jar of tips and put our money in there, coins and 20s, 50s, hundreds, and this big jar would be halfway full, then my sister would come and visit and it would be gone. We started saving again when we moved here, but I don't feel safe with my money here, to be honest with you.

As soon as I can afford to stay in Cape Town, I'm gone. Not because of the lifestyle but because my sister is such a trigger for me. I can't save money. I can't even think about saving money because somebody else is going to use it. I'm saving for someone else. I get so angry when I think about that. It has been proven over and over. I get here, look at me putting savings on the side, having money there, and then her landlord will call me and ask me to pay her rent. It's, like, why are you phoning me?

The first few months, I would end up paying the rent and said to him, 'If she pays, then pay me back. Don't tell her that I pay you.' Then I was like, 'No, I told you not to call me.'

The last time he called me, I said, 'Listen, dude, don't call me again about my sister's rent. If she's not paying rent, kick her out. She's working already.'

The scary thing is that if they kick her out, she's going to come stay with me, so I feel trapped. So I wonder, will I not give in again? Because it would be safer for me if she has her own place and doesn't come stay at my house. I have this anxiety just talking about this.

VANGILE: I'm sending you deep hugs because this sounds like a lot. Aside from refusing to pay her rent, what measures have you put in place to deal with your sister?

PRECIOUS: I have learnt about boundaries and am learning to say no. I think that has given me peace of mind and my guilt has eased a lot. I have been using your course, the Fall In Love With Your Bank Account Challenge, and it has helped me a lot.

I'll tell you why. Because when I sit down and put my values with money, this is how I look at it – my kids are the most valuable things in my life. If I were to put them in a boarding school, will I just leave them there? How will I look after them? That's how I look at money.

So whenever I think about money and where I'm putting the money, I look at it as though I'm putting the money in the boarding school. Is it going to be safe? Is it going to be valued? Is it going to be loved?

I wouldn't put my kids in a place where they are not going to be free or loved. So why would I put my money in a space where it's not going to get the same love?

I started looking at how and where I'm spending the money, and what my values are? The most important thing for me right now is myself, because if I'm not here, who's going to take care of my kids? My mental health is very important. I used to feel guilty for being alive, but I'm starting to feel like I have a reason, not just a reason, but I have a right to be alive.

VANGILE: As you have started to notice these shifts within yourself, what shifts have you noticed with your relationship with your sister?

PRECIOUS: I would say we are in a better space right now. I think mainly because I am no longer as triggered by what she does. There is less asking. When she does ask, it's no longer about, I have to – it's about how can I help? Can I help even? I'm not saying that I don't help at all, but it's no longer coming from obligation. When I do anything right now it's because I want to do it and I can do it. I've got the capacity to do it. It shifted our relationship so much. We can communicate. We talk a lot about things and our relationship is no longer based on what I can give her. We can have a conversation. She can come and visit without wanting anything. I just realised now that, whenever I got a call from her, I would always think, 'What does she want?'

There's less of that, because now I can even pick up the phone and call her. She can come to my house, and we'll have a conversation and talk about things. In December, they came for Christmas at my house. Everybody brought something. She was like, 'Okay, I don't have cash, but I'm coming. This is what I'm going to do. I'll make the salads, I'll do this, I'll do that.'

I guess there is a change in our relationship. I think she's changed with everybody else still. But now we have evolved and we have a relationship that is not based on what I can offer her. There are still moments where I know that she's going to ask for something and I will say, 'Look, I'm no longer that person.'

It's like she can sense that it's not going to happen, so why do you even try?

I had a conversation with her and I was honest and said, 'Some of the choices I've made got you here. But here's the thing – you can take it from here and relearn. Probably some of the traumas you have are because of me. But there is help out there.'

I have been very open with her about getting a coach and healing my inner child. I did what I could with the tools that I had when I was young. Right? And I take full responsibility for that. This is why I'm doing my own healing so that I don't continue that with my kids. Because I could easily have easily parented them the same way if I didn't get the help that I needed. It was the only way that I knew how to parent. I learnt to be a parent with her. I didn't know what I was doing.

VANGILE: What would you tell people who are dealing with an adult who is refusing to take responsibility for their life?

PRECIOUS: Honestly, I would say you need to heal yourself first

– the guilt, the shame, the anger, and all of that. It's not about the other person, it's about us healing. They are reflecting our wounds. We're feeding on that. That's what I figured with me. Obviously, different people have different stories. However, I would say heal yourself. I don't think there's a shortcut. When you are healed, you will see it as it is. When you are aware of what the relationship is, you're going to say, 'This is not for me.'

It's never about you changing how they do things. You can yell at them to change their behaviour. You can reason with them. You can do anything. That is never going to change unless they find healing. So you got to make peace with the fact that that person is like that, period.

You need to find your own healing because there is a beast within us that we are feeding. I was feeding that guilt. And because I had lost control when I lost my mothers, I felt then that I have no control of anything. So at least I could control being financially responsible for these human beings. I know there's been a lot of us in the family doing the same thing, but I personally take responsibility for that.

VANGILE: Thank you so much, Precious.

Ask yourself ...

1. What aspects of the Eternal Child profile caught your attention and made you think deeper about the profile?
2. Which traits, if any, of the Eternal Child profile do you see in yourself, and how have they played a role in your life so far?
3. Can you think of someone in your family who embodies the Eternal Child profile, and how does their behaviour affect the family dynamic, particularly when it comes to money?
4. How does the Eternal Child profile affect the way your

family handles their finances, positively or negatively?
5. What are three actionable steps that can be taken to support and encourage the Eternal Child in your family to develop healthy financial habits and grow in this area of their life?

Take action

1. **Take the time to re-parent your wounded inner child or teen:** As an Eternal Child, you may feel like parts of you are stuck in past traumas and experiences. It's important to integrate these parts of yourself into your psyche and provide the love and care you may have missed out on as a child. This can be done in various ways, such as inner-child meditations, journalling and therapy. By doing this, you can start to heal old wounds and create a more nurturing and loving relationship with yourself.
2. **Work on healing the mother and father wounds:** It's common for those with the Eternal Child profile to carry wounds from their childhood relationships with their parents. This can manifest in feelings of abandonment, rejection and unworthiness. However, it's important to forgive your parents and give yourself permission to stop blaming them for any faults.
3. **Spend five minutes a day studying your bank account:** As an Eternal Child, anything that involves finances may be scary to your wounded inner child or teen. To change this fear, spend time examining your bank account:
    - Go to your online banking profile, open up your bank account and go to the transactions page (personal or business, whichever one you use most).
    - Put your cellphone on silent (not vibrate).

The Eternal Child

- Set a five-minute timer on your phone alarm.
- Take a minute to scroll through your bank account and then close your eyes and observe your breathing for the next five minutes.
- Breathe normally – do *not* control your breath – and try to sit as still as possible. Just observe your breath and accept everything that happens in this exercise. If your mind wanders, just bring it back to your breathing. No judging or criticising yourself.
- Grab a pen and a sheet of paper and write down your insights and the thoughts that came up during the exercise. Question any thoughts that feel uncomfortable.

CHAPTER 12

How archetypes interact

In this section, we dive into how the different archetypes come together within family dynamics or relationships. It's crucial to grasp how these Shadow archetypes interact because understanding that provides us with valuable insights on effective communication within the family unit. When we understand each other's archetypes, we can find better ways to connect, communicate and work towards a shared financial vision that benefits the entire family.

By recognising and understanding the archetypal patterns at play, we can tailor our communication strategies to align with the needs and motivations of each family member. This understanding allows us to foster open dialogue, build trust, and gain support from others in pursuing our common financial goals. It then becomes easier to find common ground and make decisions that serve the best interests of the family as a whole.

Moreover, delving into archetypes can shed light on the hidden dynamics and unconscious patterns that may hinder effective communication and financial harmony within the family. This helps us identify areas where conflict or misunderstandings may arise and provides guidance on how to navigate them with empathy and respect.

The Sweet One versus the Sweet One

The Sweet One is constantly working on making everyone in the family and in their space feel welcome or creating a welcoming space within the family. They want peace above all else.

If two Sweet Ones are in any kind of relationship, they will focus on making sure that everything is civil and calm, strive to keep the peace and ensure that the family has a good name and reputation. They will be concerned with what others say and how the family unit is perceived externally or how the relationship appears versus what's happening below the surface. A lot of their dynamics are outward-focused to present a perfect image, so they may even swallow their truths to keep with this illusion of perfection.

When it comes to family dynamics and resolving family trauma, they may talk about it but hold back from doing the work required to process things because they both have a fear of digging deeper and shining the light on the uncomfortable.

Financially, these two profiles can achieve a lot if they work together in a family or romantic relationship. They are very likely to get to a space where they are financially comfortable and may even become wealthy in later years because they tend to do the practical financial things. Generally, they are considerate of each other's financial situation and don't have the same risk appetite of the Destroyer or Fixer.

They can be very practical and are able to do a lot with limited resources. They won't demand a lot from the other, which can have its drawbacks because sometimes expansion requires us to think big and go beyond the practical.

While this is a low-conflict relationship (romantic or family), it may stagnate because they rarely challenge each other to grow since they don't like to make each other uncomfortable. They will be overly caring, overly worried about what the other thinks, and so they are reluctant to dig deeper than surface level.

The Sweet One versus the Destroyer

The Sweet One fears the Destroyer and their crazy anger, which ironically makes them rely even more on their own sweetness. I don't see these two personalities even engaging when it comes to finances. And generally, if they do interact, it's because the Destroyer is forcing some type of financial support – either supporting the Sweet One or taking from the Sweet One.

If the Destroyer is supporting the Sweet One, the Sweet One will become powerless over time and lose their sense of self, because they are scared to upset the Destroyer in any way. The Sweet One is diplomatic so they try to avoid upsetting the Destroyer by all means, which unfortunately triggers the Destroyer even more. In fact, part of the challenge with this dynamic is that the Sweet One triggers the Destroyer. The Destroyer is generally not well liked in the family because of their propensity for revealing hard truths in the worst way and at the worst time. They feel that the only reason the Sweet One is liked is because The Sweet One is fake and the Destroyer can see some of the Sweet One's toxic traits and they try to reveal them.

The Destroyer can sense the Sweet One's suppressed anger and that drives the Destroyer insane and they can act out in the worst ways. What the Destroyer doesn't understand is that the Sweet One is genuinely unaware of their anger. To survive, they must ignore the emotions that society frowns upon. The Destroyer mirrors the Sweet One's hidden anger, which scares the Sweet One because they see how people react to that anger and, in order to keep getting the family's love and approval, they focus on being even sweeter.

In a romantic relationship, this dynamic can be toxic – the Destroyer will bully the Sweet One and it could turn very ugly. However, a romantic dynamic could work with their healed archetypes (the Boundaried One and the Renovator, see the upcoming Golden Archetypes section) because they then tend to learn from each other. The Destroyer learns how to be diplomatic and softer and the Sweet

One learns the importance of feeling their emotions (especially anger) and speaking their truth.

The Sweet One versus the Fixer

For obvious reasons, the Sweet One and the Fixer are good friends and, if siblings, get along very well and do things together financially. The Fixer will basically dictate to the Sweet One what to do and they then follow instructions and do it, which will make wealth creation easy (especially if there is no strong Destroyer energy to challenge the Fixer).

The Sweet One will always be polite and bow to the whims of the Fixer, but often feels less powerful or intelligent than the Fixer. The energy, power and wilfulness of the Fixer may leave them in awe or completely overwhelmed to the point that they start to think that the Fixer has more value to add to the relationship than they do. As a result, the Fixer tends to have a lot more control and a lot more power in this dynamic.

The Fixer can run roughshod over the Sweet One because they don't have anyone to challenge them when they are being overly controlling and demanding. This dynamic becomes more balanced if the Sweet One moves into the Golden archetype of the Boundaried One.

A marriage between the Sweet One and a Fixer can be good and financially beneficial for both parties. The Fixer is content in this dynamic (albeit bored sometimes) because they encounter no resistance from the Sweet One. The Sweet One may sometimes feel controlled, but they tend to feel safe with the Fixer because they are loyal and a visionary and don't require them to be fully visible. All the Fixer requires is for the Sweet One to go along with their ideas.

The Sweet One versus the RunAway

The RunAway and the Sweet One are two sides of the same coin, but because the Sweet One is … well, sweet … the RunAway often feels safest with the Sweet One and may depend on them financially because the Sweet One would never complain about helping them.

Interestingly, because both have checked out emotionally, they also seem to understand each other, so they get along well and the financial help the Sweet One gives the RunAway isn't resented and doesn't come with complaints.

The problem is that the Sweet One will never ask the RunAway to elevate themselves and do better and the RunAway will never ask the Sweet One to be vulnerable and authentic, which could hinder both their financial growth.

The Sweet One versus the Eternal Child

This dynamic works in the long term and can be peaceful for both parties, but it is also silently toxic and, in a way, dangerous because it's hard to spot the co-dependence when the Sweet One just looks like they are being sweet. It, however, goes deeper than that and their actions can keep the Eternal Child in their trauma state for the long term.

The truth is that the Sweet One gets validation from having the Eternal Child depend on them, so they have no real reason or incentive to help them heal or change their ways. They thus enable the Eternal Child's behaviour because helping them fits the Sweet One's view of themselves as a nice person and reinforces this image in the minds of others.

If the Eternal Child ends up in a romantic relationship with a Sweet One, their life turns out to be a rather cushy one because the Sweet One will cater to them and parent them fully. The Sweet One will emotionally, financially and psychologically support the

Eternal Child without any complaints (even though they may feel deep resentment at times). They will pay for everything and be silent about it, suppressing their anger and resentment because they are 'sweet'.

This actually causes a lot of drama in the family, especially with their kids, who often feel as though they can't rely on either of their parents. They can't depend on the Eternal Child parent because they rarely parent and will feel that the Sweet One has too much on their plate in parenting their Eternal Child parent, which could lead to them (the children) acting as a deputy parent to their siblings or a deputy spouse to the Sweet One.

The Destroyer versus the Destroyer

Two Destroyers in one space can lead to intense disagreements, passionate love and remarkable innovation.

They constantly call each other out on their issues, which can be jarring for their nervous systems, but can also hold space for one another to unravel and find their truth, no matter how dark.

They are both truthful and communicate in a matter-of-fact manner. Their focus will be on healing and, if they are not too scared of rejection, they can do this together and bring forth powerful medicine for the world.

Destroyers work well together financially, building an empire when they work together, because they understand what it's like to be the black sheep of the family and, once they are able to get over their fear of rejection, can support each other's innovative ideas.

Apart from a Fixer, only another Destroyer will understand the risk appetite of a Destroyer archetype and their drive to innovate and birth new things. If they both believe in the idea and vision, they will be able to hold each other, but if they disagree on something, they will also fight to have their views heard. The problem arises when it comes to the Destroyer's enormous risk tolerance; they are the most likely to take on loans in order to innovate, so two Destroyers working together means twice the risk, which can also delay wealth accumulation within a family. So, although the return on investment could be high, they could also end up in debt.

Destroyers usually live an unconventional lifestyle and can move the family in a new direction in terms of innovation (remember that the Destroyer is here to help us all see what doesn't work, even in society). They are thus more likely to change how families operate in terms of education, schooling, or career for instance, and they have the energy to share these changes with the rest of society.

The Destroyer versus the Fixer

The Destroyer will destroy everything the Fixer tries to fix without first consulting the Fixer and that will cause fireworks in the family. The Fixer, of course, loves telling people what to do – and often get their own way – but the Destroyer is a natural rebel and doesn't react well to being told what to do.

These two archetypes are essentially two sides of the same coin – it's just their approaches that are different. The Destroyer is also trying to fix things in the family, but they do so by first destroying what isn't working before they get around to fixing it. They want to build on a solid foundation. To do this, they will ruin Christmas, weddings and funerals, for example. They will thus be seen as the toxic ones, but it's because they don't have the language to explain that they want to tear down the system in order to start something new. And they don't have the resources to build. For this reason, the Fixer will never be able to get the family to move forward because the Destroyer will obliterate their efforts and sabotage them.

To the Destroyer, the Fixer is manipulative and in denial of the truth of the situation (this is sort of true). To the Fixer, the Destroyer is toxic, angry and self-centred (also sort of true).

In a romantic relationship, these two archetypes may be deeply attracted to each other because they hold each other's intense energy, but their relationship will be marked by intense fights because they are opposites and tend to trigger each other's wounds.

These two archetypes don't rely on each other financially but, ironically, need each other to build holistic wealth in the family or the romantic relationship, especially in their healed archetypes (the Renovator and the Sovereign One, see the upcoming Golden Archetypes section) because they are both loyal, innovative, and driven.

A Destroyer can teach the Fixer to ask for permission and honour every soul's sovereign mission and let them direct their own path so that everyone in the family becomes empowered and is not financially dependent on the Fixer. They can also teach the Fixer to prioritise themselves and stop projecting their needs and desires onto the whole family, which, interestingly, can help build generational wealth faster.

The Fixer, in turn, can teach the Destroyer how to build something – and how to keep building – instead of destroying when the going gets tough. The Fixer may also teach the Destroyer how to unite people around a common vision, and demonstrate how to be diplomatic so that the Destroyer knows when and how to speak harsh truths. The Fixer values expansion, growth and innovation, so in their healed state they give the Destroyer permission to thrive and elevate without fear of rejection, which can be life changing for a Destroyer and can help them escape their boom-and-bust cycle and build wealth.

The Destroyer versus the RunAway

The RunAway and Destroyer intuitively understand each other and why the other is behaving the way they are so they tend to be either good friends or chilled enemies.

As mentioned, the Destroyer helps the RunAway manoeuvre

family dynamics by forcing everyone to do their inner work so that the RunAway isn't overwhelmed by having to process all the emotions others refuse to feel. Without a strong Destroyer archetype (or a Fixer who can step into the Destroyer role every so often) in a family, the RunAway will be overwhelmed by people's emotions and may never go home. The Destroyer helps alleviate the RunAway's allostatic load by forcing family members to deal with their own emotions, which allows the RunAway to ground themselves and feel safe in their own body and so start to set boundaries and tap into their own power.

At times, however, the Destroyer – if they are in the darkest phase and dealing with their anger – can overwhelm the nervous system of the RunAway and trigger the RunAway to shut down or run away for good, because they don't have the capacity to process all the emotions of the Destroyer.

Because of this intuitive understanding, these two will be okay helping each other financially.

The Destroyer versus the Eternal Child

The role of the Destroyer (in a family or in a relationship) is to help others awaken to the truth and face the things they are running from. The role of the Eternal Child, on the other hand, is to help people see where they are stuck in the trauma, and to bring their attention to that block.

As you can imagine, this is a challenging dynamic because the Destroyer wants the Eternal Child to face the trauma and grow up, whereas the Eternal Child doesn't know how to grow up. As a result, the Eternal Child knows to play far away from the Destroyer, because a Destroyer will call out the Eternal Child on their issues and go nuclear on them.

In a family, the Eternal Child will try to stay clear of the Destroyer, and in a romantic relationship, it will look as though the Destroyer is bullying the Eternal Child. And, chances are, the Eternal Child will run away and head straight back home where they can be parented. The Destroyer will thus try to get the Eternal Child to grow up by fighting their resistance to adulthood, which may traumatise the Eternal Child all over again and that level of violence may make them dig into their Eternal Child survival patterns.

As romantic partners these two archetypes can thus be toxic. There will be no peace, as the Destroyer simply doesn't have the patience to nurture the Eternal Child – and nor do they want to.

The Fixer versus the Fixer

When two Fixers come together it can create a captivating dynamic and holds the potential for significant abundance within a family. There may, however, also be countless power struggles because you have two intense energies in one space. Unless they are both on the same page, they'll almost inevitably butt heads. If the two Fixers have completely different goals and viewpoints, the constant tug of war – especially in a romantic relationship – will make it hard to get anything done.

For the family to move forward financially, the Fixers have to agree on a common goal and common values. When this happens, the Fixers come together and make magic because, even if they have differing viewpoints, they can always come back to the primary goal. The result is that generational wealth can be achieved within a single generation, the level of focus they share leads to wealth creation for almost every member of the family.

But should the two Fixers fail to agree on a goal or end up having very different core values, they could end up tearing the family in half and splitting loyalties.

The Fixer versus the RunAway

The Fixer and the RunAway simply don't see eye to eye, largely because the RunAway is not engaged in anything within the family, which triggers the Fixer who is working hard to move the family forward and needs everyone involved to make this happen. The RunAway may, for instance, show up to a family function for no more than an hour and then they are out until next year or they just aren't fully sober or present.

The RunAway is often not financially stable (they haven't developed the ability to see things through), so they will often call home and ask for financial assistance, especially from the Fixer, who will often give that assistance because of their loyalty to the family and the hope that one day the RunAway will return to the family fold.

The Fixer may attempt to control the RunAway with money, but it never works, because the RunAway is not motivated by money; they are running from their trauma or from dealing with it. The RunAway is also motivated by the need to be an individual and break free to do their own thing, so the Fixer triggers them because they represent groundedness, family responsibility and control, which can feel like the very opposite of freedom to the RunAway. Except when they need something, the RunAway will avoid the Fixer as much as possible.

The RunAway also triggers the Fixer because they cannot understand how someone cannot be motivated by financial safety and a sense of belonging. And so they exhaust themselves trying to get the RunAway back into the family fold to attend family events. The RunAway thus frustrates the Fixer because they remind them that Fixers can't control everyone, that every person is a sovereign being and not everyone *wants* to be part of the family unit.

To the Fixer, the RunAway is selfish and/or irresponsible. To the RunAway, the Fixer is controlling and boring, so this relationship is tense and there is resentment on either side. As a result, in a romantic relationship, this dynamic can be a challenging one because the Fixer is stable while the RunAway is prone to leaving, which can make building anything between them in the long term very taxing. This can only work if they are both willing to compromise and change their views of the other, because in reality they have a lot to teach each other.

The Fixer versus the Eternal Child

This dynamic can work in the long term, but getting there can be extremely stressful for both parties. The Fixer is all about building and keeping the family or relationship going, even if it is not perfect. They are also prone to adopting 'projects', mainly because they believe they are responsible for everyone but also because they have a hard time understanding sovereignty.

The Fixer will scream, shout, beg, plead, reason, pay for a university education (which may never be fully utilised) and even help fund the Eternal Child's business ventures (most of which never take off) all in an effort to make them change. The Fixer thus exhausts themselves trying to fix the Eternal Child; some days they will think they're winning and convince themselves that they're making headway, but ultimately they won't win.

Small glimpses of potential will give a Fixer hope and energise them, which is a problem because they will then keep trying to fix the Eternal Child with tools of logic and other tricks, not fully understanding the root cause of the Eternal Child's resistance to growth.

In a marriage, a Fixer will take care of all (or almost all) the bills and household tasks, doing most of the emotional work required in the relationship and they will end up parenting an adult. This may then split their parenting energy and rob their kids of two parents, with one parent behaving like a child and the other parenting an adult. This can then cause deep wounds of abandonment for their children.

There may be constant fights between the two, in which the Fixer ends up using all their energy to parent the Eternal Child, trying to change them into a functional adult, rather than focusing that energy into building wealth and expansion, which affects the family's finances in the long run.

The RunAway versus the RunAway

Two RunAways in a romantic relationship or within a family can be challenging as very little gets done or resolved. When things get tough, they both flee the scene or disinvest from everything.

Often, a relationship between two RunAways in the same space can be rocky because they both tend to run away and abandon the union altogether when the going gets tough; they'll probably ghost each other or just lose interest in the dynamic. For much the same reason, two RunAways seldom last in a business partnership because neither has learnt to stay and deal with challenges, so there's no one to help get the business back on track.

RunAways run away from finances, and can actually keep themselves stuck because, unless they are using money as an escape, both may be secretly looking for a saviour and for someone to take over their finances. They tend to avoid finances, because money is an uncomfortable topic for them, and this avoidance of money makes it difficult to build generational wealth. Without a strong Fixer archetype in the mix, it can be hard to get RunAways to do anything let alone manifest their vision; they need a Fixer archetype to come in and help make it real.

Two RunAways as parents is challenging because when either of them is triggered or parenting gets tough, their natural inclination is to flee or simply refuse to deal with uncomfortable situations as they arise.

The RunAway versus the Eternal Child

The RunAway is freaked out by the Eternal Child, the adult that essentially never grew up and is constantly highlighting the very trauma the RunAway is trying to escape. When the RunAway sees the Eternal Child they are thus triggered and so flee to avoid the Eternal Child.

The Eternal Child, on the other hand, is looking for a mother or father and may try to get this from the RunAway, which is something the RunAway doesn't want. In fact, both these archetypes tend to avoid responsibility. The RunAway doesn't want responsibility because that would mean that they have to deal with their emotions and delve into themselves to start processing things that they are not comfortable processing. The Eternal Child, on the other hand, doesn't want responsibility because they don't want to grow up. As a result, these two archetypes often avoid each other because they are not able to deal with the other's emotions.

Financially, neither will be motivated enough to launch entrepreneurial ventures. The RunAway (a workaholic) may make a lot of money as they tend to use money as an escape from having to deal with their emotions, but will avoid the responsibility of parenting the partner Eternal Child. The RunAway also doesn't want the responsibility of debt and savings where the Eternal Child is concerned. As a result, the Eternal Child will often feel as though they're not seen by the RunAway. This dynamic is, therefore, not always the greatest in terms of building generational wealth.

The Eternal Child versus the Eternal Child

Children know very little about adulting, growing generational wealth, making money, saving and paying off debt, so naturally the dynamic between two Eternal Children is generally chaotic – in fact, just about anything goes. And when you have two Eternal Child archetypes in the family or in a household you can expect chaos: there's no sense of responsibility, bills are never paid, money is always scarce and they are often being supported by parents or other family members (usually a Fixer or Sweet One). A family with two Eternal Child archetypes and no Fixer or Sweet One archetype is generally in trouble because there's no adult to actually run the place.

The only way that this dynamic works is if one of the archetypes also has a Fixer or Sweet One as a Secondary archetype, because one will make sure that the household continues to run as usual. If you have Eternal Child archetypes and no Fixer or Sweet One archetypes, chances are that the family home (the Eternal Child never own a home of their own) may end up completely rundown or dilapidated; things simply fall apart, nothing is ever fixed, there is never any food, the house is rarely cleaned, and eventually the home may be abandoned as the Eternal Child goes looking for a romantic partner to parent them.

In the next section, we dive into how the Shadow archetypes transform and grow as they heal their deepest wounds. When these archetypes heal, they blossom into their Golden archetypes, and gain wisdom and strength from their healing journey and so change how they engage with family, approach parenting, and handle their relationship with money.

When we face our wounds – whether they are emotional, psychological, or spiritual – we connect with the parts of ourselves that cause suffering. It is through this conscious acknowledgement and exploration of our pain that we create an opportunity for growth and change. By shining a light on our wounds, we begin to understand their origins, effects, and the patterns they create in our lives.

The process of healing these wounds is often challenging and requires inner work, self-reflection, and sometimes support from others. As we delve deeper into the wounds, we gradually gain insight, compassion, and a greater understanding of ourselves. Through this journey, we cultivate resilience, strength, and wisdom.

This transformation changes the way we navigate life. We begin to go through life with greater resilience, make healthier choices, cultivate more meaningful relationships, and find purpose and fulfilment.

PART 3

The Golden Archetypes

The Golden archetype refers to the positive aspects of a person's personality. The harmful and destructive personalities have been acknowledged, embraced and integrated into a person's self-awareness, leading to personal growth, maturity and expansion in various areas of an individual's life.

CHAPTER 13

The Sweet One becomes the Boundaried One

While the role of the Sweet One is to be the glue that holds the family together – often at the expense of themselves – the role of the Boundaried One is to teach the family about self-love and acceptance and how to love others without sacrificing themselves or becoming bitter.

Melissa Urban (2022), also known as the Boundary Lady, defines boundaries as clear limits you establish around the way you allow people to engage with you, so that you keep yourself and your relationships healthy. She explains that boundary setting will be different for each situation and person, and that boundaries can decrease anxiety and self-doubt and increase self-confidence and emotional security.

When the Sweet One goes on their journey of setting boundaries, they go from sacrificing themselves at the expense of others to someone who still cares about other people but also knows their capacity. They still value family and friends and make them feel included, but they don't do so at their own expense. They no longer sacrifice themselves.

They no longer have the urge to keep the peace in order to make everyone comfortable. They start to understand that it is possible to have peace, but not if that peace is going to cause them heartache and sorrow. They now give themselves permission to say no when they mean no and yes when they mean yes. And, in so doing, they break the cycle of co-dependency, with all its associated toxic behaviours within the family.

Dale (2011) talks about the importance of energetic boundaries and how setting those boundaries separates us from what we don't need by letting in people, thoughts and situations that promote our healing so we can be more of our authentic selves. She also argues that a lot of our money and work problems are due to poor energetic boundaries and once we learn to set those boundaries, we will start to see a shift.

When the Sweet One starts setting boundaries (including energetic boundaries), they no longer enable the RunAway to come and go as they please. They start asserting their own rights and let others, such as the RunAway, know that they also have a role to play within the family. They also stop being taken advantage of by the Eternal Child and no longer allow themselves to be overpowered by the Fixer.

Healing the not-good-enough wound

According to Peer (2018), when we don't like ourselves or see ourselves as being enough, we build lives we don't like, but when we have unshakable self-love, we are self-confident and unstoppable, because changing the way we feel on the inside changes the way we feel about external events.

When the Sweet One establishes a connection with their inner child and inner teen, making them feel accepted and worthy by revisiting moments when they felt inadequate, and validating and permitting these inner aspects to be disliked, their adult self begins to feel at ease with setting boundaries.

They are also able to set financial boundaries with everyone around them, and so it becomes easier for them to set payment terms, decide how and when clients pay them, submit invoices on time and follow up on late or delayed payments. They are able to say no to free labour or working 'for exposure' (a huge problem for the Sweet One).

As the Sweet One, they sacrifice themselves to please everyone, but as the Boundaried One all that stops; they no longer give more than they are able to in exchange for love from those around them because they know that they have nothing to prove, which makes it easier for them to set boundaries. This frees them up and so they can take on more clients, create new streams of income and rest. They now put themselves first and seek fairness; they are fair to everyone around them and to themselves.

How does healing the not-good-enough wound affect our finances?

- **Increased income:** When we heal the not-good-enough wound, we move away from the belief that we are not enough and that we're not doing enough – in other words, we start believing in ourselves. To quote Grace Byers (2018) in her children's book *I Am Enough*, 'Like the sun, I'm here to shine. Like the voice, I'm here to sing. Like the bird, I'm here to fly and soar high over everything.'

  The Boundaried One believes in themselves, and this self-belief helps them keep going until they find solutions to their problems. They don't internalise setbacks that imply they are inadequate, which changes the way they approach their work, business and careers and increases their chances of success, which leads to increased income.
- **Decreased debt:** When we feel as though we are not enough, we often use money to buy things to make us feel

better. We therefore rely on external validation to feel fulfilled, which leads to an increase in impulsive spending, and thus increased debt.

The Boundaried One knows they are enough and are able to validate themselves more often, which leads to a sense of self-fulfilment. This means that they don't rely on material possessions to make them feel better, which then leads to a decrease in impulsive spending and in debt.

They are also able to set boundaries with their family, so they no longer sacrifice themselves by taking on debt to save others financially for validation.

- **Increased savings:** As the Boundaried One increases income and decreases debt and stops taking on debt for the sake of the family, they are able to increase their own savings and investments.

Healing the fear of being seen as imperfect

Antony & Swinson (2009) define perfectionism as having such high standards and expectations that they are difficult to meet and state that people who struggle with perfectionism may also struggle to get along with those who don't meet those standards, or find that they are not able to complete jobs on time, that their perfectionism obstructs their ability to perform their work effectively and may even compromise their health.

When the Sweet One works with their inner critic and realises that it was merely trying to shield them from external criticism, they no longer seek validation from others and so give themselves permission to validate themselves. They start to own their power and are able to free themselves by tapping into their deepest magic. And when they do this, they're able to set prices that are more reflective of the value of their products and services without needing everything to be 'perfect'.

The Boundaried One no longer denies or erases themselves because they know that being imperfect is part of life. They give themselves the same grace they've given everyone else and show themselves the same compassion. In the same way that they've held space for the imperfections or failures of others, they do the same for themselves.

They're able to tackle difficult tasks, even if it is imperfect, leading to reduced concern and quicker decision-making. This constant momentum in their lives keeps them moving forward.

No matter what's happening, the Boundaried One is able to keep going, which increases their chances of success. In business, they get over failure faster, no longer put themselves into debt to keep up a particular image, and are able to save more money because they're no longer interested in proving anything to anyone. They give themselves permission to truly be seen and embrace vulnerability, which helps them connect to their ideal clients a lot quicker, which further increases their sales in business.

How does healing the need to be perfect affect our finances?

- **Increased income:** According to a study by Kelly (2015), successful people are less likely to be perfectionists because they are aware that the symptoms of perfectionism limit success. Kelly argues that perfectionism stunts creativity, joy, inspiration and productivity. When the Boundaried One lets go of perfectionism, they let go of the fear of failure and so increase productivity, thereby improving their chances of success in their career and business, which leads to increased income.
- **Decreased debt:** When the Boundaried One is no longer concerned with fitting in and doing the right thing so that they can get praise from society or family, they are able to connect with their own truth and start spending according to their values, which leads to a decrease in impulsive

spending, and a decrease in debt.
- **Increased savings:** The Boundaried One increases their income and starts spending in alignment with their values, which leads to increased savings.

Releasing repressed anger in the womb

According to Bertrand & Bertrand (2017), when people with wombs start to connect and talk to their wombs, they are able to explore their own energy system, allow trapped energy to flow again, discover their own personal destinies, connect with their intuition and download the secrets of the universe.

The Sweet One becomes the Boundaried One by giving themselves permission to release the repressed anger stored in their wombs, which allows them to connect with the grief and sadness that that anger has been masking.

Being active participants in our own self-erasure can be painful, but as the Boundaried One starts to heal, they give themselves permission to genuinely see themselves and heal. And as they heal their relationship with their womb they start tapping into their creativity, allowing themselves to start birthing their creative ideas, which also increases their chances of business success and financial success.

Individuals who have wombs draw energy from their second chakra, which is associated with creativity and fertility. Considering the powerful energy of the womb that brings forth human life, one might wonder what could happen if that same energy is harnessed to give birth to businesses and ideas.

When the Boundaried One is no longer afraid of their own power, they can start negotiating for themselves and so give themselves permission to fearlessly expand.

How does releasing anger in the womb influence financial behaviour?

- **Increased income:** I have worked with hundreds of women to help them connect with their wombs (I have even written and published a two-part *Next Level You Womb and Money Journal*) and have seen how, when women connect with their wombs, they start to achieve intuitive wisdom when it comes to launching and growing businesses, managing money, and understanding the next steps to take for their lives, businesses and careers. I have seen how these messages defy traditional logic but always lead to magical outcomes and, ultimately, increased income. This is why the core work on healing ancestral money trauma centres on helping women heal their relationship with their womb.

   When the Boundaried One starts releasing the anger in their womb and honouring their womb, they step into their power and start following their intuitive guidance, which leads to increased income.
- **Decreased debt:** Anger leads to increased impulsive spending (Makwakwa, 2013), but when the Boundaried One releases their anger, they think more deeply before spending money, which decreases reckless spending and leads to decreased debt.

   When the Boundaried One starts to connect with their womb, they connect to themselves; they get to know themselves and start to tap into their own power, which decreases their spending and, in turn, debt.
- **Increased savings:** As the Boundaried One increases their income and decreases their debt, they tend to spend less money on material things, which leads to an increase in savings.

CASE STUDY

The Boundaried One

VANGILE: Welcome, Ayanda. Thank you for doing this interview. Can you start by telling us where you're from?

AYANDA: I am from one of the villages in the Eastern Cape.

VANGILE: What would you say your relationship with money has been and your relationship with your family when it comes to money, before you began your healing journey?

AYANDA: I had an interesting upbringing in the sense that we grew up with my dad as the primary caregiver. He had an open style of talking about money or being open about money; he would show us his salary slip in terms of how much he was earning and how much goes to our school and food in the house and assistance in the house. We also had pocket money. My dad would give us girls pocket money in case we needed anything. So I always had money, until he had a mental breakdown after buying a house. He lost his job and lost the house. I consider it one of the traumatic experiences that I had to witness because he had a full-on mental breakdown after that.

[When I] started running my business, I noticed that I was self-sabotaging financially. Even now, I think my biggest thing is around service pricing. I always want to under charge because I'm afraid of gaining so much and then losing it. I'm afraid of attaining money and then losing my mind. I think, along the years, it has felt safer to then serve without charging people. I guess my relationship with money was a bit twofold. One was that a group in the family was comfortable about money, but also then experienced trauma around money.

VANGILE: You grew up always having money and when your

dad experienced his mental breakdown, did you find yourself stepping into the role of the primary caregiver at any point?

AYANDA: Most of the time I would ... because also my dad had an alcohol problem. When he was drunk, I would take care of the family financially, based on whatever was available at that time. When he had a mental breakdown, I had to then stop studying so that I could assist the family financially. Then I became the primary caregiver in a sense. Or breadwinner.

And, interestingly enough, it still continues even now, but in different forms. I'm older now, but when a whole lot of the stuff happens at home I probably provide for it financially, including supporting my siblings and their children.

VANGILE: I know you're still supporting them, but how is that support different now to how it was a few years ago?

AYANDA: A few years ago, I would apply for a loan to support them. I would sacrifice to ensure that everyone in the house was taken care of. When I started a business, I had to resign from my job. One of the things I was stuck at was, if I resign, who's going to take care of everybody else? I had to decide to start living for me. Running a business also taught me that I was self-sabotaging a lot and therefore not creating a lot of money because I was afraid that the money is going to go back to the family. When I started working, I realised there was a complete cycle around self-sabotage that I couldn't break. And then, while doing the Wealthy Money work, I started to be more strategic around certain boundaries around choosing what is best for me, around being okay with saying no. I had to learn to be okay with being selfish and only what I'm able to give and not self-sacrifice myself to support everybody else. I had to encourage people to work and only support when I can. So the change is that I no longer sacrifice.

When I look at some of my siblings, learning to say no and not self-sacrifice has taught them to find their own way of making money, which I feel taught them to be slightly more responsible and more accountable financially because, along the line, I realised that by doing everything for them, I was indirectly teaching them to be more irresponsible. When I took back some of the responsibility for myself, it taught them to work on their ideas, to build their own careers and their own finances.

VANGILE: How do you respond to financial challenges now and has it changed over the years?

AYANDA: It has changed. In the past, it was easy for me to take on a lot of debt and then struggle to pay off the debt and then get blacklisted or reported to the credit bureaus. It became a cycle where I have an amount of debt that I pay and then recreate all over again. Now I find that I have more patience; if I don't have the money that I need right now, then I don't have it. I know I'm not going to rush to create a debt for me to service my immediate need. I feel like my approach to money has changed quite a lot. Also, in the past, it was easier for me to create a debt to assist another person. The difference now is that if I do think about creating a debt, it's usually around attaining more income within the business.

I'll give an example: My business is on an upskill trajectory and more money is needed. As much as I get frustrated about the need for money and all the bills I must pay, I do find a certain sense of calm. I'm not as panicky. Of course, I want things to move forward, but for some weird reason, there's also a sense of calm where I'm frustrated mentally, but inside there's a sense of calm where I'm now thinking, 'Okay, what am I missing? What can I do differently?'

VANGILE: How did you get to this space of calm and no longer creating debt to save others? Do you have any exercises or suggestions?

AYANDA: To be honest, I really think it's just that I don't have a lot of finance coaches. I usually just use one person. I only do

Wealthy Money finance work because I didn't want to confuse myself. Of course, people can do different things. Also, because at the end stage of my business, I was aware of the changes and shifts when I did certain meditations around my understanding of money, around my relationship with money. My go-to tips are literally around the Wealthy Money course because it was easy for me to … If I'm stuck, I go and check if there's anything in my inner self, my inner child, that is creating confusion in how I'm doing things now. So the inner-child meditations and the spirit-of-money meditations are where I go, and also understanding my relationship with money. It was important for me initially to write things down so that I can see in black and white where I'm missing things and what I can do differently.

So even now, right now, I think the calm comes from the fact that I now understand that whatever is happening in my mind is not always me having made a bad decision. It's just that there's something that I need to align properly and then be able to make different choices. I think what has also helped is being open to ask for help and to say, 'I'm not doing well financially.'

Because doing the inner work doesn't mean that everything is going to be super perfect from the get-go because we still get stuck in our ways. I think I started the inner work when I was in my mid-thirties. From zero to 30, I was doing things in a particular way. It's easy to get caught up in how you used to do things. I found that I struggled more when I assumed I knew everything, where I felt like, okay, now I'm fine, I can do this on my own.

Sometimes we become an enemy of progress for ourselves because we don't see the blind spots and we don't see where we are missing things or, just generally, we are too close to the situation to see anyway. So reaching out and asking for help, I find that it was quite useful as well.

VANGILE: I can imagine that they were quite drastic because if one's family is used to always receiving support from them and then to suddenly put boundaries in place, that can be quite a lot for your family. How did they respond to that and how did you cope with their response?

AYANDA: It was wild at first because most of my siblings and even my parents were used to a whole lot of things that I was either giving or that's just the way that I was doing things. So having to set those boundaries at first was really tough. I think we had a lot of pressures initially, but also because in my business I work a lot with family dynamics [and] I recognised that I needed to change the pattern in my family. And for me to change that pattern meant doing things differently. So all I could do was to keep asserting my boundaries and staying present with them and not disengaging just because we were going through a rough communication space. I kept communicating my boundaries and remained present until they recognised that I don't hate them, I was just changing how I do things.

VANGILE: What advice would you give to someone who is doing everything for family and sacrificing themselves?

AYANDA: Their starting point should be themselves because I find that when we take on a lot of load we can feel when it's too heavy and we can feel when it's getting too much. When we then look at how much we are carrying, it's important to ask ourselves, 'If something would happen to me today, how is this family going to function? Am I assisting them by carrying all their load or am I crippling them?'

Once you recognise that actually you're crippling them and yourself, you then start deciding which load you need to take away. Then you do that bit by bit until people get used it. One of the things I even had to do in my case is to say to my mom, 'Actually, Mom, I'm also a child in this family and therefore it's not my responsibility to take care of your kids.'

We had a huge fight about those things, but I needed to

remind myself that I'm also a child and a beneficiary in this family because what tends to happen once you become a breadwinner and the primary caregiver, you tend to forget your role in your family and your position in the family, and then everyone becomes your responsibility. Then, for you to be okay, you need to restore the order. Restoring the order sometimes might mean you being the child that you are and the mom being the mom.

I had to also teach my mom or guide my mom to interact with her children, my siblings and me, so she could go back to her role and I could go back to mine.

Start by asking yourself, 'How would life look like if I was prioritising myself?'

Once you become that person who prioritises themselves, it's easy to see when something is not serving you but serving other people you love most. Once you see that, you then let go of that because then it's not serving you. Of course, it doesn't mean that you'll be all-out selfish, but you will see things [that are] building you and those that are destroying you. Then you let go of those things bit by bit. I think the other thing is to be open to talking and communicating because we tend to refuse to talk to family about these things.

People decide to let go and leave and then they shut themselves out. Families often don't even know what's wrong or what's happening with you. I find that having these tough conversations helps us to say, 'No, I can't help you now because I must take myself to school. Or, no, I can't assist your child right now because I don't even have the money to take care of my own child.'

Having these conversations helps because then people know exactly what's going on.

VANGILE: I love this advice so much. Thank you, Ayanda.

CHAPTER 14

The Destroyer becomes the Renovator

The Renovator is the healing or healed version of the Destroyer. They know what it is to be the black sheep of the family, have left the family home (Destroyers rarely live at home), done their healing and are now back to take on their role as the one who shows the family what becomes possible when one heals their trauma and lives their truth.

The Destroyer knows how much energy it takes to fight the family and break down the house to get everyone to open the closet in order to reveal their skeletons, to get to the truth (because that's all that matters to them); as they mature and heal and step into the role of the Renovator, they realise – just like the renovator of a building – that one doesn't need to break down the entire house just to tear it down and rebuild dilapidated closets. The Renovator knows that if all buildings were torn down, there would be nothing but rubble left, so if you're going to tear down buildings, you'd better have a great constructor to help you rebuild and sometimes the walls and the foundation need to be kept for the rebuilding.

The Renovator is no longer consumed by rage (silent or vocal) and frustration at the refusal of their family, community or world to examine the truth. The Renovator is willing to lead by example and show the family what life looks like when they overcome their fears of revealing the skeletons in their closet. They also know the pain of being othered and will usually be the first to tell people who are different, 'You are okay as you are', and will often give the Sweet One and the RunAway permission to show their truth.

What I've seen in my work is how the feelings of abandonment and rejection lead many Destroyers on some of the deepest healing journeys and, when they come out on the other end, they take other family members on the journey. They have taken a page from Rumi, who says, 'Yesterday I was clever, so I wanted to change the world. Today I am wise, so I am changing myself.'

Instead of showing people the truth, they have decided to stand in their truth. They've learnt that you cannot force others to heal – all you can do is shine your light by living your truth and following your heart, and building a splendid life or a life you can be proud of, where you are not weighed down by the lies and the fear of facing yourself and your trauma. This ignites others to do the same, which sets them on their own healing journey.

Renovators have learnt the power of living by example. They have learnt that their presence, their way of being – the way they live life differently – is what influences people to change and start questioning themselves and their life choices. When family members see the Renovator's evolution, they come to ask them, 'How do we heal this? How did you do it?' They start to see what the Destroyer was trying to get them to heal and face in their childhood. So the Destroyer's light starts to shine, their energy starts to shine and even the Fixer starts to pay attention, because there's nothing a Fixer respects more than someone who is independent and getting on with their life. The Fixer might actually be one of the first members in the family to come to learn from the Renovator because the Fixer is always trying to do things better and is motivated by what will be best for the family.

Healing the wound of not belonging

About 4% of prisoners in American prisons find themselves in solitary confinement, and these make up 50% of the suicides; the loneliness and sense of rejection drive them to take their own lives (Peer, 2018), which shows just how damaging the wound of not belonging can be to us as humans.

When the Renovator heals the wound of not belonging in their family of origin, they start to realise that they always belonged – they belonged to themselves, and when they went on their healing journey, they connected with themselves. They don't have the luxury of pretending that they are accepted and that everything is okay. They must go on their own journey, and when they do, they find their own tribe and heal that wound of not belonging.

They accept and see the power of having a different viewpoint from others in the family and so start to form their own core values separate from the family. They give themselves permission to do things differently, including finances – they have diverse ways of making money, have varying spending habits and even approach savings differently. They become the pattern breakers, by giving themselves permission to go beyond their family and to innovate in how they make money, spend money, pay back debt and save. They may later bring that information back into their family of origin.

They discover who they are as individuals outside of their family of origin. They can shape their identities independent of the family and craft a life that's really their own and so start to self-actualise. This is what Anderson (2000) calls 'shattering', arguing that abandonment serves as a catalyst for profound personal growth because it offers an opportunity to go from oneness to separateness and so start to truly step into your own.

Renovators take the money that they use to distribute among the family to buy a sense of belonging, and start using it to invest in themselves and their businesses. They're not just making money –

they're making a positive impact on society by innovating and uplifting others. The Renovator within them has awoken, and they can embrace their differences and break free from the status quo. They challenge norms and so pave the way for exciting new possibilities that will push humanity forward.

How does healing the wound of not belonging affect financial behaviour?

- **Increased income and investments:** When the Renovator steps into separation, innovation, doing things completely differently – new technologies, ways of schooling, new ways of being in relationships, and parenting and working, for example. Their innovative spirit leads to boosted income and this is accompanied by increased investment in new opportunities.
- **Decreased debt:** The Renovator doesn't use money to fill the void of not belonging, so they spend less on things they don't need, which leads to a decrease in impulsive spending and so a further decrease in debt. Also, when The Renovator heals their abandonment wounds, they stop using money as a tool to buy love and are less likely to get into debt in order to help others because they no longer fear losing them.
- **Increased savings:** When they release the wound of not belonging, they start to form healthy attachment bonds with the people in their lives and also release their hyper independence, which means they ask for help from their community when they need it, which saves them money, or they hire support in their business ventures or careers, which makes them money in the long run because it frees them to focus on their core strengths. When their income increases and debt decreases, they have more money to save and invest.

Healing self-doubt

A study by Javed et al. (2017) looked at the behaviour of students in China's consumer financial market and, based on the results, they concluded that objective financial knowledge, although important for managing finances, is not enough – self-esteem plays an important role in managing finances. They even go as far as to recommend that governments and policymakers focus on both psychological traits and objective knowledge when conducting financial literacy training. So, based on this and similar research, we can conclude that healing self-doubt and increasing self-esteem will have financial benefits.

When the Renovator heals their self-doubt or fear of being seen, they give themselves permission to release their fears of judgement and criticism that stem from, 'What will other people think or say?'

Part of the Renovator's journey is to work through the shame that comes with being the black sheep, which then allows them to claim themselves, claim their identities and believe in themselves. Their journey teaches them how to have compassion for themselves, how to stand in their truth and own their stories and differences. When they stop worrying about others, they free themselves to do whatever their souls really want to do. They become free to redefine themselves to embody the identities they always wished to embody. And, in so doing, they give the rest of us permission to try out new identities, to explore new philosophies and embody them.

It's often the Renovators who give us new ways of seeing the world, who get us to question the norm and explore new ways of being. They bring forth these ideas and are willing to stand by them because they are no longer scared of being seen as 'too much' – they no longer doubt themselves. They have so much self-belief that they are also able to get us to believe in the ideas.

They have the energy to persist and the resilience to keep going no matter what. And, as they do that, they get most of us to buy in to these ideas and start testing out new ideas, to ask ourselves: What if?

What if home schooling is not so bad? What if working a four-hour day is actually good for our mental health?

They introduce new ideas, which increases their income and, which they can use to keep investing in their innovations and radical ideas and fighting the traditional ways of thinking and even starting NGOs.

How does healing self-doubt and the fear of being 'too much' affect financial behaviour?

- **Increased income:** When the Renovator heals their self-doubt, they become more sure of themselves, no longer worry and doubt themselves when it comes to their work, which leads to them negotiating higher salaries and charging fair market prices in their businesses. They know that what they're charging for their products and services is a reflection of the value of their work and what they are bringing forth into this world.

    The Renovator still runs the risk of being overconfident, which may lead to them taking on more risk.
- **Decreased debt:** Healing self-doubt and increasing self-esteem tend to impact financial management, probably because when people feel more confident about themselves and their ability they are more willing to apply the financial knowledge they've acquired, which leads to better financial management. And better financial management leads to a decrease in impulsive spending, which leads to a decrease in debt.
- **Increased savings:** When the Renovator increases their self-esteem, they become more confident in employing their financial management skills, which leads to an increase in their savings.

Healing the fear of rejection

When the Renovator heals their fear of rejection, they give others permission to reject them, but being rejected is no longer the end of the world. As Smith (2016) says in his book, *The Other Side of Rejection*, rejection can be a powerful motivator for success and a guaranteed law of success (in other words, it will happen) because it's important for visionaries, dreamers and pioneers to be rejected so that they can be isolated and delve inward to realise their greatness. He says that, in this way, rejection works for us because it helps us develop resilience, tenacity and drive, which are important characteristics for success.

It is human nature for us to want to be loved or to be liked, to want to fit in with others, but when the Renovator heals their fear of rejection, it becomes easier for them to stand in their truth and trust themselves. Overcoming that fear is what then gives them the courage to go back to their family of origin and share the lessons they have learnt on their journey.

How does healing the fear of rejection affect financial behaviour?

- **Increased income:** When the Renovator heals their fear of rejection, their level of resilience increases, which impacts their income. They no longer take rejection personally and are able to put themselves in uncomfortable positions over and over again, getting people to buy in to their ideas or buy their products and services and support their businesses, which ultimately grows their business ideas and increases their income. In business, they're able to price their products and services appropriately because they now understand that when people reject them based on their salary or their pricing, it's not personal. They give people permission to do that, and so also open themselves up to new opportunities (business and employment) as well as new clients willing to pay for their products and services, which also increases their income.

- **Increased savings:** As their businesses improve and income increases because they no longer feel the need to try to fit in with the tribe, they are able to start increasing their savings. They no longer use money as a tool to buy things they don't want or go to places they don't like in order to be liked by others. They now use their money productively and to do what they've always wanted to do, which is to bring a different way of being to the world, thus increasing their income and investments.
- **Decreased debt:** When Renovators heal their fear of rejection, they release themselves from having to prove anything to anyone. They don't use money to prove themselves, which allows them to spend in accordance with their values and so decrease their debt.

CASE STUDY

The Renovator

VANGILE: Hello, Lerato. Where are you from?

LERATO: I stay in Johannesburg.

VANGILE: How would you describe your relationship with your family before starting your money journey?

LERATO: I see how I was always trying to get rid of the money I had, and I also used money to buy love. I had this relationship with my mom where I always wanted to please her and be everything she wanted me to be. Sustaining that didn't fully work out because there are certain things about myself that I couldn't change. For instance, the fact that I'm gay and a sangoma, which are two of the things that really trigger her. I would just try to use money to buy her love and we had this strange dynamic where I was mothering her. I basically didn't have a mother because I was mothering my mother, I was mothering my sister, and at certain times I had to mother my father.

VANGILE: How did this dynamic change?

LERATO: It's from the work that I've been doing through your programme, but it was very volatile. I spent probably over a year not speaking to my mom. We've also had major fights in between, with me trying to tell her how she's treated me. It would be like speaking to a wall, basically. She would not hear me. And then weeks later, she would come back and be, like, I don't understand why you're not talking to me.

So, yeah, I had to take some drastic measures to also remember that I really am just a daughter. I'm not my mother's mother. She must sort out her own mommy issues. And it was the same with my sister – she didn't speak to me for a year. We started talking again in January and that was only because I made contact. And now my sister is studying at university.

All I did basically after reaching out to her was to find out if she's okay, ask her where she stays, who's paying for things. I haven't done anything beyond that. I haven't said, I'm going to commit to giving you this amount of money every single month. I actually don't want to be involved. I want her and my mother to just figure it out and not get me involved.

I think my mother is still very shocked. As someone who doesn't want to discuss things and take accountability, she's wondering who the hell is this person who's not trying to please her, who's not trying to make everything okay. I'm a shaman and my ndumba [sacred ancestral house] is at my mother's place. A few months ago, she sent me a picture of my door in my ndumba, and it had been destroyed at the bottom. And she asked, 'When are you going to buy a door?'

I was just like, 'I don't have the money. I don't know when we're going to get a new door.'

And I just ended it off there. And then she took the initiative and said she would pay for it. So this week she sent pictures. I have a new door. She's covered it in plastic. She said that she's still going to have it painted. And it looks very nice.

VANGILE: How did you used to feel when you mothered your mother and everyone else in the family?

LERATO: I was so stressed out. It's like I was being pulled in different directions. I had to make sure that everyone was okay. No one was making sure that I was okay. They didn't even consider me. I felt like, no matter what I did for those people, it wasn't enough. I was always trying to find better ways to do something for them. I have a sister who's very secretive. I think it's probably her personality. I would feel so rejected every time she didn't open up to me. And it was just crazy. I mean, I was like the mom with eyes at the back of her head. Even when my sister went on a date, I would Google the guy to check his profile, make sure that she's okay. And she didn't care who she was meeting. She was just happy that she was being taken out. Or she'd be hanging out with her friends, drinking, and then she'd come home tipsy, and I'd be so worried. I didn't have a life. I was basically living for my mom and my sister.

　　　Even when I thought about the idea of making money, I wasn't thinking, I want this in five years. It was more of, if I die, at least my mom and my sister are going to be taken care of.

　　　I thought things started and ended with me, and always felt like if I stopped what I was doing, then everything was going to fall apart. And I stopped and I don't know if things fell apart, but I see how life went on. My sister finally came to her senses and decided to go get a degree. I don't know what's happening with my mom. Maybe she got her life. I don't know. But life went on. It's like nobody missed me.

VANGILE: How has the way you face challenges changed as you've gone through your healing journey?

LERATO: I didn't know how to ask for help. I was not creative with my finances. I thought I had to be the one with the strategy in terms of how to make money. There was no involvement of the Divine. By that I mean God, all my ancestors and my higher self. I was on my own. I was living on a planet where I was the only person and I had to fend for myself. I had to make sure that I was okay. It was tough and stressful. I was doing a million things. I can tell you that those many things I was doing, not all of them were profitable, but they were taking up so much of my time because I was in survival mode and I wanted something to work. I needed to be okay. I don't want to depend on anyone. It was so hard. But I was burnt out and I was about to just snap.

I had a certain image that I wanted to create. I was the ideal daughter. I was the ideal sister, the ideal mother.

I worked through my inner teen stuff and realised that I felt really challenged to operate from a position of connection instead of just wanting to destroy everything. I see how I've evolved and I'm sure part of my mother has evolved too, but I actually don't want to connect with a better version of her. I'd much rather have the relationship be destroyed because I don't want to deal with the idea of her being better.

Who the hell am I going to be mad at if she's suddenly this better, evolved person? I'm fine with my anger. I feel validated. So if she decides to become a better person, that's just going to mess with me.

VANGILE: How has your anger served you?

LERATO: It makes me feel like I'm the actual victim in all of this. I just want things to burn down. But, sadly, life is really challenging me right now because people and money show up more. I'm not fighting as much as I used to with money. There's also someone that I like. I am going to start dating, whether it's her or someone else.

I'm less angry. I'm no longer trying to prove a point. It was always easier for me to just be angry. That was the dominant emotion that I felt like I could connect with best. Connecting with happiness was a very weird thing. I just felt like my happiness was probably going to be taken away at any given moment. But with anger, we're best friends. We've been together for a long time. Anger is my ride or die. It doesn't matter what the season is. Anger will always be here for me. Anger is loyal.

VANGILE: As I listen to you, I hear that your anger also comes from a space of unfairness. It's unfair to mother our parents and siblings and to not have a childhood. How has pointing out that unfairness to yourself, acknowledging that unfairness to yourself and to your family, helped you transform your finances and family dynamics?

LERATO: They actually had to figure out things themselves, and they also had to want things enough to create them for themselves. I tried so hard to convince my sister to go to university. Imagine convincing someone to fix their life? I even had to convince her to get a part-time job and stop depending on an allowance from my father because she was over 21.

I needed my family to need me. If it was possible for me to be the person that puts the air into their lungs so they could breathe, I would have done that because I just wanted to be needed.

For many years, my father said that property will make you lots of money and, because I wanted to prove a point, I decided that I could do better than him in property and I ended up doing not so well, but I got to work with Dr Miranda, who's a property coach, and we changed the way that I view property. Now I'm going to go and do it properly, not from a position of wanting to prove something to my dad but more in alignment with me and my goals.

Before, I used to feel like I would hear my mother's opinion, my mom's voice, my sister's voice, my dad's voice in my head, and

I didn't know who exactly I was because I was so stuck in that. Now I see myself. I feel like I'm living my own life. I eat things that I like. I'm no longer trying to prove myself.

VANGILE: How did your relationship with your family affect the way you spend and save money and how has that changed now that you see yourself?

LERATO: I always just felt like it doesn't matter how much money I make – my mom and my sister are going to take it from me, in any case. I would always just try to get rid of money. I would just find a way to spend it so that it's not there. I didn't feel safe with it because I had two children – my mom and my sister – and they demanded everything of mine. And sometimes I would even buy clothes and hide them. What the hell? It felt like I had to also buy things for them too. So that was so horrible. I've had to learn to make money and save money. And it's very strange having money for myself, not money that I'm going to have to split with other people. I would even go as far as sending my mother money when I got a bonus. I'd send my sister money. Imagine ... I worked hard, but I'm splitting my bonus with them. Wow, what a wild life. It was even hard for me to buy the car of my dreams because I felt like my family would be like, 'Who the hell do you think you are? You think you're so big.'

My mom would always try to make me smaller. Not talking to her for over a year was good for me because I learnt to allow myself to grow and be bigger and less fearful of what she's going to do to me if she feels like I'm becoming bigger than her. It's made the idea of making more money less scary because, before, I felt like I was being hunted by my mom and my sister.

Now I feel like money and I are getting along. It's been a long time coming, but we're getting there. We're good to each other. I'm not trying to get rid of money, even if it means I pay all my expenses and needs and I'm left with zero. But it means that I spend the money on things that are for me, not for my mom, not for my sister. I'm not using the money to try to impress people.

VANGILE: What advice would you give someone who is where you were and is angry and feeling rejected by family and is using money to buy their acceptance?

LERATO: I think it's important that people give themselves permission to be angry. I don't think anger is such a bad thing. It's just that I was raised to think that it was a horrible thing, and I was not allowed to feel my anger. My grandmother would tell my cousin and me that if you're angry, it means you're the devil's child.

Anger meant something else to me growing up because my grandmother believed that you shouldn't be angry. You must be a lady. You must be sweet. You must be happy all the time and accommodating.

The idea of being angry is possibly scary to a lot of people because you don't know what you're going to do with that anger. One of the reasons I ended up in therapy consistently when I was 20 was because I would get really angry and I'd black out. I wouldn't remember what I did. So I was, like, it's either I'm going to get so angry and end up killing someone and then I go to jail, or I'm going to commit suicide.

I was, like, let me just start going to therapy, and have been in therapy consistently. Now I'm 34 and have learnt to feel my anger in healthy ways and I've seen how my anger has transformed a lot of things. It's shifted a lot of things. I had the space and the support to know that being angry is okay. You don't have to be the sweet, perfect person who doesn't feel her emotions because I also didn't like emotions. I thought they were a lie, so I intellectualised everything.

Then I joined the Money Magic course, and you were not asking me to draw up a spreadsheet, you were asking me to meditate and feel things in my body and connect with my lineage. That was, like, oh my gosh. I would call it also an emotional intelligence course in a way because it helped me so much. I realised that it doesn't matter how smart you are, if you must fix your relationship with money, it's going to take a lot of working through emotions.

You're meant to feel all your emotions. So start by allowing yourself to be angry, but have positive outlets.

VANGILE: Thank you so much, Lerato.

CHAPTER 15

The RunAway becomes the Grounded Seeker

While the RunAway's role is to process the trauma in the family, the Grounded Seeker's role is to teach every family member to acknowledge their own feelings and to take responsibility for their emotional wellbeing and healing. Once the RunAway begins to heal, they learn how to be the Grounded Seeker. They start metabolising family trauma and their healing has wide ramifications for the family, which results in a visible shift in the family's relationship dynamics.

The Grounded Seeker stops running from their bodies and allows themselves to feel their feelings and starts becoming curious about their emotions and the sensations in their bodies. Their body is a house they've lived in for years, sometimes decades, constantly ignoring and running away from it. But when they embark on their healing journey they start seeking and going into their bodies to understand what emotions reside there. The Grounded Seeker allows themselves to fully connect with their own bodies, and may even start exploring nutrition, different forms of movement, dance, yoga and/or exercise.

As the Grounded Seeker gets to know themselves, they become

a different type of traveller or runner; they are now the one who goes within and explores their inner world, even as they continue to travel externally.

They might find themselves grounded to one particular place and living like a hermit for a while as they get to know themselves, because there's a lot of work that goes into connecting with your body. But when the Grounded Seeker emerges from their hermit journey, they come back to teach us how to connect with ourselves, know ourselves better and go on our own journey.

The Grounded Seeker starts to understand their role as an empath and they begin to set boundaries, including energetic boundaries. Initially, they can go to the extreme of filtering out a lot of people and not allowing others into their space because they need to go through a process of learning how to stop absorbing other people's emotions and learning how to allow others to process their own emotions. As the Grounded Seeker, they begin to understand that a lot of people want to be in their presence because they are able to not just absorb others' emotions, but also metabolise those emotions and help them process them.

Healing the feeling of unsafety

The more the Grounded Seeker gets comfortable with going into their body, the more they are able to integrate their ancestral trauma and regulate their nervous system, so they're no longer in a state of hypervigilance, making it less likely for them to dissociate and numb their emotions.

They start to feel safe in their bodies and in the world, and even with money. They are able to look at their own finances rather than running towards money to feel safe; they now have a neutral relationship with money, where having money is no longer scary.

As a RunAway archetype, I have seen this in my own life. I spent so much of my life running away from myself through travel (I still travel extensively but not to run away) and dissociating from my body because being in my body felt unsafe; over time, I developed digestive issues, a pain in my coccyx that made it difficult to sit down, terrible womb pains that would sometimes make me faint, and then the right side of my body would go numb. It took physical pain to get me to focus on my body, to start feeling the sensations and develop my interoception skills – the ability to feel what's going on in our bodies – so that I could start regulating my emotions and learning to regulate my nervous system.

Nothing in my life felt safe – not relationships, not money and definitely not expressing myself. I suffered panic attacks whenever I had to deal with money (invoice people, pay for things or even withdraw money at the ATM), abandoned relationships at the drop of a hat, and left anything I started at the first sign of a challenge or a trigger.

The first time I attended a 10-day vipassana meditation course, I started to delve into my body and to sit with the physical and emotional pain stored in it; a lot of memories and emotions came up for me, which helped me see for myself that trauma does indeed live in the body.

After 10 days, I began to feel safer and started regulating my nervous system and something incredible happened – I felt a deep sense of inner peace and calm and started to fall in love with my own company and being in my body. Over time, the more I meditated, the more I learnt to persevere through challenges and tackle difficult tasks like budgeting, writing, running businesses and paying off my US$60,000 debt. I learnt to hold myself and stay in my body when I was triggered, and to grow in relationships even when things got hard and I got scared. And I started to see a change in my finances too – I felt safe enough to make money, to pay off my debt, to start investing and to charge fair market prices for my products and services. I was also no longer travelling just to escape my debt and other money issues; I started using only cash (no credit cards) and travelled for fun and pleasure. In short, I was now operating from my Grounded Seeker archetype.

How does feeling safe in our bodies affect financial behaviour?

- **Increased income:** When the Grounded Seeker feels safer in their bodies, they feel safer about charging for their products and services. Making money no longer feels unsafe and they don't have an excessive need to work continuously to make lots of money to feel secure, which changes their relationship with money. They're able to achieve balance in the way that they make money and can make money in ways that allow them to stay connected to themselves.
- **Decreased debt:** When the Grounded Seeker starts feeling safe they are no longer threatened by bills or creditors. Because they now have uncomfortable money conversations, they are able to regulate their nervous systems and manage their finances better because they no longer swing from one extreme to the next in an attempt to run from their finances.
- **Increased savings:** As the Grounded Seeker delves into their body, they feel safe enough to increase their money set point and start increasing how much money their nervous system can hold, which increases the amount of money in their bank accounts.

Setting boundaries

The Grounded Seeker must set boundaries to feel safe and protect their energy. They begin to understand that they easily absorb the emotions of others by co-regulating or co-dysregulating to other people's nervous systems. They also begin to understand how people in their space impact their mental health and their growth.

Like the Sweet One, they start to set financial boundaries; they are clear on how, when and how much they're going to be paid, and are able to stick to those boundaries.

They also begin to set boundaries with their family, which means family members have to start processing their own emotions and doing their own emotional labour, which actually leaves the Grounded Seeker with more energy than they've ever had, since they are no longer using their energy to process other people's emotions. They feel more rested physically, which impacts both their mental health and finances because they can think clearly and have more energy to deal with challenges.

If I can offer some advice ... The Grounded Seeker needs to move out of home and have their own space, even if they have a good relationship with their family, because they can easily fall back into old patterns of absorbing family members' trauma while they stay within the unit.

Healing the sense of powerlessness

In an effort to understand burnout or emotional exhaustion, a study by Zhou & Chen (2021) collected data from 226 MBA students who were also employees in Western China, and found that the more psychologically empowered and emotionally safe a person felt, the less emotionally exhausted they were. They also concluded that feeling empowered leads to positive work performance and an ability to cope with stress more positively at work. Given the results of the study, we can conclude that when the Grounded Seeker heals their sense of powerlessness and feels empowered, their exhaustion levels go down, their capacity to handle stress goes up and they are less emotionally exhausted.

When the Grounded Seeker begins to heal their trauma and integrate that into their nervous system, they find that they have more capacity to handle day-to-day activities as their allostatic load decreases. And as their static load starts to decrease, they find they have more capacity to do things and handle even the most complex of tasks. They are no longer overwhelmed by small things, and this increases their staying power and resilience.

This is how they become the Grounded Seeker – they can stay in one place and keep going into their body and even change the way that they travel, because they not only tap into their own power, but also *see* their own power. They start to see their own strengths and capitalise on these and, in so doing, realise that they are more than enough – that they are good enough.

They begin to manage small daily tasks very well, develop their resilience and stay in their power, which helps them trust themselves. And as they start to feel their own power and see that they're good enough, they are able to start new projects, stick to them and even handle the challenges of entrepreneurship and/or employment.

This resilience becomes a superpower that can be used to start building successful careers and profitable businesses and to inspire those who work with them and motivate them to have the same kind of staying power, resilience and persistence. They also bring that same sort of staying power into their families.

How does feeling powerful affect financial behaviour?

- **Increased income and investments:** When the Grounded Seeker feels more empowered, they are better able to cope with stress, especially work-related matters, and build their resilience so that they persevere in the face of challenges. This increases their chances of succeeding in business, as well as their careers, which leads to increased income.

  Also, when the Grounded Seeker understands they are good enough and that the prices they charge for their products and services are not a reflection of their value as individuals they are less likely to take rejection personally. They're able to charge a fair market rate for their products and services and even negotiate for better salaries at work. They may also explore new ways of making money, especially as they dive into areas of mental health, energy work and body work. Through their journeys of self-discovery, they start to push the envelope and bring forth incredible knowledge from within themselves and from the ether. They are able to launch new industries or start to marry the work that they do with their journeys of self-discovery, which can move us forward as a society.

- **Decreased debt:** Grounded Seekers have very little debt because they no longer use money as a tool to fill a void and no longer avoid money because they are finally able to sit with the uncomfortable emotions and sensations their finances bring up.

    When the Grounded Seeker feels empowered, they handle stress better so they have less need to spend money or to use money as a tool to buy experiences or material goods to help them escape from themselves, their emotions or their bodies, which leads to a decrease in impulsive spending and debt.

- **Increased savings:** Having done the healing work they require, Grounded Seekers become curious about their finances. They look at their finances in a different way and start building a relationship with money because they are no longer running from discomfort and uncomfortable situations, which leads to a change in spending habits and increased savings. And when the Grounded Seeker feels empowered, they are more likely to increase their income and decrease their spending and debt, which leads to increased savings.

Part 3: The Golden Archetypes

CASE STUDY

The Grounded Seeker

VANGILE: Hello, Priyanka, where are you from originally?

PRIYANKA: I'm from Bangladesh, but I currently live in Canada.

VANGILE: How would you describe your relationship with your family when it comes to money?

PRIYANKA: I felt like we have to tiptoe around it. Money was something we never talked about with my dad. It was always through my mom. I remember I had to wait for the end of the month to ask for something. Money was the reason there were a lot of fights, a lot of chaos. I was the peacekeeper, the Sweet One. In my mind, my brothers were shameless because they would want this toy, that toy, and it would cause my mom so much anxiety. I remember my brother just rolling on the floor and crying in the middle of the market. My mom would have a panic attack because she couldn't afford to buy that toy. I was like, 'No matter what happens, I'm going to be that good kid and make sure my parents are not upset.'

I would wait until the end of the month when my dad got paid because there would be a different energy in the home. I remember my parents would take me to the art shop, I would get art supplies and then we'd go to the bookstore and we'd get books. I remembered that from my childhood. We all moved around my dad's emotions and my mom was the sponge.

And if we ever needed something, my mom had to ask my dad and sometimes had to lie.

VANGILE: What do you think your financial role in your family has been and how has it changed?

PRIYANKA: I had no needs, I had no demands. And then I remember my first job – I got US$20 equivalent. I remember buying gifts for everybody and I remember spending it all in one day. Then I moved to the US and I remember one time I bought US$200 worth of Bath & Body Works things for everybody in my family, including my extended family, people I'd never met.

I would overdo gifts. Even when I was making $800 salary, I would spend $200 on a friend's birthday.

Then I remember when we have Eid, I bought a cow for my parents. A cow!

My brother went on a honeymoon and my mom was, like, 'Can you give me US$300?' I gave it. Then my brother took money from me. He never returned it. My mom was, like, 'Forget about it, it's okay.'

I would always give money. Every month when I received my regular salary, I would give a certain portion to my mom, which was fine. I would buy my friend, my co-worker, a trip, flights, hotel. And then it changed when I started doing my own work, since 2018 – I started having boundaries and spending money on personal-development stuff.

I stopped engaging with my family. I would not ask what they needed, if they had a problem. My mom would say, 'Oh, it's end of the month. You don't have money, you don't have this.'

Before, I would immediately spend money, but I don't participate any more. I moved and I disengaged completely. The same people I bought this entire suitcase worth of bath and bodyworks, lotion, perfume and body spray from, I blocked them. I cut them off.

VANGILE: You blocked them and cut them off? Was there a specific incident that triggered this?

PRIYANKA: Yeah. I think it was my divorce, my first divorce. In my mind, I expected people to be there for me because I bought stuff for them. Or I thought I had friends because I was there for everybody, solving everybody's problems.

Then nobody was there. And if somebody was there, they

would say such terrible things. So I just started cutting people off left and right. I went on Facebook, blocked people, deleted people's numbers and stopped talking to them. And that was a big deal for me because I used to think that, without these very people, I have no identity. I have nobody. That was a hit on my nervous system. But I continued to live.

At this time, I also ran away from my family. I had had a fight with my mom. The next day I woke up at 5am. I packed my bag, I called an Uber and I left. I didn't tell my parents where I went.

I got an Airbnb in the city, somewhere randomly, and I moved there. My parents had no idea where I was. I blocked them everywhere. Then I think, after days, they found my number. They could contact me but running away was my way of punishing them.

VANGILE: Did you ever go back?

PRIYANKA: I did, but a lot of other stuff happened. I got married a second time because of money, because I didn't have a house. And, back home, it's really hard for a woman to find a place to rent. Long story short, I married someone and it was a disaster. When I met that guy, I was, like, 'Okay, at least I have a roof over my head.' He had schizophrenia that I had no idea about. And then I was homeless and my parents had to come rescue me. I had to move in with my parents again in a matter of five months. So it was bad. I also had a stroke.

I had really low self-esteem, low confidence because I was unable to walk properly, not type, not write with my hand properly.

Then I was back with my parents in the pandemic and I was, like, 'Okay, let's stop running. Let's start meeting these people.' And I went deeper into my healing work and I manifested my move to Canada and came here. I have pretty much been running away for the last five years.

One of the reasons why I went to college in the US is because, in fourth grade, a teacher told me, you can go abroad if you get a scholarship. I was, like, 'Great, I can run away from my family if I study well and get a scholarship.' So I did that.

But when I came back and I got married, first time, second time, all that stuff happened, then I was, like, 'Okay, I'm leaving this time for Canada.' But there's a grief in me because part of me wants to go back, but part of me really wants to run constantly.

I'm really going against that urge. I'm, like, 'It's okay to be here. Just stay here for six months. Seriously, stay in this space. For six months, you're allowed to just rest, not move.'

VANGILE: Having worked with you, I know it has been a huge thing for you to return back to your body. Can you talk to us about what you realised about running away from situations and also dissociating from the body?

PRIYANKA: Yeah. I think it was through my work with Misa [Wealthy Money coach] that I got to know that I don't feel my feelings, that I'm always running from them. I remember, in a session with her, I had to sit with my feelings and my body. It was the most difficult thing ever. In that meditation, my inner child was there, my grandma was there, and I was there, Misa was there. It was hard. But since that day, things moved, shifted. I was, like, 'Okay, I'm going to give myself permission to feel. Okay, I feel anger right now. Can I feel anger? If I feel rage, I feel rage.'

I'm not going to say it's majority, still it's minority times that I feel my emotions. Last night, this was literally my thought before I went to sleep: I want to experience my body. I went to the doctor yesterday and I told him, 'Look, please give me a prescription for physiotherapy. I want to go get help for my movement problems because I can't walk properly for too long or I can't run.'

I used to be a very active person. I want to feel better in my body. This is a major shift for me. The fact that I daydream about looking better, in the sense, because I was considered stereotypical pretty, so I experienced sexual molestation as a kid.

For me, adorning myself with earrings or putting make-up on or loving on myself, expressing myself was a major problem for me. I hated that feminine energy but lately, since doing the Wealthy Money safety work, all I want to do is experience that feminine energy in me. I want to be creative in the way I dress. I look at people who are dressed nicely – how they put together their outfit, what shoes they're wearing, what earrings they're wearing, the scrunchie they've put on. You can see the difference. Somebody who put five minutes into their outfit versus somebody who just put something on. For the majority of my life, I would not even brush my hair properly. I would just make sure I look really not put-together, really ugly.

Today, after our call, I'm going to go to a thrift store and I'm going to find an outfit. I don't care. It's going to be under $10 – before, I would never spend money on that. I would give that money to somebody. I want to experience my body, experience taking up space. I want to express myself. I want to go for a walk. I want to go for a swim. And I'm, like, where is this coming from? Because I don't have any memory of experiencing this. I feel like I am returning to myself with this embodiment work and this safety work.

VANGILE: How is your relationship with money changing as you start to feel safer in your body?

PRIYANKA: The government sent me $1100. When I looked at it, my immediate reaction was panic. Then I was, like, 'It's okay. I have money. It's all right. It's okay.' It was uncomfortable. So, still, making more money is uncomfortable.

When I started working with you, my average income was $300 a month. But then since working with you and doing the safety work, I got a job and now, on average, I make $1500 a month, and with that, I pay you, other coaches, rent, groceries and my phone bill, and I would be left with no money in my bank account. That's okay because, for me, it's a big deal that I went from asking money from my parents to making my own money. I still can't allow money to just exist in the account. It's a very tricky thing for me because that never happened for my family.

I'm at a point where it's a big deal that I'm able to pay for living expenses because, ancestrally, women in my family had to experience abuse to have someone pay for their expenses.

My dad has always hidden how much money he made from my mom. That was constant grief from my mom that she had no idea how much my dad made monthly. She would have so much anxiety asking for money for groceries because she didn't know if he had money.

My mom would often say, 'The only reason I haven't left your father is because he provides for me.' And I was just so upset with my mom for that because she's so talented, she's so qualified. She has written two books and she is a self-taught artist, but she has no confidence in herself.

She didn't have childcare support and, as a single woman, she can't rent an apartment. I'm turning 33, but even at this age, I can't find an apartment to rent as a single woman back home. How could my mom do it 30 years ago? It's not easy for her to leave her husband. But in my mind, my child mind, my teenager years, I didn't consider this, but it's systemic.

For me right now, it's a massive disruption to be able to exist without having somebody else pay for my things. I talk to my dad once a month to ask him to pay for my tuition. Now my master's programme is ending and I'm, like, I would have no reason to call my dad. That's another reason why I want to stay poor – I saw that I have a reason to call my dad. If I'm financially fully abundant and self-sufficient, I have no reason to call my dad. For me, that's so painful.

There have been months when I made $5,000, but it went away in a flash because I had debt to pay off. I would make sure the money runs out. But through doing this safety work, I try to keep the money in my account for three days at least and then I spend it.

VANGILE: What's your understanding of safety and how does feeling safe in your body help you cope with challenging situations?

PRIYANKA: For me, safety means allowing feelings to pass through my body like a waterfall, just allowing it to pass through me and rinse my body through that emotion and let it flow through me. That's number one, safety. Number two, safety, I think, is having more peace with being able to trust God.

Remember how scared I was to be homeless and I would tell you, 'What if I'm homeless?'

That fear of homelessness has left my body. It doesn't come. Now I have to work really hard to feel that fear of homelessness. I don't feel it because, over and over, over and over, God has shown up. Money has shown up. Since moving to this apartment, 95% of the things in this apartment have shown up at my doorstep. People came by, people dropped off something that I needed.

There's a statement you say to me, 'Can I allow myself to feel safe right now? For one minute, can I allow myself to feel safe?'

Since doing this work, people just show up with things. I would tell somebody else, 'I was thinking of getting this coffee machine,' and they would just bring it over. I'm, like, 'How is this happening?'

Nothing is accidental, but it seems like it's very serendipitous.

I used to keep my clothes in bags and suitcases and then one day a dresser showed up on my stairs outside. Somebody had left it for me in perfect condition. I slept without bed sheets for two weeks. I didn't have money to go buy a bed sheet. I felt so bad because I was spending so much money on my personal development, yet I had no money for a bed sheet. I remember telling my friend, 'I'm thinking of going to a thrift store and buying a bed sheet,' but I didn't tell her I didn't have bed sheets. The next day, she showed up with new bed sheets she hadn't used, including a comforter.

When I came into this house, I didn't have a fork. I didn't have a spoon. My roommate gave me a fork and a spoon. And then, out of nowhere – I didn't tell this to my friend – she came with all these spoons, these plates, these bottles, these cups, a whole box of things. I never told her. I just asked and I received it in a matter of a day or two.

That's when I started realising, okay, there's something else happening beyond my 3D, beyond my body, beyond my conscious energy, [my] consciousness that is looking after me. I think that has really helped me.

There's an invisible force around us. There are beings around us who are listening to us as we speak, caring for us. I feel my spirit guides, my ancestors, and really doing the work with you calling in the energy of my grandma. It's powerful. For me, safety is being able to trust that I don't have to know everything and that my safety is inevitable. My safety is not negotiable and that it's going to be okay.

VANGILE: How have things changed between you and your family as you have been coming into your sense of safety, also setting boundaries, really prioritising yourself?

PRIYANKA: I don't know what it's going to be like in six months because this work is so intense – six months can have a different outlook. Before, I would call my parents and I would say, 'Oh, I'm so poor. I don't have money for this and that.' My whole conversation with them would be about not having money. These days, when I call them, I don't talk about that. I just listen. I'm more present. I listen to them talk about not having money and people stealing our money and money just leaving us in a very unjust way.

I let them be. I let them be who they are. I think that's one thing Misa told me: 'What if you let your father be who he is? What if you don't have to change your mom? What if you just let them be who they are?'

I let them be who they are. Sometimes I can't. Sometimes it just triggers me to say something, but most of the time I just let them be. I don't go and offer them money.

That's how it is with my family now – learning to establish my boundaries, but also acknowledging that the humanness in me is showing up. Drama responses are showing up, which is, like, I don't want them to know I make money. Even if I make money through my clients, I don't tell them. I've had one or two clients [and] my parents have no idea I got paid.

VANGILE: What advice would you give to someone who is always running away and has a hard time feeling safe in their bodies?

PRIYANKA: Reduce the over-explaining. If somebody has not asked me something, I don't go and offer and tell them. My parents have not asked me, 'Do you work two extra days?'

I don't feel safe telling them I work five days. They know I work three days. It's okay. They don't have to know everything about my life. Those little things, those boundaries, they're so abstract, but these are some of the ways I've started creating this container of safety within me.

Finally, having that courage, having that inspiration to feel my body, is the next step. Understanding that my body is a house and I want to feel this house. I want to go to every corner of my house and live in it. That's what my goal is now for safety, which is to experience my body. Which I think will open up the next chakra, which is a sacral chakra, which makes sense. Sacral can only open up if you're feeling safe.

VANGILE: Thank you, Priyanka.

CHAPTER 16

The Fixer becomes the Sovereign One

While the role of the Fixer is to help the family move forward and grow financially as a unit, the role of the Sovereign One is to show everyone that individual growth should not come at the expense of collective growth and that honouring our individual wants, needs and desires is also important and can improve how we show up for other family members.

When the Fixer goes on a healing journey and starts to embody the Golden archetype of the Sovereign One, they give themselves permission to go from fixing the lives of family members, being involved in their family's lives and controlling their family to exploring themselves and looking after their own needs. And, in so doing, they begin to release any resentment and anger they feel towards their families.

They give themselves permission to focus on re-parenting their inner child and teen and to find the things that make them happy, which allows them to let go, to surrender, and give family members an opportunity to take control of their own lives and make their own mistakes. And, as family members start to take control of their own lives, the Sovereign One learns the valuable and slightly painful lesson that everyone has always been able to survive without them. They realise that people are able to make plans for themselves financially, that they're able to figure out the complexities of life on their own, and that, if left alone, family members will eventually find their own way.

When the Sovereign One steps back from the family matters, it gives family members breathing room to embark on their own journeys, find themselves and understand themselves as individuals. It must, however, be noted that this can lead to a lot of family members' lives falling apart in the short term (they rebound in the long term), since the Sovereign One no longer behaves like the Fixer by stepping in to save family members.

The Sovereign One starts to learn new things about their family because they're able to sit down and have conversations with them without feeling as though they have to fix the problem or save them, which allows them to truly hear their family members, making them even more effective as a support system. As a result, they are met with less resistance within their families and can support members from a knowledgeable space because they understand what people truly want and need and how they want to be supported. While the Fixer would rush to fix family members' problems, the Sovereign One honours boundaries and only steps in when requested.

And when they start supporting their families instead of dictating to them, it becomes easier for others to buy into their vision and they may just find that everyone has the same goal – they just have a different idea of how they're going to reach that goal.

Re-parenting the inner child or teen

The Sovereign One gives themselves permission to go on a journey to heal and re-parent their inner child and teen, and when they finally do that, they stop being the parent to others in the family. They take all that parenting obsession and the need to parent everyone else and give it to their inner child and teen, the versions of them that needed the parenting they were actually giving to everyone else.

When the Sovereign One re-parents their inner child and teen, they gain a greater understanding of their emotional and behavioural patterns, which increases their ability to handle stress and difficult emotions. Increased self-awareness also changes the way we relate to ourselves with kindness and compassion, which boosts our self-esteem and self-confidence.

Re-parenting the inner child or teen requires us to go into our past memories and to start processing our emotions and experiences from the past, which leads to a decrease in stress hormones, a more regulated nervous system and reduced anxiety. As our inner child heals, we learn how to love and respect ourselves, and so increase our confidence and self-esteem and learn to manage our emotions (Davis, 2020).

As their inner child and teen heal, the Sovereign One starts to practice self-compassion, play more, rediscover joy and remember how to have fun, which activates the parasympathetic nervous system and further reduces stress. As their levels of self-compassion increase and they start to understand their inner child better, they become more relaxed and understanding as parents, which changes the way they show up for their children, reducing the trauma their children inherit.

How does healing the inner child affect our finances?

- **Increased income:** Re-parenting their inner child leads to an increase in their self-esteem, which leads to more confidence in financial decision-making, the ability to forgive past financial mistakes and keep going (Makwakwa, 2013), which increases the changes of financial success,
- **Decreased debt:** Re-parenting the inner child or teen increases self-awareness and their understanding of their

emotional and behavioural patterns, which allows them to make more informed buying decisions and avoid reckless spending (Makwakwa, 2013), which in turn decreases the Sovereign One's debt. The more self-aware they become, the more alert they are to the amount of risk they are taking on, which decreases their debt even further.

When the Sovereign One re-parents themselves, they stop trying to parent their family members or to rescue them financially, which means they stop creating debt in order to help other people, which leads to decreased debt.

- **Increased savings and investing:** As the Sovereign One's income increases, expenses and debt decrease, so they find that they have more money for saving and investing. They are also then more likely to invest in new business opportunities.

Healing the God wound

The God wound speaks to our inability to see our own Divinity and feel our own connection to the greater source regardless of religion. The term refers to our ability to surrender to what is, to trust our life and ourselves, and that we are held, if not by a higher source, then at least by our higher selves, regardless of what is unfolding in the moment.

Ozcan et al. (2021) conducted a study among female aid workers who work in stressful and unsafe environments and found that having a faith-based or spiritual approach helped the workers feel grounded, calm, resilient and present in difficult situations; they also felt more of a community, with a sense of belonging.

It is important to note, though, that studies do show that religious coping mechanisms are *not* ideal for people struggling with depression or anxiety and can actually make the situation worse (Bryan et al., 2016). Nevertheless, although studies may suggest that religion and spirituality cannot heal or help us overcome complex trauma or mental health issues, a relationship with the Divine may indeed affect the way we process and view traumatic events.

Healing the God wound, therefore, has nothing to do with religion (I have never subscribed to religion), but is focused on the relationship between ourselves and the Divine so that we can start changing the way we see our past and so begin to heal it. When the Sovereign One starts to heal the God wound, their connection to themselves starts to deepen and they begin to trust themselves a lot more. They connect with their own power and acknowledge the power of others.

They release the need to control the outcome of events and feel calm in the face of challenges. They start giving themselves permission to live and they start to surrender to how their life wants to unfold.

When the Sovereign One starts trusting themselves, they release the fear of what will happen if things go wrong because they know they can find the answers they need within themselves or get the help and support they want and need. Self-trust improves self-awareness, which helps us understand our own motivations, values and behaviours, which leads to improved relationships with others in our circles. In this way, the Sovereign One starts to release control and opens up to life, new people and new experiences, which may even lead to new business opportunities.

They realise that they too need support and they start calling in people who are able to offer that support, which helps them reach their financial goals so much faster. With more support, they are able to build wealth portfolios and generational wealth faster than they could have imagined because they're now open to receiving.

This affects their finances in the following ways:

- **Increased income and investments:** As the Sovereign One starts to trust themselves and others, they are better able to understand their key strengths, make financial decisions faster and ask others for support, especially in their weak areas. This helps them get more things done – and quicker too – which can be beneficial in a job and business. It also helps them reach their goals faster and increase their income. They can focus on their zone of genius and find new investment opportunities in places that they never would have imagined.

- **Decreased debt:** When people trust themselves or believe in themselves, they are more likely to make informed decisions and avoid impulsive behaviour (Makwakwa, 2013). When the Sovereign One starts healing their God wound and trusting themselves, they are more deliberate in how they spend money, which decreases both their spending and debt.

  When the Sovereign One trusts themselves, they begin to trust not only others, but also their own ability to save themselves and find financial solutions; they start helping their family members help themselves by finding long-term solutions rather than creating further debt to assist them.

- **Increased savings:** Increasing self-awareness can bring attention to our values and financial behaviour, which can lead to an increase in savings (Makwakwa, 2013).

Increasing the pleasure set point

According to Dietrich (2017), increasing pleasure in our lives increases our general wellbeing because we find ourselves noticing the sensations in our body and, ultimately, feel better. So, when the Sovereign One starts to re-parent their inner child they allow themselves to have more fun and experience more pleasure. They stop carrying the world on their shoulders, believing that their family's success depends on them, and that gives them permission to embark on a journey of self-discovery and connect with their inner child.

Play teaches children how to use their creativity and develop their imagination and emotional strength and also aids in healthy brain development (Ginsburg, 2007). Research also shows that playing (sports, games and hobbies, for example) activates the release of endorphins and happiness hormones, as well as dopamine, a neurotransmitter that helps us regulate our emotions and moods and reduce our stress and anxiety levels (Wang & Aamodt, 2012).

Playful activities also stimulate the activation of the parasympathetic nervous system, which helps the body relax and reduces our stress responses. Play (and rest) has also been shown to improve sleep quality, which leads to mental clarity, which has a further impact on the Sovereign One's finances.

Increasing the pleasure set point impacts finances in the following ways:

- **Increased income and investments:** As the Sovereign One increases their fun and pleasure set point, their stress levels drop and they become more relaxed, which leads to mental clarity, which then leads them to make more informed financial decisions as well as improved financial decisions.

    Increased relaxation can also lead to increased energy levels, leading to greater work efficiency and productivity, which in turn leads to increased income and even promotions at work. In fact, being more relaxed and responding to situations in a calm manner may mean improved relationships, which can lead to increased networking and collaboration opportunities.

    I would also argue that the Sovereign One has, over time, trained themselves to see financial opportunities, so as they start to focus on fun and may turn hobbies into businesses,

which actually increases their streams of income and offers new investment opportunities.
- **Decreased debt:** When the Sovereign One increases their fun and pleasure, they tend to spend money on themselves rather than deny themselves. They give themselves permission to spend on things they enjoy, which changes their spending habits but doesn't lead to an increase.

   This may seem counterintuitive, but I have worked with hundreds of people from around the world and have seen how creating a fun account and spending a percentage of our income on ourselves and the things that make us happy, leads to a decrease in expenses and debt. This is because we're now aware of how we spend money and are actually budgeting for fun, instead of impulsively spending when the need arises. As a result, this leads to a decrease in spending and decreased debt.
- **Increased savings:** Play improves stress levels, which reduces stress-related spending and increases savings. In addition, as the Sovereign One's income increases and debt decreases, their savings increase.

Healing the abandonment wound

Abandonment trauma is rooted in the fear of losing love. When the Sovereign One heals their fear of losing love, they give their family members permission to simply live their own lives. They stop trying to control love and forcing people to love them and stay in their lives. As a result, they themselves start healing their abandonment trauma and give themselves permission to keep growing.

The fear of abandonment can cause anxiety that activates the body's chronic stress response, leading to nervous system dysregulation, so healing abandonment trauma can help regulate the system by reducing stress, anxiety and the impact of stress on the body. This reduces the root cause of the trauma, which is the fear of losing love. As the fear of losing love diminishes, the feelings of insecurity and anxiety also diminish, which reduces the body's stress response.

Chronic stress increases our allostatic load and thus risks our mental and physical health, as well as our ability to think clearly. When the Sovereign One heals their fear of losing love, their allostatic load decreases. This increases their capacity to process emotions and builds up their resilience over time.

The Fixer's fear of losing love also shows up as being overly involved in their family's business, overdoing for family members and over-giving to family members to keep their love, which can also lead to them creating debt to help others. But when the Sovereign One releases this fear, they begin to set boundaries on how much they give to family and how much they do for family, including how much time they dedicate to family.

So, how does healing the fear of losing love impact finances?

- **Increased income and investments:** Healing abandonment trauma reduces anxiety, and when we're less anxious, we concentrate better, are more productive and make better decisions, which leads to increased income.

    Reduced anxiety also leads to better job performance, because when we're less anxious we second-guess ourselves less and that leads to higher levels of performance, better chances for promotion, bonuses and rewards. It can also lead to increased entrepreneurial success because people feel more confident following entrepreneurial opportunities.

    When the Sovereign One finally releases their fear of losing love, they start to set boundaries with family members, which frees up their time and energy. They can use this free time to focus on resting, playing or building their business or careers, which leads to an increase in income. They can also use this time and energy to research and invest in new opportunities, which increases their investment portfolio.

- **Decreased debt:** Where the Fixer would have gone into debt to help their family members, the Sovereign One has boundaries when it comes to how they help family. When they heal the fear of losing love, they start to understand that they don't have to sacrifice themselves in order to help others. Their wants and needs also matter and they understand that they need to have something left over for themselves. They no longer get into debt to save others because they've learnt that they don't need to save family members in order to be loved.

    They also honour their own boundaries and that of others – they no longer seek validation by making themselves overly useful in their family's lives by forcing people to rely on them or forcing them to accept their help. They start to teach family members to help themselves rather than centring themselves in family stories and being the go-to person.

- **Increased savings:** When the Sovereign One heals their fear of losing love, they increase their income and decrease their debt, which leads to an increase in savings (Makwakwa, 2013). Healing abandonment trauma also reduces anxiety, thus decreasing an individual's allostatic load and increasing their capacity to deal with financial stress. This, in turn, decreases avoidance behaviour when it comes to money and allows them to be more open to adopting new financial behaviours and habits.

CASE STUDY

The Sovereign One

VANGILE: Hello, Sibongile. Can you tell us where you're from?

SIBONGILE: I grew up essentially in Soweto.

VANGILE: How would you define your relationship with money when it comes to family?

SIBONGILE: Oh my goodness. It's a subject that we skirt around. How you see that we are talking about money is when there are little things that we need to address – making a contribution for somebody's birthday, or there's the funeral coming up and whose car we're going to use and if we will collectively put gas in your car, but we don't discuss money in terms of, 'What are your future plans? The big plan,' or 'What's your generational wealth plan?' Oh, no, not that big.

    I talk about it with them, which is something that has changed immensely. I put it on the table. I throw it on the table and I know it's going to shut most people up. They either walk away or they're just like, 'You like talking about money.'

    I talk about trusts, I talk about the family house and how I cannot stand it when they try to sell me products that I have no interest in, I'm like, 'No, I don't see how it's going to add to my financial future.' So everyone just thinks, You've taught your daughter to talk like that, and my daughter talks about money all the time.

VANGILE: How has your role with money in the family evolved?

SIBONGILE: I used to be the constant Jesus Christ, the saviour. I was the go-to person whether you were looking for R100 000 or R10 000. I am so glad I shed that role. Now I watch people struggle and I'm, like, 'So what are you going to do about that?'

    I used to be the one who would plug that gap when somebody's car rental or lease is behind. I'm the one who pays up. And how would I pay it up then? It meant overdraft credit card.

I see it now in retrospect, of course, that everyone felt that I should have money. I felt like I would be accused of being a miser if I don't. My role was to plug that hole and constantly make people feel better.

VANGILE: How did this start to change?

SIBONGILE: I think, firstly, it came when I acknowledged that I have been a millionaire many, many times. Every million has been spent in a way that I couldn't account for. When I met you at the first workshop I attended with you, the first thing I declared was I've been a millionaire many times, but I'm not. I remember that very, very well.

I think when my daughter was born, that's when I started counting money. And, yeah, four or five years into her life, I was like, 'This is not going to work for the ambitions and aspirations I have for her. I need to have the million and keep my million. And stop having to chase and close gaps for other people whenever I get my bonus or whenever I get a well-paying short job or something like that.'

So that was the first thing. But I think the very next thing was learning to ask for my money back because people would borrow money and never return it. I was too afraid to ask for my money myself, which was, for me, devastating because I would have anxiety attacks thinking, How am I going to ask for my money from this person? And you'll find that it's the third and the fourth loan in.

VANGILE: How do you think that this affected your income and how has that changed?

SIBONGILE: In the past, my old self would not have a plan for my money. I had all this money sitting in the bank and it was almost always waiting for someone else's emergency. You know what I mean? I didn't have my own financial plan.

And when my daughter was born, I had new financial goals. I wanted overseas trips for her. Suddenly I had plans and a very set menu of how our lives are going to go. So that's how I noticed that we were short of money. And what has changed now is that there is set money for living expenses, for medium term and for our future travel plans, because, for me, travel and education just fall in the same bucket. To me, it's not even a separate thing. And then I have my own wealth-creation goals.

I help with what I have. When there's a family funeral I quickly declare that I will contribute R500 before someone tells me what to contribute. If I have R500, that's the money I have. When I have R1000, I don't say I have R8000. And tomorrow I find that the relationship is still intact. I think most of my need to save people was with my own stories in my mind.

So when you ask for money, even when there is R10 000 that's sitting in my bank account, it's got a plan. And you are not part of the plan. It's a no. I'm not just saying no to the person, but I'm saying yes to my own future plan and my own generational wealth-creation plan. So the guilt has eased off. I don't have it.

VANGILE: Would you say your income-generating activities were driven by your family's needs?

SIBONGILE: I don't even think I had generational wealth plan in that way. I thought a generational wealth plan is to help family. Your family is your wealth. And until I discovered that, family will just consume. They have no plan of their own, but they don't have a plan for you either. It's not like, on the day when they are flush with cash, you become part of their plan.

VANGILE: How has focusing on your generational wealth-building for your daughter changed your family and their money story?

SIBONGILE: A few of them, only a few, are willing to speak honestly about money. They're like, 'So how do you do it? How did you even plan to get your daughter to Disney?'

They will ask you a direct question about, 'How do you do

long-term planning like that?'

I'm, like, 'I just do. I find out how much it's going to cost, and then I bank towards it. And then I let her know what we are saving towards so that even when she wants to demand little things that are short- term and consumables, she also realises that, okay, we've got a bigger plan with Mommy, and it gets her excited.'

So there are two or three people that have asked me – they don't know how to do long-term planning like that. They find it hard and they hate it, and it almost feels restrictive to them. And I'm, like, 'Well, travel is more exciting to me than buying a handbag.'

So that's the difference. But I have the younger generation and I find they really want to know how they are going to get financially independent. I find the older folk are stuck. They can't. They just don't see it. I don't share my big future goals with them because I find that it freaks them out. They seem to think that's not possible: 'It's not possible for a Black woman to have that money.'

VANGILE: Do you think people ever felt controlled by your financial behaviour and your need to save them?

SIBONGILE: They did. It caused a lot of resentment. They want your help, but they don't. So you are damned if you do and damned if you don't. We would be talking about cutting up a pineapple and a person will fly off the handle and tell me how I think I'm better, 'just because you helped me out that other year'.

Also you find that older folk would ask me about big decisions just because, 'Remember Sibongile brought R10 000 to that event.' So I ended up being part of big decisions in the family.

Now people leave me alone. They know I've got my daughter's fees, I've got my stuff and the relationships are better, actually.

VANGILE: How have your savings and investments changed?

SIBONGILE: I find that whatever financial hurdles I have, I caused them myself. It's much easier to track back and say, 'Where did we go wrong here? How come this income came in but we don't see it translating into savings and the stuff that we thought we would pay off?'

I'm not totally an expert in my own money right now, but I find that it's also easier to forgive myself because there's only one person involved. When I decide that I'm going to buy a luxury item, I consciously go to buy a luxury item, knowing that I have a plan for how it's going to be paid.

I now have multiple streams of income and various investments, including property.

VANGILE: What advice would you give someone who has been in your shoes where you're everything doing for everybody?

SIBONGILE: I wish there was a button that just clicked. I would give it to them if there was. But I think what really helped me was doing the Bank Account Challenge Course. I'll tell you why: the bank account challenge is a limited course of five days. And you have three or four exercises in the five days. I found it manageable. So what I did, if you can recall, I kept repeating the bank account challenge.

I just did a series of them because I remember the first thing that we had to do after the workshop at the Apartheid Museum was choose three people who owe you and write them via text or email or call them and just ask for the money without expectation and see what happens. I think, for me, that exercise was the most powerful thing. Just stepping into honouring my money and calling it back. Not all of them paid me back. But two of them made plans. They were like, 'Hey, yeah, it's been long.'

They felt bad and I didn't know that they could. I became the advocate for my money, and they made a plan. The feeling of guilt was left with them. Suddenly, it left my body and it freed me. So I'm more deliberate about asking for my money. And I think the portion of ask for it, no expectation, the latter part is what has been the most powerful thing that I've always told everyone. I'm, like, if you are so scared, write a WhatsApp message. And I know that lump in the throat, that was the one thing. But my most powerful, which I have just done again with the business I went into with the family, was to get back to the notebook. Not Excel sheet, none of that. Notebook. And I wrote the expenses down. And they start looking at the real numbers.

There's power in seeing the real numbers because you get a lump in your throat, you close it off, you walk away, you come back, [and] it's still looking at you. And you're, like, I can't believe I've got overheads of R28 000 and I haven't made R28 000. What now?

And sometimes it's just the knowing. And, yes, it panics me. I don't have it, but I have Wealthy Money tools, I have tapping and I have breathwork. I need that because I think my first emotion, my only biggest emotion in my whole life, is anxiety. I'm very impulsive and then I get anxious. So having the tools of appeasing my own anxiety has been probably the most powerful thing I have done.

My third last thing, not that it's the last thing, I have a tracking app. I track on my bank app. I track spending of every little thing because I'm an Aries. If you left me alone, I would just spend and I get giddy as a child. So tracking is my thing. And my banking app tells me when I am overspending.

VANGILE: Thank you, Sibongile.

CHAPTER 17

The Eternal Child becomes the Evolving Adult

While the role of the Eternal Child is to mirror to everyone in the family the parts of them that were denied love, parenting and compassion, the role of the Evolving Adult is to remind us that we are not defined by our trauma, to show us that healing and growth are indeed possible, and to remind us to be compassionate with ourselves on this life journey. When the Eternal Child starts to heal the parts of themselves that were denied love, parenting and compassion, they begin to embody the Evolving Adult.

Sometimes the decision to start adulting is one they make themselves, but often it's because those around them have had enough – parents start to set boundaries and other family members stop looking after them. As frustrating as it is to take care of the Eternal Child, I don't recommend just cutting them off because it could retraumatise the Eternal Child, making them feel that they have truly been abandoned and are being punished not only for their pain but also for being in pain, which could lead them to abandoning the family and getting lost in the world (literally). But it can also give them the wake-up call they need to get their stuff together and start stepping into adulthood.

Once the Eternal Child makes the decision to step into adulthood, they begin to give themselves space to feel whole, held, heard and seen, which creates safety for their wounded inner child and inner teen to start integrating and healing the trauma they are holding onto. As these wounded parts start to heal, they stop hijacking their adult self and the adult is able to accept that they've grown and that their parents cannot be responsible for parenting them any further or that they did the best they could with the resources they had. And if they want to heal, they will have to re-parent themselves.

It takes a lot of tears, anger, blame, screaming and grieving the childhood they had (and never had) for the Eternal Child to start feeling safe enough to stop hijacking the Evolving Adult. As children, they simply didn't have the resources to process events rationally and logically. The pain of feeling as though you've been denied love, weren't adequately parented and/or weren't given what you needed as a child can cut any child to the bone, so it's important to grieve what was or what never was. In order to heal, it is important for the Evolving Adult to grieve what was or what never was as they go through the process of re-parenting their inner child and inner teen.

Most Evolving Adults may feel like they are behind on this adulting journey and are now playing catch-up because they must look after themselves for the first time as they move out of home, learn how to cook and learn how to do laundry and pay their own bills.

They will have to be patient with themselves because they are new to this game of adulting and one of the key lessons they must learn is financial management: how to make money, how to manage their bank accounts, how to budget and how to increase their income. And for a while they may struggle with financial management. This may very well be a continuous journey for them because they've always been supported financially. As a result, their financial journey may be frustrating at first, simply because they are learning new things that up until now have been entirely foreign to them, and their peers may or may not know about the journey on which they have now embarked.

If the family sees the Evolving Adult struggling, I recommend that they offer non-financial support in the form of guidance and information and encourage them to keep going, because this evolution does take courage. The person to support the Evolving Adult on their financial journey is the Boundaried One, because they probably have a good relationship, built on trust and respect, with them.

Regulating the nervous system

When the Evolving Adult starts to grieve all that happened and didn't happen in their childhood, they start to process and make sense of the experiences, which decreases their allostatic load, reduces symptoms of anxiety and depression, and regulates their nervous system. And when the nervous system is not in a constant state of hypervigilance, it becomes easier to focus and concentrate, leading to improved cognitive functioning.

The process of grieving can also increase self-awareness and help us understand our own patterns of behaviour and thought, which can help us form better relationships with other people. Processing traumatic experiences can reduce the risk of being re-traumatised in the future, which means the inner child and the inner teen stop hijacking the Evolving Adult whenever they feel unsafe or have to do anything that requires them to be an adult, such as getting a job, paying off credit-card debt, or buying a house, for instance.

The wounded inner child or teen can relax and allow the adult self to step forward, take over, make decisions, build their resilience muscles and learn persistence so that they can continue to show up, even when things get uncomfortable.

They may have moments when they slip up or they regress into inner-child or -teen mode, but this happens to all of us at some point.

The problem isn't the trigger – we are all triggered on this journey; the important thing is that we are able to find our way out, beyond the trigger.

When the Evolving Adult regulates their nervous system, it changes their finances in the following ways:

- **Increased income:** It may take the Evolving Adult a while to figure out what they want to do to make money and start earning a consistent income, but as they keep healing and regulating their nervous system, they become comfortable with uncertainty and exploring new possibilities.

    Grieving their childhood can help the Evolving Adult improve their emotional and mental wellbeing because it helps them process feelings about their childhood and find closure about how it played out. This can reduce their feelings of blame and anger, especially towards their parents, which could lead to increased happiness and peace. And when a person is in a state of happiness or peace, they tend to be more focused, motivated and productive, leading to better decision-making, problem-solving skills and communication, which then leads to job promotions or increased business opportunities.

    Happy people also tend to make calculated business and financial decisions, which increases their chances of success (Makwakwa, 2013).
- **Decreased debt:** Because they've always had someone looking after their finances, the Evolving Adult may struggle with managing debt and other aspects of their finances, but the more they regulate their nervous system, the easier it will become for them to sit with the uncomfortable sensations that money brings up and the better they become at managing debt.

    When the Evolving Adult heals the grief of their

childhood trauma, they improve their mental wellbeing, which reduces stress-related spending. When people are in a state of emotional turmoil, they may engage in impulsive spending or overspend to get temporary comfort or emotional release. Healing grief helps people reduce stress-related spending, so they prioritise their spending habits, leading to a decrease in debt.
- **Increased savings:** As the Evolving Adult starts regulating their nervous system and increasing their income as they decrease their debt, they eventually learn to start saving and increase their savings as well. There are times, though, when the Evolving Adult may find themselves falling back on old habits, where they demand that family members support them when they are broke or face an emergency. In such cases, the family may offer non-financial support to help them find solutions.

Healing the Vengeful Child

Anger often masks grief and sadness; the Vengeful Child is the inner child who hasn't acknowledged their grief about the trauma they experienced and so they are stuck in their anger. Holding onto feelings of anger and the desire for revenge can result in a continuous state of chronic stress, leading to the repeated activation of the fight-or-flight response, which keeps us in a constant state of hypervigilance, further dysregulating our nervous systems.

When we feel vengeful, we tend to punish others in a way that forces them to look after us, so we keep ourselves stuck in the trauma or the unhappy situation to punish others and guilt trip them (Makwakwa, 2013). When the Evolving Adult starts to heal their resentment and releases their need to punish their caregivers, they can start to give themselves permission to utilise their anger constructively.

The Evolving Adult no longer uses their need for vengeance to stay stuck in one place to punish their parents; instead, they start to connect with their anger and grief and so let their parents and/or caregivers off the hook. The minute they do that they start to take responsibility for their own healing and give themselves permission to release their anger and vengeance and start adulting.

Some of the first steps that may take include: moving out of the family home, no longer relying on their parents financially, paying their own bills and paying attention to how they spend money. All these steps will help them become fiscally responsible adults. They also get out of debt because now they know that no one else is going to pay their bills for them. So they start to decrease their debt, and increase their income by getting a steady job. More often, they will look for a traditional job just to get themselves off the ground, but may also venture into entrepreneurship.

Healing the Vengeful Child affects the Evolving Adult's finances in the following ways:

- **Increased income:** The sixteenth-century poet George Herbert once said, 'Living well is the best revenge.' When the Evolving Adult releases their need for revenge, they give themselves permission to get unstuck and start living their lives, perhaps their best lives.

   Releasing the need for vengeance reduces stress and improves emotional and mental wellbeing, allowing us to perform at our best and make informed and effective decisions, which means we are better able to take advantage of promising business and career opportunities, which leads to increased income.
- **Decreased debt:** Releasing the need for vengeance can decrease the Evolving Adult's debt – they stop using their indebtedness as a way to punish their parents or caregivers; instead, they choose to prioritise their own emotional and

mental health, which leads to better financial decision-making and reduced stress-related spending, which leads to decreased debt.
- **Increased savings and investments:** When the Evolving Adult increases their income and decreases their debt, they can start to increase their savings and the amount of money they invest.

Healing the God wound

When the Evolving Adult starts to heal the God wound they reclaim their own power because they realise that we're all responsible for our own lives, no matter how raw a deal we got. Regardless of how unfair life has been, at the end of the day, the life we were given is the life we have to work with and make the best of. And it's true – life can be brutal, but if we get stuck in this story, lamenting how unfair life is, we spend our energy looking for someone or something to blame or stay angry at, which can stagnate us.

The Evolving Adult makes the difficult choice to release anger and blame and to love what is by accepting the things they cannot change, to accept and love the body they were born in, the circumstances of their birth, their sexuality and their messy childhood so that they can heal, make peace with the past and move forward. And when the Evolving Adult makes peace with the things they can't change, they stop waging war with the Divine and learn to surrender. They allow themselves to be Divinely supported and start trusting the Divine and, in the process, learn to trust themselves as they embark onto adulthood. They learn that the Divine is not outside of us, but within, and forgiving the Divine means forgiving ourselves and letting ourselves off the hook.

In her book *Change Me Prayers* (2015), Tosha Silver says: 'When we invoke the Divine to "shift" us, we invite the Highest part of ourselves to take over.'

Healing the God wound impacts the Evolving Adult's finances in the following ways:

- **Increased income:** The God wound manifests as blame and an inability for the Eternal Child to take responsibility for their finances, which keeps them in a childlike state, unable to earn an income and so forcing other family members to take care of them. Blaming others for our problems can shift the focus away from personal accountability and prevent us from taking action to change the situation, and thus keeps us from taking responsibility for ourselves and so achieve financial freedom (Makwakwa, 2013).

    When the Evolving Adult starts to heal their God wound and they release the need to blame others and/or the Divine for their problems, they increase their personal responsibility and self-awareness, leading to improved decision-making and confidence, which in turn leads to making informed decisions in their career and/or business and so increase their income.

- **Decreased debt:** When we lack accountability and avoid taking responsibility for our finances, it becomes difficult for us to examine our financial behaviour and spending habits, which can keep us in a cycle of impulsive spending and debt.

    When the Evolving Adult stops blaming others, including the Divine, they become more self-aware and start exploring how they are contributing to their financial issues, which can reduce their impulsive spending habits and lead them to focus on debt reduction, leading to a decrease in debt.

- **Increased savings:** When the Evolving Adult starts to take responsibility for their lives, they stop justifying why their parents or other family members should be looking after them and start taking responsibility for their finances and saving for things they want, as well as for emergencies, which leads to increased savings.

CASE STUDY

The Evolving Adult

VANGILE: Hello, Dudu, where are you from?

DUDU: I am from Cape Town – born, bred, and buttered in the township of Gugulethu. Gugulethu is one of the townships that came about in the time of apartheid South Africa. My mom beat the odds that were available to young people during the time and managed to get property in an up-and-coming area, which is now huge.

VANGILE: I am interviewing you because you have a generational pattern of Eternal Children in your family and have mothered the adults around you. What is your relationship with money when it comes to family?

DUDU: It's shifted so much. Right now, I feel like I'm a spectator to my own money movements within my family because I'm, like, 'Oh girl, you can say no now.'

I've come a long way, from a point when I didn't know there was a relationship to be had with money. Money was just a thing that people either had or didn't have. And, to me, it looked like my family didn't quite have. But when we had it, it had to do what it had to do. So it was never really mine. And I think I was mimicking my mom's footsteps because she was the breadwinner. I grew up wanting to be my mom.

She would take her last and sacrifice it for the family. There was a point when I did that too. My granny passed away in 2017;

she was never formally educated but she was a brilliant lady. Her academic education stopped when she became a mother to my mom, [then] she lost her sister and inherited her seven boys.

And, in her lack of formal education, she could never become a professional in anything. And thanks to capitalism, if you're not a professional in anything, the thinking is that you can't really generate income. So she had a crèche, which did well. People would want her specifically to look after their kids. We lived in competition, with everyone in our street claiming her as their mother. I always said to her that I think she was born to be a mother, literally. She was everyone's mother.

But that crèche went up in smoke. I think when I was born, she was, like, 'My focus is on you now. I'm not looking after the other children.'

VANGILE: How has your financial role in your family evolved?

DUDU: I was my mom's deputy breadwinner. That was my relationship with money. It wasn't mine, or it was mine, but I would be using it to cover all the bases she couldn't cover. Being a breadwinner does not stop at ensuring that we have lights, we have electricity in the house, and we have food in the house. There are things like death in the family. There are things like traditional ceremonies that require a whole cow. And someone has to buy that cow. And, for most of my life, it would be my mom and I, just together, carrying the family until I tapped out, until I was, like, 'Look, I don't know if I want to do that any more.' In fact, thinking back, I think it was my grandmother who stopped me, but I don't know if she knew what she was doing. I remember when I started working, I wanted to renovate her house and build on extra rooms so I could stay home and she was, like, 'I don't want you to do that.'

And I couldn't understand because I was embarrassed of this house. And she would say, 'But when I'm gone, you won't be able to claim this house.' And I think the seed might have been planted at that point of her saying, 'This is not your cross to carry. This is not for you to do. You go on and you do what you need to do with your own life.' And that's what I'm doing. And it hasn't been so well received in the family.

It's not as smooth as I'm saying it because sometimes I'll still want to take on things because: habits.

VANGILE: Yes. I wanted to talk to you precisely because you are the child who was mothering adults who never grew up. I know from working with you that you saw your grandmother go through the same thing with seven people. Can you talk to us about the dynamic of being a mother to grown adults and how that affects your finances?

DUDU: It's so heavy because you owe it to yourself to do life to the best of your ability. But it feels like you are held down by all that weight. I've seen my mom do it. These people are her cousins, but because that's not really a thing in our African homes, they are her siblings. She had to play a parental role, even to the ones who are close to her in age as well. Things like going to initiation school. I have only one brother. Technically, that should have been the first time she got involved in such, but she had done it so many times before my brother came along that by the time my brother came along, she was so experienced in that she ... The cost involved, what the process entails, all of that. So it feels like this weight holding you down. But it's not. And you feel resentment. You feel resentment. And I often wonder if I am the one who woke up my mom's resentment when I started speaking up, stepping away and saying, 'I don't want to carry this anymore.' It's almost as though she noticed that, hey, okay, maybe I don't want to either.

There's a sense of obligation that you have. Even when you start feeling like the weight is heavy, there's so much guilt that is with you, because how dare you be exhausted when for two generations before you, this has been how we roll. This is how we do it. The more messed-up thing about it is that these are people who are older than you. These are people who should, in essence, be parenting you. Now, if I am sacrificing my last, as I would for my child, I start being disrespectful because I am playing a parenting role for those people. It creates confusion, because who's the elder here, really?

Every now and then, they'd remind me to not forget my place because I am a child and I'm just a grandchild. I'm like, 'Okay, so I'm a grandchild until what point exactly? I'm a child until what point? Until it is me who has to switch the lights on. Then I'm no longer a child. Until people need to eat, until someone dies. Then I'm no longer a grandchild.'

I've even been reminded to not forget my place. But my place is for you to parent me. And if I need to parent you, then there's nothing I'm forgetting here. You're the one who's not recognising your role. It's complicated relationships where I'm certain I'm seen as disrespectful. I'm certain I'm seen as entitled.

VANGILE: How has taking on the parental role at such a young age affected you?

DUDU: I've got mega abandonment issues; I've got mega neglect issues. I'm so sensitive to you not wanting to be around me at any given moment. It can be in the slightest way. It can be the smallest annoyance, and I'm able to pick that up. I think it stems from a sense of neglect and abandonment, which I only noticed when we started doing the Wealthy Money work. I realised later, probably in my thirties, that, 'Hang on, but my mother's role to me had not been completed. She outsourced the mothering to my granny and only took the easier section.'

It's also what's complicated our relationship to an extent, because in my feeling that she hadn't mothered me, before I was aware of it, I was still idolising her, wanting to be everything she was. And, therefore, I could see nothing wrong with her if I wanted to be with her.

And because nothing was wrong with her, I literally mimicked the way she spoke, the way she talked, hence taking on all the admin that she had taken on in the family as well. I had worked so hard to mimic even ailments that she had. I grew up with my mom suffering from a hectic case of sinusitis. As a little girl, I'd ask her, 'But why are you sneezing so much?'

And she'd tell me, 'I have sinusitis.'

And in my heart, I would think, 'I want to be you, I want to have sinusitis too.'

I remember being in primary school and telling people that I suffered from sinusitis. I didn't have sinusitis. I was one hundred per cent healthy, but I wanted to be like my mother. And the price of that is that today I have a very bad case of sinusitis that's had me hospitalised, and I was almost under the knife. They called it 'complicated sinusitis', where my eyes were just bulging out of my face because the mucus pulled up was too much. It got bad. I think I held on to anything that would get me close to my mother, whether it was illness or not, for the most part of my life, because only then would I feel her being closer than just providing the material things.

It's the weirdest thing because even when I was attending treatment after I was discharged from hospital for my complicated sinusitis, when I'd go for check-ups, the doctor's room would be full of little children, literally infants and toddlers, because most people who suffered from those things were infants and toddlers. According to my immune system, I'm a toddler or an infant, an eternal child that needed to be mothered.

The same with my eczema. I don't know how many times I was hospitalised for a bad case of eczema. When I go for outpatient treatment and check-ups, I encounter little kids because, technically, these are conditions that you have as a kid and then you outgrow them. I never did.

And of course my mom had to take me to the doctor, so there was some special attention happening there. The last time I was hospitalised was in, I think, in May 2018. I had to move back home and my mom took time off work to look after me. Girl, when I tell you I had the time of my life being sick because she was there and she was mummy.

Once I started doing the work, I realised what was going on ...

VANGILE: This is really fascinating. You're the second in your family to move out of home and to adult on your own – how did you make that shift, especially when you have been dealing with people who have been struggling to grow up?

DUDU: I literally attempted to move out of home three times before finally getting it right two years ago. The first time was at university; I lived in a commune close to campus. Then I fell pregnant and my mom was, like, 'You are not having a grandchild of mine in a commune, so come back home.'

The second attempt, I was about 26, I think, and I moved all the way to Johannesburg. I secured a job there and was living my best life. One Sunday night we were driving to a party, and my grandmother calls, and I put her on speaker. The first thing I said, because my granny had no filter, 'You are on speaker, watch what you say.'

She asked, 'Why are you in the car this late? Where are you off to?'

I'm like, 'Oh, going to a party in Soweto. I've been invited.'

She responded, 'You're off to Soweto? This late? The way I see it, you are going to come to Cape Town. What's with your madness in that Johannesburg, because it looks like your life is a one-way party. It must be time for you to come back home.'

Believe me when I tell you that the very next day I received a call from Cape Town for a career move that I could not resist. My grandmother sabotaged my second move directly, literally.

The third time, which is this period now, is when I had started doing inner work. I was aware of things like people in my lineage don't really move out of home. People in my lineage don't generally get their own property. My mom was an exception to the rule.

My granny's sister had done it, but it had been decades ago. It's not a norm. As a result, all my uncles still stay in my grandmother's house. The same with my father's side of the family. No one has property. It's a rare thing. People have done it. And, interestingly, it's the women, but it's very rare. And it could be decades and decades.

Usually one person moves out, then everyone else just stays at home and dies at home until the next person does it in the next generation. So this time around it was heavy because I knew what I was dealing with. I knew that, in terms of my lineage, this is not a normal move. There are vows that I'm going to have to break because I don't think I was one of the people who were supposed to move.

My mom had done it. If you're looking at family history, when your mom does it, then you don't do it until two generations or something like that. For me to do it immediately after, to be the next person to do it after my mom. Because I've got aunts who are my mom's cousins, but they've never really left. One of them did. She went and found a rental property somewhere. But she's back home right now.

And to avoid that fate, you literally need to set fire to the rain, so to speak.

We carry people's trauma, we carry people's joy, successes inside of us, people who we've never even met. So if these people who I may or may not have any knowledge of never made it out of home, there's a high chance that I may move in the same direction. So, in order to think in my own path, to cover my own path, the inner work helped a lot.

First, I didn't tell anyone that I was viewing a place because I thought that was another pitfall where you discuss it with your family and there's an inner rumbling of who do you think you are? Sometimes it's said to your face, and I didn't grow up the most confident of people. I remember you advising me to just go about viewing places and not mention anything to anyone.

So then I started viewing places and place came up out of nowhere, really in the area I never even considered. Money came through. I paid up the deposit. I was meant to move on the first of April 2021. That entire weekend leading up to that date, I couldn't sleep. I cried. I didn't even know why exactly I was crying but was I feeling uncomfortable in my life.

The step felt too big. How was I going to furnish the place? Would I be able to look after my daughter? It was a lot.

I now realise that at that point, that's when the vow of loyalty to stay home was being broken. Because after that the property manager called me and she gave me some furniture as well.

My then fiancée, now husband, came down and he furnished the entire place from scratch with new stuff. Now it's a full-on, warm, beautiful home.

The universe was, like, 'Girl, I got you.' I got a house and furniture and all-in-one man.

I love it.

I've got a husband, I've got a daughter, and everything is new for him too. Everything is new for the three of us because my daughter has never had a present father before. There's the whole getting to know her stepdad, and there's the relationship between them. But there's also the maintenance in the relationship between myself and my daughter in that I now stay with my best friend.

There's been a lot going on and very little space to show up as I used to at home. When I tell you, my mom and I have fought – she will understand it to a certain point. And then she's throwing childish tantrums. I think, subconsciously, I am aware that she's an Eternal Child too, because the way I just sit still when she throws her tantrums, like a real mother, I sit still and I let her be.

VANGILE: What shifts have you seen since making the move and choosing to no longer parent the adults around you?

DUDU: Correct me if I'm wrong, but I would think that Eternal Children are mostly born from an environment where one of the parents doesn't show up for the parenting, right?

I feel that my parents birthed Eternal Children, but they, excuse me, in a sense, are Eternal Children too. If my dad shows up and he's looking good, Mom told him what to wear. That's childlike. This is why I became a deputy parent, because I'd say to myself, 'But who is then going to help my mother if I don't?'

Where I have seen a change in me becoming the Sovereign One is, I remember, 2021 when my uncle passed on; he was one of the seven cousins my grandmother adopted. He passed on and he's got a daughter who's older than me and one who is slightly younger than me, but everyone on my mom's side is used to my mother carrying the load in the family.

We went to a family meeting to discuss the funeral and, because I've been doing the work for a minute, so I was comfortable with saying, 'I'm contributing this little and this is all I'm doing. And whether you approve of it or not, it's not my story.'

My mother was expected to champion the whole thing, but she sat there and she was, like, 'This is my little that I'm contributing and I am not willing or able to do more.'

When I tell you that there was silence in the meeting … Even I looked at her shocked. It caused an uproar. There was physical violence a couple of days later because we refused to part with more money than we contributed. I've never seen such a thing.

We were able to simply get into the car and leave. And the leaving was a big thing for me because it was home that we were leaving. Up until that point, we'd all had difficulty leaving that space. Child, we walked away, leaving the mess behind us.

My mother didn't go to the funeral; she said, 'The disrespect was too much.'

People were now forced to show up. My uncle's children were forced to show up. My other uncles were shocked because in my mom they believe.

I'm also finding that my mom is doing more age-appropriate things – I hate to use that term. She used to be friends with my friends and do things I used to do with me. Now she's friends with people who are her age, people she was in Varsity with, she grew up with. It's just looking so tasteful. She recently went on a spa date and slept over at the hotel with her friend. I suppose I was her crutch because we even hung out together.

I have a younger brother, too. He's 30 this year, and I still refer to him as my baby brother. Often, when I'm being honest with myself, I'll say, I'm contributing to this one not growing up because I view him as my baby brother. When I tell you how much he's grown since I left home.

We had my mom's sixtieth last year. And my brother and I contributed, we went 50-50. It was a first. My brother and I don't go 50-50 on stuff. I go one hundred. It was amazing.

Last December, my mom was telling me she got surprised by my brother giving her grocery shopping vouchers. And it was a whole lot of money. They had groceries for months.

I'm, like, 'What? He's able to do that? He never did that when I was around.'

I had to carry the baggage of the entire family's groceries from a young age and he was able to help? He does that now. He shows up.

My brother will complain about my mom's manipulation and all the things she does and how unreasonable she is. And I'll say to him, 'So why do you get involved? Let her have her tantrum. After her tantrum, she'll come right.' And she really does.

My mom is throwing all the tantrums at the many steps I am now taking. But, at the end of the day, she comes around. She has her tantrum, she rolls on the floor, and then she sits back up and we speak like adults because that's how our boundaries have been formed now.

VANGILE: You no longer being the Fixer or deputy parent has shifted something in the lineage, and he's starting to step into his adult role. Also, your brother is now left with essentially two Eternal Children. So he now has to step up. Someone has to be the adult.

Thank you, Dudu. This has been an enlightening interview on generational money profiles and how one person's decision to do the healing work can change everything.

CHAPTER 18

Using ancestral money wisdom

Until now, I've been talking about the impact of ancestral trauma and Black Tax. But in this chapter I focus on something positive: ancestral wisdom. I'll share a small example of how we can break the cycle of Black Tax and even create family legacies using our ancestors' tools. One tool my paternal family has used is the lekgotla. This is a traditional African gathering where elders, leaders and community members come together to talk about important things, share ideas, and make decisions as a group.

When I was growing up, I saw my dad Daniel Phori Maelane, and other relatives in the Maelane family use the lekgotla to start a burial society. They supported each other emotionally and, together, saved money to cover funeral costs. Now, as an adult, I see how the lekgotla has become a place where the next generation receives mentoring and advice in order to succeed in their careers and learn about our culture and ancestors.

I've seen how the lekgotla helps us save money, and in the future, it could even become a way to invest and create a family trust. Some of the older generation are starting to consider this idea. To give you a better understanding, I sat down with my dad and asked him to explain how our lekgotla works:

VANGILE: Thank you for agreeing to do the interview, Daddy. How did the lekgotla start?

DAD: It started when we had a funeral of one cousin of mine, a Maelane. And one old man, who happened to also be a Maelane, suggested that we meet regularly because he last saw me when I was a kid, about five years old, and he could not recognise me as an adult. Then he realised that we need to meet regularly so that we can keep contact and bond. We realised that, for us to do that, we needed something to keep us together. The idea was born in 1979, but the real lekgotla started in 1984. And after our first meeting, we realised that, to meet regularly, we would need to have something to discuss so we decided to start a burial society. The idea being that we should not have a problem such as having to collect money when one family member dies. Rather, we should have a special fund that can help the family in case of problems such as that, because funerals tend to be very expensive. That idea was welcomed by the most of us. And we carried on up to this day.

VANGILE: How did you decide who to let into the lekgotla and how does it work?

DAD: All we wanted is that you must be a Maelane. It's mainly male members of the Maelanes and you have to contribute a certain amount every month. Our contribution starts in February of every year, and it ends annually at the end of November. Then in November, that's when we have our general meeting. We actually have an executive committee, and we make sure that everyone is regarded equally so members of the executive do not have to be people who hold high positions in society. We also have a constitution, which governs us. We are quite formal. We take minutes and we send out invitations, especially for the Annual General Meeting (AGM), which normally takes place on the last Sunday of November.

VANGILE: How many families of the Maelane clan, so to speak, are part of this?

DAD: It's difficult to tell as to how many. All that I know is that our membership is about between 60 and 70. Some of the Maelanes don't join it, but nevertheless, even if they don't join us, we keep them informed of what we are doing and we always invite them to our meetings, especially the AGM. The AGM helps us carry on with our philosophy of keeping ties. The idea is to know one another, assist one another in terms of trouble. Normally, we just collect money and give to whoever is collecting, especially in case of a funeral. But if you are not a member, we just give voluntary contributions as individuals. So you don't get as much benefit as you get if you're a member.

VANGILE: What is the structure of the lekgotla?

DAD: We have an executive committee. Any member can have a position in the leadership. We have a chairman, a deputy, we have a secretary, a deputy, a treasurer, a deputy. And that makes six members. When it comes to transactions like withdrawal of money, we need at least two signatures – it should be the treasurer and the secretary and/or the chairman.

VANGILE: And how often do you guys meet?

DAD: We are supposed to meet regularly every two months, but because of other personal commitments, sometimes the AGM becomes the fifth meeting instead of being the sixth. Even though it's not in the constitution, we rotate our venues, but in August the meeting always happens in Witbank, and because I happen to be the only one in the Witbank area who can accommodate them, I always host them in August.

VANGILE: Do different members get chances to host the meetings?

DAD: Yes. It's the AGMs that we rotate, but we prefer that we hold them in the rural areas of Limpopo because that's where the Maelanes are concentrated. There are three regions where they are concentrated, and we are able to rotate our meetings around there so that when we come to a particular village, all the Maelanes can come and we can all get to know one another. When we started the AGMs we used to slaughter an ox and invite everyone in the village, but over time we realised that that was very expensive so we changed how we did things.

The AGM is where we make all the necessary amendments to our constitution. All our members can recite the constitution off by heart.

VANGILE: What do you guys talk about mainly at the AGM?

DAD: We market our lekgotla to the other Maelanes who have not yet joined, review our constitution and also share our financial statements and give our annual reports as a society.

We also go around the circle so members can share who they are and what their family tree is, so we can all know how we are related.

VANGILE: Not everybody has the same financial resources, so do you guys have options on contributions?

DAD: Yeah, there are three options. It's A, B, and C. C is the lowest contribution. And then B is for those who feel they are a bit better financially and can contribute more. And then A for those who can afford to pay the highest. In any case, the option is not decided for a member. The member chooses the option that works for them.

VANGILE: Does it work like funeral policies? Is your pay-out linked to your contribution?

DAD: That's exactly how it is. You also have to be a member for six months before you can claim. It normally covers the family. That is to say, if you are a member, you and your spouse are covered, then children who are still dependent are covered. Your in-laws are also covered – father-in-law, mother-in-law are also covered, as well as your parents. Other than that, we don't cover any other person. We will also help out pensioners and disabled members even if they are no longer able to contribute financially.

VANGILE: That's fine because, for the most part, most of the extended family is already in the lekgotla. So do you pay per person, like in a funeral policy, the more people I add, the more I contribute, or do you just pay a fixed amount based on your class A, B, C option?

DAD: You just pay a fixed amount. The member pays for 10 months in a year, from February to November, because in December we accommodate the festivities. People spend money during that period. And in January people with kids of school-going age are preparing for school expenditures. We don't want to burden people with extra expenses. We assume that by the end of January, all the educational needs are covered, then there will be money left for the lekgotla.

VANGILE: How did you guys come up with the amount that should be given by people, like your A, B, C contributions? Did you do calculations or did you just have an idea of this is how much people need to pay to be covered for a funeral?

DAD: We calculated funeral expenditures, and we looked at what amount of money can cover 10% of the funeral expenditure, and if we can come up with that money. Then we decided we need to have reserves, and how much reserves we would need at the end of each year if 60% of us were to make a claim that year. Then we asked ourselves, 'Can we still have this minimum after we spend 60 % and after 60 % of us have made that claim?' After that we decided that, in order to reach that amount, this is the contribution you have to make.

VANGILE: What are the emotional benefits of the lekgotla?

DAD: Actually, the financial thing is just a vehicle of keeping us together. It is more the emotional benefit. It really brought us closer because we get to be intimate. We inform one another about our situations and challenges. When you have somebody in the family who is not well, you know who you can talk to and it helps.

VANGILE: Are there any benefits in terms of mentoring and succession planning for the next generation?

DAD: Yeah, we have that thing. For instance, recently we decided that we need more youngsters to get into the executive and take a leadership role and get skills. Last year we had elections and we have more young people in the executive because the idea is to try to get as many young people as possible joining. And the other thing is, as I said, you get to be intimate. It's easier to know who is doing what. And if you have a youngster who has an interest in a particular field, then it's easy to connect him to someone in the family who is doing something in that field. One of your nephews (cousin-brother's son), who is doing medicine at university, is now shadowing a cousin of yours who is a doctor. This is happening in different fields such as law as well.

VANGILE: I think that's beautiful. Can you please explain why the lekgotla is made up of mainly Maelane men and not the women?

DAD: We're talking mainly of men because women may get married, and if they get married, they change their surnames and join their husbands' families. And we don't want to have our sons-in-law and brothers-in-law coming in because they have their own philosophies and value systems. Now, that can cause problems. And, again, it's not that we don't want women. Women can join. You are welcome to join. We would love to have you. But when women get married, we have a package (money) that we give them and they have to resign.

VANGILE: Why have you guys never gone the way of other burial societies and invested the money from the lekgotla, like most funeral-cover companies do?

DAD: We had that idea, but most of our guys don't believe in investing money. They fear that if you put the money in a stock exchange and it crashes, you will have to have a lot of explaining to do. Those of us who are not well informed about stock exchange crashing will think you've stolen their money.

VANGILE: Do you ever foresee a future where the money is invested?

DAD: Oh, yes. I believe the new generation will be well informed to do that. We are the first generation to do this, but the youngsters are studying in various fields. Some are working with finance – we even have a cousin of yours who has done his master's in corporate law; they will be able to give better direction on investments than we have. And maybe even start a family trust. We always tell them that if they have business ideas and need funding, the lekgotla is the first place they should come to because this is where their investors are. But we have done our work, now it's up to the next generation.

VANGILE: You guys have done great. Thank you, Daddy.

Conclusion

I hope that this book has given you some insight – and at least one Aha! moment – as to why you behave the way you do with money and how you came to behave that way. Understanding our archetypes gives us insights into our behaviours and how our family's money stories, beliefs and actions influence us as individuals.

In this book, we have explored various archetypes: the Sweet One, the Destroyer, the RunAway, the Fixer, and the Eternal Child. Each represents a different response to trauma and plays a different role within the family structure, shaping the family's financial habits and interactions.

The Sweet One archetype often emerges as a result of shutting down and numbing oneself as a coping mechanism in response to childhood experiences. This profile is sweet and accommodating, avoiding conflict and always willing to give money when asked. They struggle to set boundaries and may experience difficulties in expressing their own needs and desires, which often leads to anger, frustration and fear. While they are well liked within the family and society, their financial independence may be compromised due to their reluctance to assert themselves.

On the other hand, the Destroyer archetype manifests as the external embodiment of toxic behaviour within the family. This profile may act out their trauma with anger (repressed and overt) and a desire to tear down what is not working before attempting to rebuild. They disrupt family gatherings and confront hidden truths, often leading to conflict and strained relationships. The Destroyer rebels against societal expectations and may find it challenging to maintain financial stability due to their unconventional choices.

The RunAway archetype represents individuals who have checked out of the family structure as adults. They avoid family events, may immerse themselves in distractions such as partying or substance abuse, and struggle with emotional and financial independence. Their disengagement from family dynamics protects them from further trauma, but also affects their ability to develop healthy relationships and build wealth.

In contrast to the RunAway is the Fixer, who assumes the role of the responsible caretaker within the family. They take on the burden of fixing problems and often parent their parents and siblings. Fixers strive for perfection and constantly give unsolicited financial support in order to build generational wealth in the family. Despite their well-intentioned efforts, they may experience pushback or feel unappreciated, leading to exhaustion and resentment.

Lastly, the Eternal Child (or Spoiled Brat) archetype represents family members who never fully grow up and rely on continuous financial support, resist taking on adult responsibilities, and exert power through their powerlessness. This profile often struggles to attain financial independence and may perpetuate the cycle of being parented even in their own marriage and parenting roles.

Understanding these archetypes and their interactions can help us understand our family dynamics and the root cause of conflict in our families. For example, the relationship between the Sweet One and the Fixer often involves financial support and a shared understanding of family values so they tend to work well together and provide financial stability to the family unit.

The Destroyer's desire to tear down and rebuild clashes with the

Fixer's efforts to fix problems, leading to tension and sabotage of the Fixer's initiatives. The Sweet One may be caught in the middle, often experiencing fear and anxiety as a result of the Destroyer's explosive (or even restrained) anger.

Similarly, the relationship between the RunAway and the Fixer tends to be strained because the Fixer attempts to intervene and fix the RunAway's issues without fully acknowledging the root cause of the situation. The RunAway's disengagement frustrates the Fixer, who relies on involved individuals to enact their fixes. The RunAway and the Destroyer, on the other hand, often understand each other's behaviours and may form a supportive bond, acknowledging the pain and trauma that led them to their coping mechanisms.

As we begin to heal and stop reacting as a result of our trauma we are able to move from our Shadow archetypes into our Golden archetypes. The Sweet One can transform into the Boundaried One, learning to set healthy boundaries and help family members without sacrificing themselves. This transformation allows them to maintain loving relationships with family members without enabling their toxic or destructive behaviours. The Destroyer becomes the Renovator and learns to hold onto the things that are working, rebuild the things that don't work, and replace dying systems with new ones, instead of destroying everything. The RunAway becomes the Grounded Seeker and learns to find safety in their own body and, in so doing, learns resilience and to stick it out through gruelling challenges. The Fixer becomes the Sovereign One and allows others to take responsibility for their own lives, showing us all how to honour individual wants, needs and desires. The Eternal Child becomes the Evolving adult and shows us that healing and growth are possible and that forgiveness and letting go of childhood wounds are imperative.

It is important to note, however, that these archetypes are not fixed in stone; they evolve and more money archetypes have been presented and will continue to be presented as society changes. In fact, we may identify with various characteristics of multiple archetypes, but the key is to recognise these patterns within ourselves and our families and to practice compassion.

Exploring our family's ancestral stories, traumas and beliefs, and understanding how they have shaped our own financial behaviour can help us break free from generational patterns and create healthier family and money dynamics. Healing our relationship with money requires us to acknowledge and address the wounds that have been passed down through generations. This may involve seeking therapy, engaging in inner work, journaling, healing ancestral trauma, or engaging in various healing methodologies.

It is also important for us to create a family environment that allows for open and honest communication. By sharing our experiences and stories within our families, we can deepen our understanding of each other and cultivate empathy and support. This communication can also help break the cycle of secrecy and shame that often surrounds money, allowing us to approach financial topics with transparency and collaboration. We may even be able to start programmes such as lekgotlas – part of our ancestral wisdom – when it comes to money and building generational wealth.

By understanding and working with these archetypes, I hope we will be able to change our own money stories and break the cycle of trauma and dysfunction within our families. It may take time and effort, and there may be resistance and challenges along the way, but each of us can change our family dynamics. As we have seen in the case studies, it only takes one person.

I hope this book helps you reflect on your money behaviours, family dynamics and patterns of trauma, and that you continue to use it as a tool to heal and transform your relationship with money, family and yourself – and by so doing, create a new financial legacy for future generations.

If this has resonated with you and you want to dig deeper in order to understand how you can heal your ancestral money trauma and tap into your ancestral money wisdom, check out some of the

Conclusion

following resources available from Wealthy Money:

- Free 7 Day Tapping Into Ancestral Money Wisdom Training: wealthy-money.com/training
- Money Magic Podcast: Search on Apple, Spotify and Podbean
- Bank Account Challenge: Change your spending habits by working with your body and ancestors: wealthy-money.com/bankaccount
- Creating Money Magic – our signature course to help you heal ancestral money trauma and double your income: wealthy-money.com/moneymagic

If you're interested in learning more about building a relationship with your ancestors and understanding yourself in the context of your ancestors, check out the Sangoma Society's course, Answers From Our Ancestors: https://www.sangomasociety.com/

Glossary

Allostatic load: The toll that chronic stress takes on the body over time.

Divine, The; Divinity: God in the traditional sense; your higher self; nature; or the universe.

Energetic boundaries: The personal and subtle barriers we create to protect our energy, emotions, and wellbeing from negative people and external influences.

Father wound: The emotional pain and unresolved issues that people carry as a result of their relationship with their father; often comes from unmet needs and experiences in childhood.

God wound: A term coined by Vangile Makwakwa to explain the wound that originates as a result of trauma, which causes an individual to completely forget their power and their own divinity or God nature, thus leading to a person betraying themselves, their values and their mission.

Golden archetype: A person who has acknowledged, embraced, and integrated their harmful or destructive qualities and traits and is now self-aware and is experiencing continuous personal growth, maturity and expansion in various areas of their life.

Healed archetype: A Shadow archetype that has integrated and brought their unconscious harmful behaviours to light and as a result, making different choices and decisions.

Hypervigilance: A heightened state of constant alertness to potential threats or dangers in people or external environments as a result of past trauma.

Mother wound: the emotional pain and unresolved issues that people carry as a result of their relationship with their mother; often comes from unmet needs and experiences in childhood.

Primary archetype: The predominant/main profile (personality) that you identify with.

Sacral chakra: Energy centre located in the lower abdomen of our bodies, it is associated with creativity, passion, emotions, and the ability to experience pleasure and joy.

Sangoma: A spiritual healer, found in southern African cultures, that has the ability to connect with the spirit world and use this connection to provide healing, divination and guidance to individuals and communities.

Secondary archetype: Another profile or personality that you identify with that influences your behaviour.

Second chakra: Another way to define the sacral chakra.

Set point: A predetermined level or value that we hold. Example: a money set point is a predetermined amount of money that we make or tend to hold in our bank account.

Shadow archetype: The hidden and unconscious part of a person's personality that includes traits and emotions they may not want to acknowledge or show to others because they have been deemed undesirable and shameful.

Shaman: A spiritual healer, usually found in traditional societies, who has the ability to connect with the spirit world and uses this connection to heal and guide people and communities.

Womb health: Uterine or reproductive health, refers to the wellbeing and health of the female reproductive system, including the menstrual cycle.

Womb pain: Any sensations of discomfort or pain experienced in the lower abdominal region, specifically in the area of the uterus or womb.

References

At the time of recording, all the website and article links provided in the book were live.

Adonis, CK. (2016). 'Exploring the salience of intergenerational trauma among children and grandchildren of victims of apartheid-era gross human rights violations.' *Indo-Pacific Journal of Phenomenology* 16, No. 2, 1–17. http://dx.doi.org/10.1080/20797222.2016.1184838

Anderson, S. (2000). *The Journey from Abandonment to Healing: Turn the End of a Relationship into the Beginning of a New Life*. Berkley.

Antoni, X. (2023). 'The role of family structure on financial socialisation techniques and behaviour of students in the Eastern Cape, South Africa.' *Cogent Economics & Finance*, 11:1. 10.1080/23322039.2023.2196844

Antony, MM, and RP Swinson. (2009). *When Perfect Isn't Good Enough: Strategies for Coping with Perfectionism* (2nd ed.). New Harbinger Publications.

Baker, MR. (2018). 'The Phenomenon of Belonging.' *Counseling and Family Therapy Scholarship Review*, Vol. 1(1), Article 1. https://doi.org/10.53309/LLFK1193

Bennett, M, and J Lagopoulos. (2018). 'Grey matter changes in the brain following stress and trauma.' *Stress, Trauma and Synaptic Plasticity*. Springer, Cham. https://doi.org/10.1007/978-3-319-91116-8_1

Berckmoes, LH, V Eichelsheim, T Rutayisire, A Richters, and B Hola. (2017). 'How legacies of genocide are transmitted in the family environment:

A qualitative study of two generations in Rwanda.' *Societies* 7, No. 3:24. https://doi.org/10.3390/soc7030024

Bertrand, A, and S Bertrand. (2017). *Womb Awakening: Initiatory Wisdom from the Creatrix of All Life* (3rd ed.). Bear & Company.

Bleiweis, R, J Frye, and R Khattar. (2021). *Women of Color and the Wage Gap.* Center for American Progress. Retrieved 8 July 2023, from https://www.americanprogress.org/article/women-of-color-and-the-wage-gap/

Bloom, S. (2001). 'Commentary: Reflections on the desire for revenge.' *Journal of Emotional Abuse*, 2, 61–94. https://doi.org/10.1300/J135v02n04_06

Bombay, A, K Matheson, and H Anisman. (2014). 'The intergenerational effects of Indian Residential Schools: Implications for the concept of historical trauma.' *Transcultural Psychiatry*, 51(3), 320–33. https://doi.org/10.1177/1363461513503380

Booth, J, SL Ayers, and FF Marsiglia. (2012). 'Perceived neighborhood safety and psychological distress: Exploring protective factors.' *The Journal of Sociology & Social Welfare*, Vol. 39, Issue 4. https://scholarworks.wmich.edu/jssw/vol39/iss4/8

Bremner, JD. (2006). 'Traumatic stress: effects on the brain.' *Dialogues in clinical neuroscience*, 8(4), 445–461. https://doi.org/10.31887/DCNS.2006.8.4/jbremner

Briggs, A. (2019). *Overcoming Perfectionism: Release the lies, experience the liberation of giving yourself grace, and become who you were meant to be.* Alice Arlene, Limited Company Press.

Bryan, JL, S Lucas, MC Quist, MN Steers, DW Foster, CM Young, and Q Lu. (2016). 'God, Can I Tell You Something? The Effect of Religious Coping on the Relationship between Anxiety Over Emotional Expression, Anxiety, and Depressive Symptoms.' *Psychology of Religion and Spirituality*, 8(1), 46–53. https://doi.org/10.1037/rel0000023

Budlender, D, and F Lund. (2011). 'South Africa: A legacy of family disruption.' *Development and Change* 42, No. 4, 925–946. https://onlinelibrary.wiley.com/doi/10.1111/j.1467-7660.2011.01715.x

Burger, JM. (1985). 'Desire for control and achievement-related behaviours.' *Journal of Personality and Social Psychology*, 48(6), 1520–1533. https://doi.org/0022-3514/85/

Burgess, L, and T Legg. (2017). 'Hypervigilance: What you need to know.' *Medical News Today*. Retrieved 20 December 2022, from https://www.medicalnewstoday.com/articles/319289

References

Byers, G. (2018). *I Am Enough*. Balzer + Bray.

Callaghan, BL, A Fields, DG Gee, L Gabard-Durnam, C Caldera, KL Humphreys, B Goff, J Flannery, EH Telzer, M Shapiro, and N Tottenham. (2020). 'Mind and gut: Associations between mood and gastrointestinal distress in children exposed to adversity.' *Development and Psychopathology*, 32 (1):309–328. https://doi.org/10.1017/S0954579419000087

Camille, C. (2021). 'Working on your relationship with pleasure can help you be happier.' *Medium*. Retrieved 19 June 2022, from https://camille-grady.medium.com/your-relationship-with-pleasure-can-help-you-be-happier-4beacaa56ea5

Cooper, A. (2021). 'Why we blame.' *The Family Institute at Northwestern University*. Retrieved 10 January 2023, from https://www.family-institute.org/behavioural-health-resources/why-we-blame-0

Dale, C. (2011). *Energetic Boundaries: How to Stay Protected and Connected in Work, Love, and Life*. Sounds True.

Davids, MN. (2018). 'Ideology critique as decolonising pedagogy: Urban forced removals as a case study.' *Educational Research for Social Change*, 7(spe), 16–30.

Davis, S. (2020). 'The wounded inner child.' CPTSD Foundation. Retrieved 1 May 2022, from https://cptsdfoundation.org/2020/07/13/the-wounded-inner-child/

Davis, S. (2020). 'Reparenting to heal the wounded inner child.' CPSTD Foundation. Retrieved 27 December 2022, from https://cptsdfoundation.org/2020/07/27/reparenting-to-heal-the-wounded-inner-child/

DBT and Mental Health Services. (2020). 'How does trauma affect the parasympathetic nervous system?' *Mental Health Services Journal*. Retrieved 20 December 2022, from https://www.mhs-dbt.com/blog/parasympathetic-nervous-system-and-trauma/

DeAngelis, T. (2019). 'The legacy of trauma.' *Monitor on Psychology*, 50(2). https://www.apa.org/monitor/2019/02/legacy-trauma

Diamond, J. (2017). '5 surprising ways the father wound harms women.' *Good Men Project*. Retrieved 10 September 2022, from https://goodmenproject.com/families/5-surprising-ways-father-wound-harms-women-wcz/

Diamond, SA. (2008). 'Essential secrets of psychotherapy: The inner child.' *Psychology Today*. Retrieved 30 April 2022, from https://www.

psychologytoday.com/us/blog/evil-deeds/200806/essential-secrets-psychotherapy-the-inner-child

Dias, B, and K Ressler. (2014). 'Parental olfactory experience influences behaviour and neural structure in subsequent generations.' *Nature Neuroscience* 17, 89–96. https://doi.org/10.1038/nn.3594

Dibdin, E. (2022). 'Need to control everything? This may be why.' *PsychCentral*. Retrieved 8 June 2022, from https://psychcentral.com/blog/why-you-need-to-control-everything

Dietrich, M. (2017). 'What is your relationship with pleasure?' Retrieved 18 June 2022, from https://madelinedietrich.com/blog/single/what_is_your_relationship_with_pleasure

Fernández-López, S, S Castro-González, L Rey-Ares, and D Rodeiro-Pazos. (2023). 'Self-control and debt decisions relationship: Evidence for different credit options.' *Current Psychology*. https://doi.org/10.1007/s12144-023-04251-7

Firman, J, and A Russell. (1994). *Opening to the Inner Child: Recovering Authentic Personality*. Psychosynthesis Palo Alto.

Fishman, R. (2018). 'Overcoming the fear of being too much.' *My Meadow Report*. Retrieved 10 September 2022, from https://mymeadowreport.com/reneefishman/2018/fear-of-being-too-much/

Gaba, S. (2019). 'How our relationships with our mothers affect our codependency.' *Psychology Today*. https://www.psychologytoday.com/za/blog/addiction-and-recovery/201910/the-mother-wound.

Geronimus, AT, M Hicken, D Keene, and J Bound. (2006). '"Weathering" and age patterns of allostatic load scores among blacks and whites in the United States.' *American Journal of Public Health*, 96(5), 826–833. https://doi.org/10.2105/AJPH.2004.060749

Goldner, L, R Lev-Wiesel, and G Simon. (2019). 'Revenge fantasies after experiencing traumatic events: Sex differences.' *Frontiers in Psychology*, 10. https://doi.org/10.3389/fpsyg.2019.00886

Guidi, J, M Lucente, N Sonino, and GA Fava. (2021). 'Allostatic load and its impact on health: A systematic review'. *Psychotherapy and Pyschosomatics,* 90, 11–27. https://doi.org/10.1159/000510696

Hahn, H, and M Simms. (2021). 'Poverty results from structural barriers, not personal choices. safety net programs should reflect that fact.' Retrieved 24 November 2022, from https://www.urban.org/urban-wire/poverty-results-structural-barriers-not-personal-choices-safety-net-programs-should-reflect-fact

References

Hantsoo, L, E Jašarević, S Criniti, B McGeehan, C Tanes, MD Sammel, MA Elovitz, C Compher, G Wu, and CN Epperson. (2019). 'Childhood adversity impact on gut microbiota and inflammatory response to stress during pregnancy.' *Brain, Behavior, and Immunity*, 75, 240–250. https://doi.org/10.1016/j.bbi.2018.11.005

Hendricks, G. (2010). *The Big Leap: Conquer Your Hidden Fear and Take Life to the Next Level*. HarperCollins.

Holz, NE, R Boecker, E Hohm, K Zohsel, AF Buchmann, D Blomeyer, C Jennen-Steinmetz, S Baumeister, S Hohmann, I Wolf, MM Plichta, G Esser, M Schmidt, A Meyer-Lindenberg, T Banaschewski, D Brandeis, and M Laucht. (2015). 'The long-term impact of early life poverty on orbitofrontal cortex volume in adulthood: results from a prospective study over 25 years.' *Neuropsychopharmacology*, 40(4), 996–1004. https://doi.org/10.1038/npp.2014.277

Javanbakht, A, and L Saab. (2017). 'What happens in the brain when we feel fear.' *Smithsonian Magazine*. Retrieved 30 April 2022, from https://www.smithsonianmag.com/science-nature/what-happens-brain-feel-fear-180966992/

Javed, MK, M Degong, and T Qadeer. (2017). 'Importance of financial knowledge and self-esteem in determining individuals' financial behaviour.' *International Journal of Management and Applied Science* (IJMAS), 3(10), 46–50. https://doi.org/http://iraj.doionline.org/dx/IJMAS-IRAJ-DOIONLINE-9707

Kelly, JD IV. (2015). 'Your best life: Perfectionism – The bane of happiness.' *Clinical Orthopaedics and Related Research*, 473(10), 3108–3111. https://doi.org/10.1007/s11999-015-42799

Kenneth RG. (2007). 'The importance of play in promoting healthy child development and maintaining strong parent-child bonds.' *Pediatrics* 119 (1): 182–191. 10.1542/peds.2006-2697

Kim, A W, RS Mohamed, SA Norris, LM Richter, and CW Kuzawa. (2022). 'Psychological Legacies of intergenerational trauma under South African apartheid: Prenatal stress predicts greater vulnerability to the psychological impacts of future stress exposure during late adolescence and early adulthood in Soweto, South Africa.' *Journal of Child Psychology and Psychiatry*, Vol. 64, No. 1, 110–124. Accessed 11 April 2023. https://doi.org/10.1111/jcpp.13672

Kraemer S. (1991). 'The origins of fatherhood: An ancient family process.' *Family Process*, 30(4), 377-392. https://doi.org/10.1111/j.1545-

5300.1991.00377.x

Kwate, NO, and MS Goodman. (2015). 'Cross-sectional and longitudinal effects of racism on mental health among residents of Black neighborhoods in New York City.' *American Journal of Public Health*, 105(4), 711–718. https://doi.org/10.2105/AJPH.2014.302243

Leary, MR. (2015). 'Emotional responses to interpersonal rejection.' *Dialogues in Clinical Neuroscience*, Vol 17(4), 435–41. 0.31887/DCNS.2015.17.4/mleary

Leary, MR, and RF Baumeister. (2000). 'The nature and function of self-esteem: Sociometer theory.' In MP Zanna (ed.), *Advances in Experimental Social Psychology,* Vol. 32, 1–62. Academic Press. https://doi.org/10.1016/S0065-2601(00)80003-9

Lejoyeux, M, C Richoux-Benhaim, A Betizeau, V Lequen, and H Lohnhardt. (2011). 'Money attitude, self-esteem, and compulsive buying in a population of medical students.' *Frontiers in Psychiatry*, 2, 13. https://doi.org/10.3389/fpsyt.2011.00013

Leman, K. (2019). *When Your Best Isn't Good Enough: Breaking Free from Perfectionism*. Revell.

Lewis, TT, and ME van Dyke. (2018). 'Discrimination and the health of African Americans: The potential importance of intersectionalities.' *Sage Journals*, 27, No. 3. https://doi.org/10.1177/0963721418770442

Lo, I. (2018). 'Feeling intensely: The wounds of being "Too much".' *Psychology Today*. Retrieved 10 September 2022, from https://www.psychologytoday.com/us/blog/living-emotional-intensity/201805/feeling-intensely-the-wounds-being-too-much

Lynch, MM, and DD Schwartz. (2014). *Tapping Into Wealth: How Emotional Freedom Techniques (EFT) Can Help You Clear the Path to Making More Money*. Tarcher/Penguin.

Lynch, MM, and R Thomas. (2011). *The 7 Levels of Wealth Manifestation*. Margaret Lynch.

Madigan, T (2021). 'American Terror: A century ago in Tulsa, a murderous mob attacked the most prosperous black community in the nation.' *Smithsonian Magazine*. Retrieved 8 August 2023, from https://www.smithsonianmag.com/history/tulsa-race-massacre-century-later-180977145/

Makwakwa, V. (2013). *Heart, Mind & Money: Using Emotional Intelligence for Financial Success*. Jacana Media.

Makwakwa, V. (2021). 'The most basic fear that stops us from thriving and expanding.' *Wealthy Money Blog*. Retrieved 22 December 2022, from https://www.wealthy-money.com/blog/the-most-basic-fear-that-stops-us-from-expanding

Mangoma, A, and A Wilson-Prangley. (2019). 'Black Tax: Understanding the financial transfers of the emerging black middle class.' *Development Southern Africa*, 36:4, 443–460, https://doi.org/10.1080/0376835X.2018.1516545

Mannor, M, A Wowak, VO Bartkus, and LR Gomez-Mejia. (2016). 'How anxiety affects CEO decision making.' *Harvard Business Review Home*. Retrieved 29 July 2022, from https://hbr.org/2016/07/how-anxiety-affects-ceo-decision-making

Mauger, L, S Remael, and B Phalen. (2016). *The Vanished: The 'Evaporated People' of Japan in Stories and Photographs*. Skyhorse.

McDermott, R, AC Lopez, and PK Hatemi. (2017). '"Blunt not the heart, enrage it": The psychology of revenge and deterrence.' *Texas National Security Review*, 1(1). https://tnsr.org/2017/11/blunt-not-heart-enrage-psychology-revenge-deterrence/

Mcleod, S. (4 April 2022). 'Maslow's Hierarchy of Needs.' *Simply Psychology*. Retrieved 21 July 2022, from https://www.simplypsychology.org/maslow.html

Moeini-Jazani, M, S Albalooshi, and IM Seljeseth. (2019). 'Self-Affirmation reduces delay discounting of the financially deprived.' *Frontiers in Psychology*, 10. https://doi.org/10.3389/fpsyg.2019.01729

Murphy, LK. (2020). *Co-Regulation Handbook: Creating Competent, Authentic Roles for Kids with Social Learning Differences, So We All Stay Positively Connected Through the Ups and Downs of Learning*. Linda K Murphy.

Murray, DW, K Rosanbalm, C Christopoulos, and A Hamoudi. (2014). 'Self-regulation and toxic stress Report 1: Foundations for understanding self-regulation from an applied perspective.' OPRE Report #1 Washington, DC: Office of Planning, Research and Evaluation, Administration for Children and Families. US Department of Health and Human Services.

Ozcan, O, M Hoelterhoff, and E Wylie. (2021). 'Faith and spirituality as psychological coping mechanism among female aid workers: a qualitative study.' *Journal of International Humanitarian Action* 6, 15. https://doi.org/10.1186/s41018-021-00100-z

Pearce S, and Pickard H. (2013). 'How therapeutic communities work:

Specific factors related to positive outcome.' *International Journal of Social Psychiatry*. Vol. 59, No. 7, 636–645. doi:10.1177/0020764012450992

Peer, M. (2018). *I Am Enough: Mark Your Mirror And Change Your Life*. Marisa Peer.

Pong, HK. (2022). 'Money attitude and spiritual well-being.' *Journal of Risk and Financial Management* 15, No. 10, 483. https://doi.org/10.3390/jrfm15100483

Porges, SW. (2022). 'Polyvagal theory: A science of safety.' *Frontiers in Integrative Neuroscience*, 16. https://doi.org/10.3389/fnint.2022.871227

Preedy, VR. (2015). *Coffee in Health and Disease Prevention*. Academic Press. https://doi.org/10.1016/C2012-0-06959-1

Rakoff, V. (1966). 'A long-term effect of the concentration camp experience.' *Viewpoints* 1, 17–22.

Rouault, M, GJ Will, SM Fleming, et al. (2022). 'Low self-esteem and the formation of global self-performance estimates in emerging adulthood.' *Translational Psychiatry* 12, 272. https://doi.org/10.1038/s41398-022-02031-8

Rucker, DD, and AD Galinsky. (2008). 'Desire to acquire: Powerlessness and compensatory consumption.' *Journal of Consumer Research*, 35(2), 257–267. https://doi.org/10.1086/588569

Ryder, G. (2022). 'The fawn response: How trauma can lead to people-pleasing.' *PsychCentral*. Retrieved 28 December 2022, from https://psychcentral.com/health/fawn-response

Salami, IA, and CIO Okeke. (2018). 'Absent fathers' socio-economic status and perceptions of fatherhood as related to developmental challenges faced by children in South Africa.' *South African Journal of Childhood Education* 8(1), a522. https:// doi.org/10.4102/sajce

Schauer, M, and T Elbert. (2010). 'Dissociation following traumatic stress etiology and treatment.' *Zeitschrift Fur Psychologie [Journal of Psychology]* 218, 109–127.

Silver, T. (2015). *Change Me Prayers: The Hidden Power of Spiritual Surrender*. Atria Books.

Smith, DG. (2020). 'Why unfairness makes you rage.' *Medium*. Retrieved 30 April 2022, from https://elemental.medium.com/why-unfairness-makes-you-rage-d7f684ae3de

Smith, JP. (2016). *The Other Side of Rejection: Healing The Damaged Soul* (2nd ed.). CreateSpace Independent Publishing Platform.

Smith, RJ. (2016) 'Perceptions of Money: Relationships between remembered parental rejection, extrinsic life aspirations and maladaptive attitudes toward money.' CUNY Academic Works. https://academicworks.cuny.edu/gc_etds/1547

Tanasugarn, DA. (2020). 'Healing from the past and living in your present.' *PsychCentral*. Retrieved 1 July 2022, from https://psychcentral.com/lib/healing-from-the-past-and-living-in-your-present#1

Teicher, MH, and JA Samson. (2016). 'Annual research review: Enduring neurobiological effects of childhood abuse and neglect.' *The Journal of Child Psychology and Psychiatry*, 57(3), 241–66. https://doi.org/10.1111/jcpp.12507

Thomas, E, and S Savoy. (2014). 'Relationships between traumatic events, religious coping style, and posttraumatic outcomes.' *Traumatology: An International Journal*. 20.84.10.1037/h0099380

Titus, SL, PC Rosenblatt, and RM Anderson. (1979). 'Family conflict over inheritance of property.' *The Family Coordinator* 28, No. 3 (1979): 337–46. https://doi.org/10.2307/581946

Torgerson, CN, HA Love, and A Vennum. (2018). 'The buffering effect of belonging on the negative association of childhood trauma with adult mental health and risky alcohol use.' *Journal of Substance Use and Addiction Treatment*, 88, 44–50. https://doi.org/10.1016/j.jsat.2018.02.005

Tull, M. (2022). 'What is dissociation?' *VeryWellMind*. Retrieved 21 December 2022, from https://www.verywellmind.com/dissociation-2797292

Urban, M. (2022). *The Book of Boundaries: Set the Limits That Will Set You Free*. The Dial Press.

Van der Kolk, BA. (1994). 'The body keeps score: Memory and the evolving psychology of post traumatic stress'. *Harvard Review of Psychiatry*, January 1994, Vol. 1, No. 5, 253–265

Van der Toorn, J, M Feinberg, JT Jost, AC Kay, TR Tyler, R Willer, and C Wilmuth. (2015). 'A sense of powerlessness fosters system justification: Implications for the legitimation of authority, hierarchy, and government.' *Political Psychology*, 36: 93–110. https://doi.org/10.1111/pops.12183

Verbeke, W, and RP Bagozzi. (2000). 'Sales call anxiety: exploring what it means when fear rules a sales encounter.' *Journal of Marketing* 64, No. 3, 88–101. http://www.jstor.org/stable/3203489

Villines, Z. (2023). 'What to know about abandonment issues.' *Medical News*

Today. Retrieved 21 January 2023, from https://www.medicalnewstoday.com/articles/abandonment-issues

Wang, S, and S Aamodt. (2012). 'Play, stress, and the learning brain.' *Cerebrum* (The Dana Forum on Brain Science), 12. https://www.ncbi.nlm.nih.gov/pmc/articles/PMC3574776/

Watanabe, S, M Iwanaga, and Y Ozeki. (2002). 'Effects of controllability and desire for control on coping and stress responses.' *The Japanese Journal of Health Psychology*, 15(1), 32–40. https://doi.org/10.11560/jahp.15.1_32

Weinberg, M, S Gil, A Besser, and J Bass. (2021). 'Personality traits and trauma exposure: The relationship between personality traits, PTSD symptoms, stress, and negative affect following exposure to traumatic cues.' *Personality and Individual Differences*, 177. https://doi.org/10.1016/j.paid.2021.110802

Weinreb, K. (2019). 'Behavioural hypervigilance in a normative population'. CUNY Academic Works. https://academicworks.cuny.edu/hc_sas_etds/523

Weir, K. (2012). 'The pain of social rejection.' *Monitor on Psychology*, 43(4). https://www.apa.org/monitor/2012/04/rejection

Williams, MT, AM Haeny, and SC Holmes. (2021). 'Posttraumatic stress disorder and racial trauma.' *PTSD Research Quarterly*, 32(1), 1–9.

Zhou, H, and J Chen. (2021). 'How does psychological empowerment prevent emotional exhaustion? Psychological safety and organizational embeddedness as mediators.' *Frontiers in Psychology*, 12. https://doi.org/10.3389/fpsyg.2021.546687

Acknowledgements

Writing this book has been a challenging and transformative journey, and I am deeply grateful to all the people who have made it possible and have held me as I was battling with the overwhelm and confusion of putting pen to paper.

First and foremost, I want to express my heartfelt gratitude to my family, especially my mother, Nomvula Kellina Makwakwa, for letting me move back home so I could finish writing this book in total peace with no distractions. Parking my nomadic lifestyle for six months and retreating into my own world was a game changer for my writing.

I am grateful to my sister, Honey Makwakwa, and my dad, Daniel Phori Maelane, for their support with the book, for listening to my ideas (even though I refused to tell them exactly what the book was about), and then for saying yes to being interviewed by me and trusting me with their truth. I am also grateful to my brother, Leago Papo, for his support on this journey.

To my friends and colleagues who have cheered me on and have believed in this book completely – thank you. A special thanks goes to Khanya Malungelo Ngonyama, who helped me through so many meltdowns and would send daily messages and call to ask how the writing was going, and would have to sit through cryptic stories about the book because I refused to talk about the book.

Thank you to Dr Miranda Moloto, Nomvelisa V Mbanga, Zandile Mazwayi Selepe, Jo Ntsebeza, Nileema Khan, Analise Torres, John Griffith, Agnieszka Zausz, Brittany Williams, Soufia Rhabha, Vuyi Qubeka, Loren Kabosha and Tshego Mpete, you guys really caught most of the drama and the tears and convinced me that this book was worth writing even though you had no clue what I was actually writing about and sometimes you just sat and watched me cry or jump around in excitement. It really takes a global village. If I missed anyone, it wasn't intentional.

I am also indebted to my assistant, Pearl Egam-Hermosilla, and my assistant coach, Ncumisa Ncama, for holding down the fort in the business so I could research and write this book.

I am thankful for my wonderful clients in the Wealthy Money Mastermind for holding space for me whenever I shared something about writing or lamented how I didn't have the words to describe what I wanted to really say.

I am indebted to my editor, Sean Fraser, and the publishing team at Pan Macmillan South Africa, especially Zodwa Kumalo-Valentine and Andrea Nattrass, for their patience and insightful feedback and guidance. To see what this book has become is a wonder and I am in awe.

My sincere appreciation goes to all the people who trusted me with their stories and who said yes to being interviewed in the case studies. Your openness and generosity have enriched the content of this book.

Lastly, thank you to all the readers who will embark on this adventure with me. I hope this book has a positive impact in your life and transforms your relationship with money and your loved ones.

Thank you all for being a part of this transformative experience.

www.ingramcontent.com/pod-product-compliance
Lightning Source LLC
Chambersburg PA
CBHW031420150426
43191CB00006B/334